In loving memory of my mother, Teta Gravari-Tamboukou

Martial P

Sewing, Fighting and Writing

Radical Cultural Studies

Series Editors: Fay Brauer, Maggie Humm, Tim Lawrence, Stephen Maddison, Ashwani Sharma and Debra Benita Shaw (Centre for Cultural Studies Research, University of East London, UK)

The Radical Cultural Studies series publishes monographs and edited collections to provide new and radical analyses of the culturopolitics, sociopolitics, aesthetics and ethics of contemporary cultures. The series is designed to stimulate debates across and within disciplines, foster new approaches to Cultural Studies and assess the radical potential of key ideas and theories.

Sewing, Fighting and Writing: Radical Practices in Work, Politics and Culture,
    by Maria Tamboukou
Radical Space: Exploring Politics and Practice, edited by Debra Benita Shaw and
    Maggie Humm (forthcoming)
Science Fiction, Fantasy and Politics: *Transmedia World-Building Beyond Capitalism,*
    by Dan Hassler-Forest (forthcoming)

Sewing, Fighting and Writing

Radical Practices in Work, Politics and Culture

Maria Tamboukou

ROWMAN &
LITTLEFIELD
─────INTERNATIONAL─────

London • New York

Published by Rowman & Littlefield International Ltd
Unit A, Whitacre Mews, 26-34 Stannary Street, London SE11 4AB
www.rowmaninternational.com

Rowman & Littlefield International Ltd. is an affiliate of Rowman & Littlefield
4501 Forbes Boulevard, Suite 200, Lanham, Maryland 20706, USA
With additional offices in Boulder, New York, Toronto (Canada), and Plymouth (UK)
www.rowman.com

British Library Cataloguing in Publication Data

A catalogue record for this book is available from the British Library
ISBN: HB 978-1-7834-8244-3
       PB 978-1-7834-8245-0

Library of Congress Cataloging-in-Publication Data

Names: Tamboukou, Maria, 1958–
Title: Sewing, fighting and writing : radical practices in work, politics and culture /
    Maria Tamboukou.
Description: Lanham : Rowman & Littlefield International, 2015. | Series: Radical
    cultural studies | Includes bibliographical references and index.
Identifiers: LCCN 2015028352| ISBN 9781783482443 (cloth : alk. paper) |
    ISBN 9781783482450 (pbk. : alk. paper) | ISBN 9781783482467 (electronic)
Subjects: LCSH: Women dressmakers—France—Paris—History—19th century. |
    Radicalism—France—Paris—History—19th century.
Classification: LCC HD8039.C62 F87 2015 | DDC 331.4/887094436109034—dc23 LC
    record available at http://lccn.loc.gov/2015028352

Contents

Acknowledgments

One of my earliest memories is lying in bed through some childhood illness and losing myself in the colourful world of my mother's fashion magazines. My mother was a seamstress, the best seamstress in town people thought, and her atelier was in our own house where I grew up, surrounded by colourful fabrics, *patrons*, beautiful toilettes, dressmakers' dummies, threads and needles. My fashion education was strict and rigid: I knew the difference between a morning, an afternoon and an evening dress, a winter coat and a spring *manteau;* I learnt that I should not confuse summer and winter colours, and I was always afraid (I still am) of what my mother would think about my garderobe choices. But growing up with a seamstress, I also knew about the hard labour of sewing, its pressures and anxieties, the many *veuilleras*, as my mother would call her late night shifts, but also the delight and satisfaction when a dress, a suit or a coat turned out to 'fall' perfectly in the final fitting. Writing the genealogy of the seamstress was thus more than just a component of my overall project of writing feminist genealogies, and there are no words to carry the intensity of my feelings in doing this research and writing this book.

But a book is not just an assemblage of memories, ideas and scholarly work, but also a material project that requires many peoples' contribution. I want to thank Maggie Humm and Debra Shaw for enthusiastically embracing the book project from the beginning and including it in their fab series of Radical Cultural Studies. The Rowman & Littlefield people were excellent throughout the process. I felt from the beginning the importance of having a rigorous academic publisher, which gave me the opportunity to write the book I wanted. My special thanks go to my editor Martina O'Sullivan for her overall guidance and advice and to Sinéad Murphy for unfailing support in the production process.

The book draws on intensive research from a number of archives in Paris. I want to thank the archivists and librarians of the *Archives Nationales de France, Bibliothèque de l'Arsenal, Bibliothèque Historique De la Ville de Paris, Bibliothèque de l'Hôtel de Ville,* and the *Bibliothèque Marguerite Durand,* for facilitating my research, helping me to trace and identify lost documents and for kindly giving me permission to quote from them. Last but not least, I want to acknowledge my gratitude to the *Bibliothèque Nationale de France* for their wonderful project of *Gallica,* a digitized library that has radically democratized the archive project across the world.

I am lucky to work at the Centre for Narrative Research, University of East London, surrounded by colleagues and research students who know how to challenge narrative conventions, canons and histories, thus creating an intellectual milieu wherein new adventures in thought are set in motion. I want to thank them all for supporting me throughout the years. I benefited from a sabbatical period from the University of East London in the spring of 2014, which gave me the opportunity to delve in the richness of my archival data and formulate the final proposal for the book, for which I am grateful. I also want to thank my School of Social Sciences for supporting me with small grants and most importantly with research time that has allowed me to go on working for this project beyond the sabbatical period.

My final thanks, as always, to the people I love and who have unfailingly supported me through harsh and happy times: my partner Mihalis Zervos, my daughter Ariagni Adam and my sister Anna Tampoukou. But this book would have never been written without my mother's presence, both real and imaginary: it is hers more than it is mine.

Introduction

Charting Lines of Flight

The Parisian Seamstress

On November 14, 1850, a strange dialogue took place between the president of a criminal court in Paris and Jeanne Deroin, who was on trial for political conspiracy against the government:

- What is your profession?
- Teacher and journalist.
- You have also said that you are a seamstress [...]
- Please write that I have also been a seamstress.
- You are then a teacher, a journalist and a seamstress.[1]

Taking the judge's final sarcastic remark as my starting point, in this book I want to explore a world of multiple 'ands' in women workers' lives, particularly focusing on the extraordinary figure of the Parisian seamstress, her passions, her actions and their effects on the social, political and cultural formations of modernity.

'More than a woman worker, a seamstress is part of a social and cultural enterprise that we have come to consider distinctively feminine', Judith Coffin has argued in her influential study on the politics of women's work in the Parisian garment trades (1996, 19). But apart from her distinct position in the history and political economy of women's work, the seamstress is a well-recognized cultural image, mostly depicted as a destitute figure to be pitied and protected: she has motivated a range of historical and sociopolitical studies that span more than two centuries[2]; she has been sung in popular culture[3] and has inspired novels, poems, paintings[4] and even operas.[5] But she has mostly been the object of study—the social problem of female labour par

1

excellence (Simon 1860), the muse or the model—very rarely the thinker, the actor or the creator—with the exception of autobiographical accounts of seamstresses who have also become writers.[6] Such autobiographical narratives have revealed that the seamstress is inextricably entangled in the sociopolitical and cultural movements in modernity as a revolutionary, a unionized worker, a militant feminist, a thinker, a writer and a creator. It is these submerged histories that I will excavate in this book by writing a feminist genealogy of the seamstress.

As I will further discuss in Chapter 1, the Foucauldian approach of writing genealogies as histories of the present is a critical way of problematizing the present we are part of, by excavating and deconstructing its conditions of possibility. In the case of the seamstresses, their dreary working conditions are not simply a 'tale of the past', but very much a contemporary issue, geographically displaced in the so-called developing countries of the global east and south, but with equally globalized consequences and questions that need urgent attention.[7]

What has therefore enabled a genealogical investigation of the figure of the seamstress is the archive of their radical practices inscribed in their personal narratives and political writings. Action as something we do always evades us, Hannah Arendt (1998) has famously argued, particularly so if we are the actors and we have to concentrate on the doing rather than the thinking or the understanding of what we do. But thanks to stories that carry traces of past actions as 'words and deeds', we have the chance to grasp some remnants of the fleeting present and by putting them into stories we gradually write History, with all its omissions, silences, gaps and margins. Narratives are thus *a conditio sine qua non* for the writing of history, particularly so when the grand discourse of History has ignored, downplayed, marginalized or erased histories of 'the other'. In this light, Arendt's take on the political nature of narratives has made connections with Foucault's genealogical insights in rewriting the seamstress into history, creating an assemblage where narratives and discourses have been studied in their interrelation.

But although narratives and discourses have been central in this study what has also emerged as a catalytic event is the question of 'how matter matters' (Barad 2007) in the excavation of the conditions of possibility for the seamstress to emerge as a labour activist, a political subject, a writer of history and a creator of culture. Here, Alfred Whitehead's (1985) critique of the separation between the material and the mental, as well as his philosophical thesis that everything is process is crucial in informing an analysis that takes as its starting point the materiality of the seamstresses' work in understanding the multiple becomings of feminist ideas in nineteenth-century France and beyond.

MAPPING PARIS: FASHION INDUSTRIES
AND THE REALITY OF UTOPIAS

It is to Paris that I put my hopes, there men and women are more advanced than
in the little villages of the provinces, where life is so uniform and so monoto-
nous. [...] I have faith in the future, I count upon Paris and I know about the
influence that the capital exercises upon the provinces.[8]

In charting the material matrix of radical ideas and practices, Paris emerges
as the geographical location par excellence for the seamstress to emerge in
the historical stage—*le grand foyer du travail féminin* (Coffin 1996, 44).
Paris, alongside Rouen, was one of the first French cities in pre-revolutionary
France, where seamstresses established independent and all female guilds in
1675. Although clandestine production was part of the labour economy in
the clothing industries,[9] being a member of the guild system was a precondition of the trade, which as Clare Crowston has persuasively shown gradually
became 'both a major actor in the urban economy and a quintessentially
feminine occupation' (2001, 2). What was also distinctive about Paris was the
coexistence of a wide range of trades in response to the demands of a diverse
market that included among others tailors, seamstresses and linen-drapers,
as well as clothing and textile merchants. It goes without saying that there
was a strict sexual division of labour within these various sections in the garment trades, charted within a matrix of hierarchies, antagonistic power relations and gendered discourses at play, famously epitomized in Jean-Jaques
Rousseau's *Emile*: 'The needle and the sword cannot be wielded by the same
hands. If I were a sovereign I would permit sewing and the needle trades only
to women and to cripples reduced to occupations like theirs' (1979, 199).

It was in this context that the seamstress emerged as a modern urban figure
in the gendered histories of the labour movement and there has been a rich
body of feminist scholarship around her, on which I will draw throughout the
book.[10] Indeed, by the end of the eighteenth century, there were around 10,000
seamstresses in Paris, a number that rose to 60,000 by the 1860s, comprising more than half of the female workforce in the French capital, while their
craft had become one of the largest in France (see, Sullerot 1968, 91–92).
The nineteenth century brought significant changes in the Parisian clothing
industry, including the radical technological changes that culminated in the
invention of the sewing machine,[11] as well as the entry of free market forces.
The latter came into play after the abolition of the guild structures in 1791, the
emergence of the ready-made clothing—what the French called *confection*—
as well as the establishment of the first department stores.[12] Thus, although
there was a significant rise of the workforce in the garment trades throughout

the nineteenth century, this was accompanied by mass proletarianization, while the strict hierarchies and divisions of the Old Regime still remained in place: 'Seamstresses, fashion workers, and linen-workers continued to constitute self-consciously distinct occupations and to regard each other with little sisterly solidarity', Crowston has pithily noted (2001, 385).

Moreover, the garment industry was strange in terms of its base, which was never factories, but rather ateliers and workshops dispersed in different urban sites, usually drawing on unskilled or semi-skilled cheap labour force and therefore difficult to unionize. It goes without saying that home-based work or what the French called *le travail à domicile* was at the heart of this labour-intensive, seasonal and exploitative industry. It was, however, its seasonal character—busy in spring and autumn, while slack for several months in winter and summer—that created unbearable conditions of tiredness and exhaustion during the high season, but also opportunities for cultural and political activities during the dead season, particularly so for the skilled and therefore more highly paid workers, whose writings I will analyse and discuss throughout the book.

In this light, the two decades between 1830 and 1850, also known as the *July Monarchy*,[13] were not only marked by fierce political uprisings and constitutional changes but were also a period of intense labour activism. During the 400 strikes that have been recorded in this period,[14] workers came together to demand higher wages, nationally organized labour training and educational opportunities for the people. They also fought against the 1791 *Chapelier Law,* which forbade workers' associations and suppressed their freedom until 1884 when it was finally abolished. It was within such organized political and labour activism, that seamstresses, or *les femmes prolétaires* as they called themselves, took central stage and constituted themselves not only as unionized workers, but also as militant activists in the wider world of republican and later socialist politics.

The July Monarchy, as the historical time of this study, is thus a period where dramatic transformations were initiated in the garment industry, a time of important passages from craftwork to industrialized mass production, from specialized workplaces to home-based work and from highly skilled masters and mistresses to low-paid wage earners. As Joan Scott (1988) has influentially discussed, gender differences were crucial in how seamstresses and tailors reacted and responded to such transformations. More widely the history of the trade has been much more discontinuous, messy and contradictory than the Marxism-influenced analyses of the industrial formations in modernity have been willing to admit. In this context, Coffin has argued that the unruly histories of the garment industry open up ways to problematize linear approaches in the process of industrialization and 'to reflect on the manifold role of gender in that process' (1996, 7).

What has also been downplayed in the complex historical processes of the early industrialization are the multiple links between the seamstresses' activities within the workers' associations and their passionate entanglement in the revolutionary events of the 1830s and of 1848. There is of course an important body of literature on nineteenth-century French feminism,[15] but although the majority of its protagonists were indeed seamstresses, their identity as workers has been stifled by their political identity as socialist utopian feminists, be they Saint-Simonians, Fourierists or Owenites. It is the seamstresses' involvement in these movements that I will discuss next, particularly taking issue with a tendency in the literature to identify the nineteenth-century feminist movement in France as 'Saint-Simonian feminism' and its protagonists as 'Saint-Simonian women'.[16]

Romantic Socialisms

The Saint-Simonian movement and its influences on the political and social movements of modernity have been the object of numerous studies both in French and English historiographies.[17] As I will further discuss in Chapters 1, 3 and 4, what has been highlighted in these studies is the movement's egalitarian position vis-à-vis women, its focus on social issues and questions, including the unique notion of 'social love', as well as its pragmatism in relation to a new organization of work beyond class and gender divisions of labour. The movement's overall ideas were systematically gathered in *The Exposition of the Doctrine of Saint Simon*[18], which included among other principles, peaceful relations between social classes, recognition of the value of work, as well as the abolishment of the inheritance of wealth.

Their egalitarian and peaceful principles notwithstanding, the Saint-Simonians supported private ownership of property but regarded it as a public trust rather than an individual right; they suggested that the means of production should be at the disposal of workers, opposed laissez-faire market modes and asked for central planning and state control over the economy. The social aspects of the Saint-Simonian ideas and visions unsurprisingly became particularly popular among women workers in general and seamstresses in particular, in their double struggle against economic and sexual exploitation. As Scott has noted,

> Dressmakers and seamstresses were amongst those who responded to the Saint-Simonian gospel, outnumbering other categories of the movement's working class disciples and contributing importantly to the *Tribune des Femmes*, a newspaper edited in 1832–1834 entirely by Saint-Simonian women. (1988, 95)

But although the first feminist newspaper, which went through a series of name changes, firstly emerged in the Saint-Simonian publishing circles, it was not 'entirely edited by Saint-Simonian women'.[19] As I will further discuss in Chapter 3, the newspaper's founder Désirée Véret explicitly detached herself from Saint-Simonianism in an article published in the seventh issue of the newspaper on November 4, 1832.[20] Jeanne Deroin, one of its first contributors, had also criticized the religious character and organization of Saint-Simonianism from the very beginning and withdrew from the newspaper and the movement after its fourth issue in September 1832. Her 'Profession of Faith'[21] has become one of the most cited texts in the nineteenth-century feminist literature. In this light, she can nowhere be registered as 'Saint-Simonian'; instead she has been theorized and discussed as an early socialist feminist.[22] Marie-Reine Guindorf, the first editor of the newspaper, who remained on the editorial team throughout its first year, had also turned to Fourierism by the end of 1833 and all her articles are distinctively different from those written by Saint-Simonian contributors. Even Suzanne Voilquin, the Saint-Simonian disciple par excellence, who joined the editorial team after Véret's withdrawal and remained as one of its editors till the end, distanced herself from Saint-Simonian restrictions when she decided to write openly about the conditions of her divorce.[23] A careful reading of this feminist newspaper—the first to be written and edited by women only—thus reveals the diverse ideas of the early socialist feminist movements: although they were significantly influenced by Saint-Simonianism, they cannot be kept within its ideological and organizational boundaries.

As I have already noted above, many of the politically active seamstresses, including Désirée Véret, Marie-Reine Guindorf and Jeanne Deroin were also involved in the Fourierist circles, an equally important social and political movement in nineteenth-century France, which has also attracted a rich body of literature.[24] Although Saint-Simonians and Fourierists shared many egalitarian ideas, there were also some important differences between the two movements. Women in the Saint-Simonian dogma were in need of spiritual guidance in order to attain equality and live in harmony. There was no such need in Fourier's ideas: men and women were born equal and they had the same rights and needs. In this context, sexual freedom for Saint-Simonians was a prerequisite of women's liberation, since women were sexually enslaved; for Fourier, however, sexual freedom was a requirement for both men and women, since their liberation depended on the possibility of expressing emotions and passions. The two movements also had different ideas about the new social order: Saint-Simonians believed that human progress would advance through industrial production and capital accumulation. Despite the many differences among them, Fourier and his followers rejected urban and industrial relations and put forward the project of phalansteries, self-sustained co-operative communities.[25] Finally, although association was a crucial notion for both movements, association bonds were hierarchically and religiously configured for Saint-Simonians, while they were purely economical for Fourierists. Most importantly, Fourier's ideas were tremendously influential for feminist thought as developed in the nineteenth and twentieth centuries:

> As a general thesis: *Social progress and changes from one era to the next are brought about in proportion to the progress of women toward freedom, and social decline is brought about in proportion to the decrease in women's freedom.* Other events influence political change; but there is no other cause that produces so rapid a social improvement or so rapid a social decline as the change in women's lot. (Fourier 1808, cited in Moses 1984, 92, emphasis in the text)

Throughout the book, I will return to the ideas and concepts of the romantic socialist movements of the nineteenth and twentieth centuries and particularly the way we have accepted their 'utopian' character—a label that Marx and Engels (2002) attached to these movements—but which, as Barbara Taylor (1983, 19) has persuasively argued, they have persistently rejected. As I will further discuss in Chapter 3, feminist historian Michèle Riot-Sarcey (1998) has rigorously defended 'the reality' of the nineteenth-century socialist 'utopias', having made an important intervention in the thorny issue of the relations between the social and the political.

The book contributes to this field of theoretical debates by drawing on neo-materialist approaches and particularly Whitehead's (1985) process philosophy. In doing this, the analysis goes beyond the dualistic separation of the material and the spiritual as a way of understanding early socialist feminism. Moreover, it does this not through some abstract theorization, but through a nuanced discussion of women workers' political and personal narratives—an alternative route of political analysis that counterpoises the abstraction of philosophical discourse according to Arendt (1998). But how are these documents to be understood?

LIVES, DOCUMENTS AND NARRATIVE PERSONAE

There is a rich body of literature around early socialist feminism, already highlighted above, but what I argue has been problematic in this scholarship is the way the seamstresses' personal, political and creative narratives have been read, presented and used. As I will further discuss in Chapter 2, the seamstresses' narratives have not been properly analysed as 'documents of life' (Plummer 2001). They mostly appear in a fragmented way, as 'data', as rhetorically powerful quotations, as evidence of the researcher's/writer's argument as well as discourses to be deconstructed. In this context, the reader rarely has an overview of their life as documents, their order of discourse, or their position within the wider archive that they are part of.[26] But as Liz Stanley has pithily noted, 'The idea of "documents of life" is part of the spectrum of narrative and biographical inquiry and it involves an approach or methodology, not just a particular kind of data' (2013, 5). A serious attention to 'how a document is' thus initiates conceptual, methodological and ethical moves that Stanley argues have a decisive impact on the research process, its 'findings' and its 'outputs'.

It is such important gaps in the literature that the book addresses: its aim is to write a feminist genealogy of the Parisian seamstress, exploring her agentic intervention in the sociocultural and political formations of modernity. As a Foucauldian genealogy, the analysis excavates marginalized and submerged documents in the archive and focuses on entanglements of material and discursive practices as inscribed on autobiographical and political writings. There are four areas of radical practices that are particularly highlighted and discussed in their interrelation: work, love, agonistic politics and creativity through writing. These themes have become the topics of the six chapters of this book as outlined below.

Chapter 1 delineates the theoretical framework of the book, bringing together insights from Michel Foucault, Hannah Arendt and Alfred Whitehead. Chapter 2 maps the archive of the research and makes connections between archival research and narrative analysis as a process of knowledge and understanding. The seamstresses' political writings are discussed and analysed in Chapter 3, which particularly focuses on a range of newspapers and pamphlets that they published between 1830 and 1843. Chapter 4 explores questions around love, sexuality, emotions, affects and passions drawing on a range of personal writings and particularly letters. Chapter 5 looks at the seamstresses' involvement in the Parisian uprisings, strikes and insurrections and most importantly in the revolutionary events of 1848. Chapter 6 presents and discusses the seamstresses' creative writings, exploring links between autobiography and fiction. Finally, the conclusion reassembles women workers' radical practices and discusses them in the light of process philosophy.

All chapters draw on different genres of political writings and autobiographical documents including journal articles, political brochures, memoirs, letters and autobiographical fiction. Many of these documents have never been published or translated into English before; I address some of the problems, challenges and pleasures of translation in Chapter 2. In bringing all these diverse documents together I have created a plane of consistency, the 'narrative assemblage' of my genealogy (Tamboukou 2010a). But my analysis is not restricted in discourses and documents; it is also attentive to the authors of these documents, the *narrative personae* of my research: these are conceptual figures that I have come up with over the years that I have been analysing discourses, narratives and authors in their interrelation (see Tamboukou 2010a, 2014a).

In configuring the seamstresses as *narrative personae,* I have followed Deleuze and Guattari's (1994) notion of the 'conceptual personae'—quite simply figures that the philosophers create to stage critical dialogues—but I have also made connections with Arendt's (1990) take of the persona as a theatrical mask, as well as a legal figure. In this context, the *narrative personae* are conceptual figures, whose actions leave behind them storylines to be followed in the pursuit of meaning and understanding. But the fact that we retrace their narratives does not necessarily mean that we find the answer to the burning question of who these seamstresses 'really' were. This is not to deny that they were real persons, but to denote the limitations of stories to convey the essence of who their author is. It is important to note that the lack of essence does not necessarily lead to 'the death of the subject', be it Barthian or Foucauldian. In his late work, Foucault conceptualized the self as a form and looked at the genealogy of its technologies (1988b). Instead of a unified and autonomous subject, there are instead technologies of the self, nomadic passages and subject positions that the *narrative personae* of my inquiries take up and move between, while writing personal and political stories.[27] Moreover, it is through their stories that certain concepts, ideas and events can be expressed, rehearsed and dramatized so that their enactment can create a scene for dialogic exchanges, communication, understanding and action.

Further considered within the realm of rights, the *narrative personae* of my research take up a position in discourse and become figures with whom one can be in dialogue, but also to whom one is responsible: as a feminist narrative researcher I am accountable to them, having taken up the responsibility of presenting their stories as a meaningful form of the self. The latter is open to interpretation and negotiation between you as audience/readers, myself as an author and narrative researcher and my *narrative personae*: although dead many years ago, they are still alive, active and very much among us as their 'words and deeds' still shape feminist histories in the making and therefore the archives of the future. What I therefore want to do now is to briefly sketch the pen-portraits of the three *narrative personae,* Désirée Véret-Gay, Marie-Reine Guindorf and Jeanne Deroin, whose writings will be analysed throughout the book. Other *narrative personae* will also be considered, most notably Suzanne Voilquin (1801–1877), whose memoirs will be discussed in Chapter 6 and thus she is not included in the pen-portraits below.

Désirée Véret-Gay (1810–c.1891)

'I was born on April 4, 1810',[28] Désirée Véret-Gay wrote to the old friend and lover of her youth Victor Considerant,[29] on June 21, 1890, from Place

St Gudule in Brussels. Her twelve letters to Considerant, sent between 1890 and 1891 are 'among the most beautiful and moving documents in the whole Considerant archive', historian Jonathan Beecher (2001, 441) has noted in his extended studies of the Fourierist social movement, wherein Considerant was a leading figure.[30] It is from her extant letters that we have also learnt that Véret-Gay outlived her husband and her two sons: 'I have a free spirit and I am independent due to the little fortune that my beloved sons and my husband have left me',[31] she wrote to Considerant in the same letter above. Looking back at her life, while living in solitude and almost blind, Véret-Gay remembered the revolutionary activities of her youth and her admiration for the apostles of the Saint-Simonian ideas:

> I was searching the light and a thick veil was hiding it from my eyes. However,
> I never despaired, I had faith [...] in a different world [and] here I am in this
> new world, the veil has fallen [...] my eyes have opened, I have seen a beautiful
> picture in the future.[32]

Disillusioned by the way the Saint-Simonian hierarchy marginalized women, despite the egalitarian principles of their doctrine, Véret detached herself from the movement as early as in 1832: 'There is different work to be done. For me all social questions depend on women's freedom',[33] she wrote in *La Femme Nouvelle,* the first feminist newspaper that she had founded with Marie-Reine Guindorf only months before, in August 1832. It was around this time that Véret turned to Fourierism, and in spring 1833 she decided to move to London where she worked as a seamstress for almost two years. Her letters to Charles Fourier reveal that she did not enjoy her life in England: 'My nature has been broken and twisted by civilization. There is in me a chaos I cannot clarify; the longer I live, the more incomprehensible I find myself',[34] she wrote from 37 Duke St, Manchester Square in London.

But despite her difficulties in England, Véret got involved in the Owenite circles and worked closely with Anna Wheeler, 'who was like a second mother to me'.[35] On returning to France in 1834, Véret worked in Dieppe first in the women's clothing industry and then in Paris again, while remaining active in the Fourierist and Owenite circles. It was during this time that she had a brief affair with Considerant:

> I guessed from the beginning your defects and your qualities and in spite of
> myself I loved everything about you. Nothing has escaped my memory: from
> your arrival at Paris in 1832 and your visit with Fugère up until the last time I
> saw you in 1837 at Robert Owen's rooms in the Hôtel de l'Angleterre.[36]

In 1837, Véret married Jules Gay, who was Owen's translator and close follower, and had two sons, Jean in 1838 and Owen in 1842. Together they tried to found an infant's school at Châtillon-sous-Bagneux in 1840; the school was to be based on Owen's pedagogical model of educating children in freedom,[37] but the project did not succeed in the end, perhaps it was too much ahead of its time.

Désirée Gay, as she signed herself after her marriage, immersed herself in labour activism, and later in the fierce politics of the 1848 revolution. Together with Jeanne Deroin she contributed to Eugénie Niboyet's daily newspaper *La Voix des Femmes* between March and June 1848. She then became editor of the *Politique des Femmes,* which only published two issues and was closed down in the aftermath of the June 1848 uprising.

After a second attempt to run the school at Châtillon-sous-Bagneux in 1848, Gay resumed her work as a dressmaker and opened an atelier in the Parisian fashion street par excellence, *rue de la Paix*—a successful enterprise as her 'honourable mention' in the 1855 Paris international exhibition testifies.[38] However, in 1864 Gay had to emigrate once more as her husband's editorial activities were too much ahead of their time: they faced a series of censorship attacks and they finally chose exile to avoid imprisonment. After a short time wandering in Europe, including Belgium, Switzerland and Italy, they eventually settled down in Brussels. During this period, she got involved in the international labour movement and served as the temporary president of the women's section in the central committee of the First Workers' International, held in Geneva in 1866,[39] while in 1868 she published the book *Éducation rationnelle de la première enfance: manuel à l'usage des jeunes mères* in Geneva and London (Gay 1868). Her ideas and impressions about labour politics in general and Belgium in particular are vividly expressed in her letter to Considerant below:

> The movement seen up close here as a whole, in this little Belgian country, is a curious thing to study insofar as it is a mixture of enthusiasm, sentiment and above all, the positivity that typifies the Belgian character. [...] Once upon a time I used to say jokingly that Belgium was a mere baby. Now it is entering its virile passionate stage.[40]

Véret-Gay must have died sometime after July 1891, the date of her last extant letter, but we will never know for sure. Although the seamstress, who signed as Jeanne-Désirée, Désirée Véret, Désirée Gay and also Désirée Véret, veuve Gay, lived a fully active political life, she did not reveal much about her inner thoughts and passions, with the exception of a few letters that I will discuss in Chapter 4. Her political writings in the form of petitions, journal articles and letters have become a significant body in the archive of feminist history that cannot be restricted within the boundaries of Saint-Simonianism, Fourierism, Owenism, utopian socialism or any other labels that have been

attached to the European social movements of the nineteenth century. As I
will further argue throughout the book, it was her entanglement in the material conditions of her work as a seamstress that created conditions of possibility for her political ideas and practices to emerge and unfold, making
connections with, but not reduced to the ideas and discourses of nineteenth-
century romantic socialism.

Marie-Reine Guindorf (1812–1837)

Since we have started our Apostolate, weak, isolated and without any other
resources than those of our needle, we have experienced many difficulties. The
greatest was to make ourselves known, to make the world learn who we are and
finally to appeal to women to help us reach our goal.[41]

In addressing the readers of the newspaper that she co-founded with Véret
in 1832, Marie-Reine Guindorf highlighted the fact that she was writing from
the subject position of a needle worker: indeed, throughout her involvement
in the newspaper it was the proletarian women's rights that she wrote about
with passion and commitment. Like Véret, however, Guindorf was soon
disillusioned by the Saint-Simonian decision to exclude women from its
hierarchy, but unlike her friend and comrade she remained as co-editor of the
newspaper for the whole first year of its publication alongside Voilquin, who
had joined the editorial team after Véret's withdrawal. It is from Guindorf's
articles in the newspaper, as well as Voilquin's published memoirs, *Souvenirs
d'une fille du people,* first published in 1866, that we can have some glimpses
in Guindorf's life and work.

As already boldly stated in her editorial above, Guindorf worked as a seamstress, which was how she got involved in the Saint-Simonian circles. After
the *July* revolution of 1830, many workers, women among them, felt disillusioned by how the French bourgeoisie took advantage of their battles in the
barricades. They thus turned to the Saint-Simonians, who were talking about
real social issues and most importantly the problem of work that was downplayed and ignored in the abstractions of republican politics and discourses:

Oh, I understand, for you writers, the misery of the people is not but a theory,
and you believe that political rights will improve their condition; but don't make
a mistake, it is not this that the people demand, Lyon[42] can teach you better.
Once the people there revolted, [...] have they asked for political rights? No
they have demanded bread and work! Yes, bread and work, this is the motto of
the people! They feel their sufferings and know well that these rights which you
scribble every day in your papers will not give to their children a better education or to them work rewarded enough to make them exit from the misery they
find themselves in.[43]

In responding to the letter of a worker in the journal *Bon Sens,* urging its editors to abandon sterile political discussions and consider ways of material improvement for workers' lives, Guindorf bitterly criticized the intellectuals' ignorance of the situation of the working classes: 'What would you say of a man who seeing one of his peers dying from lack of essential needs was given a nice lecture on the freedom of the press, instead of being given necessary support? No doubt you would find it ridiculous',[44] she wrote. The need to be practical and help workers improve the material conditions of their lives was thus at the heart of Guindorf's ideas and actions and what had initially attracted her to their circles. Indeed after the *July days* Saint-Simonians had organized outreach programmes in the working-class Parisian arrondissements, which as Moses has noted included weekly lectures, 'a special teaching programme and two cooperative workshops, one for tailors and one for seamstresses' (1984, 45). Guindorf was very active in the debates around public education between 1833 and 1834, the years that the *Loi Guizot* that established state primary schools was implemented.[45] As she wrote in February 1833:

> Public education is a question that at the moment preoccupies all advanced people, reasonably so, because the future of society depends on its solution. It is education that will transform gross and ignorant people to human beings who are calm, know their duties and their rights and accomplish the first so as to have the right to demand the latter. In this important question I think that it is useful that women should make their voice heard.[46]

Guindorf participated actively in a series of conferences that *The Society for Educational Methods* organized in Paris between 1833 and 1834 on the problem of 'improving the great intellectual movement which is manifested among women' and wrote critically in the *Tribune des femmes* about it: 'Here we have arrived at the sixth conference on the same question, and is the solution more advanced than in the first day? I don't think so. On the contrary, the question has turned: instead of searching ways to use women's intelligence, we now search for ways to develop it. This constitutes the fact that the question was badly posed',[47] she wrote in January 1834. By that time, she had left the editorial team of the *Tribune des Femmes* to throw herself as a volunteer to women workers' education. In writing a tribute to Guindorf in the last issue of the first feminist newspaper, Voilquin noted:

> Marie-Reine, my co-editor for a long time stopped only to satisfy her life sympathy for the people, in 1833 she was accepted as a member of the Association for Peoples' Education; since then her days have been devoted to work and her evenings have been employed for the education of women and the daughters of the people.[48]

It is in Voilquin's *Souvenirs* that the tragic details of Guindorf's suicide in July 1837 can be traced.[49] By that time, Guindorf had been married to Flichi, a young Saint-Simonian, who had also become a Fourierist like her; they had a son born in 1835 and were making plans for a phalanstery. In Voilquin's view, who had lived with the couple for six weeks in January 1837, Guindorf had everything that a young woman might have desired: a husband who loved her, an adorable baby boy and a nice Parisian apartment given to the couple by an unexpected inheritance of her parents. And yet her body was retrieved from Le Pont de Grenelle of the river Seine on July 1, 1837, after she had gone missing for some days. Voilquin's speculation is that Guindorf had fallen in love with a Fourierist intellectual and proponent of free love and that she eventually chose death as a solution to the emotional impasse she had found herself in, but we will never know. Her suicide was not the only one among the feminist women of the early socialist movements, a theme that I will further discuss in Chapter 4.

Jeanne Deroin (1805–1894)

'I was never familiar with the joys of infancy or the games of early childhood. From the time I learned to read, reading became my sole occupation and the charm of my every moment. I felt a vague desire to experience and know everything',[50] Jeanne Deroin wrote in her *Profession of Faith* a rich and powerful text sent to the Saint-Simonian newspaper, the *Globe,* where she boldly lays out her beliefs, her thoughts, her hopes and her fears. It is from this document that we can trace some autobiographical inscriptions since Deroin never wrote a memoir.[51] It is also from archival documents of the City of Paris that Michèle Serrière (1981) has found that Deroin was born on December 5, 1805. Although nothing is known about her parents, it is again from a letter that Deroin wrote towards the end of her life to Hubertine Auclert, a young feminist delegate of the Workers' Congress in Marseilles in 1879, that we know that she grew up in poverty: 'Born in the beginning of imperial despotism, I was profoundly moved by the mists and anxieties of mothers and the massacres of the war victims. Poor me, I saw from a very close distance the sufferings of the disinherited'.[52] Growing up as a working-class woman, Deroin had to put aside her dream for education and she became a seamstress as she had to earn her bread:

> Still too young to appreciate my social position, I was happy. The future seemed bright and gracious. I saw myself rich with the treasures of knowledge, unique object of my wishes, but these gratifying dreams would soon fade away. The necessity of work, made me understand that deprived of wealth, I had to renounce knowledge, happiness, I resigned to myself.[53]

But Deroin did not really resign. Like many of her contemporaries, she got involved in the Saint-Simonian circles and although deeply critical of their religious character she tried to see the advantages of the movement:

> I ignored the existence of Saint-Simonism, but the reading of some passages of the *Globe,* have excited my attention. My preventions against all religious institutions have not disposed me favourably in welcoming a new religion. [...] The explications that were given to me by a member of the society, Monsieur Deroches and the conscious examination of the principles of the Doctrine dispelled my suspicions. I have got the conviction that the real goal of Saint-Simonism is the happiness of humanity, and this persuasion was sufficient to inspire in me a most lively sympathy.[54]

It was indeed through her friend Antoine Ulysse Desroches, who eventually became her husband, that Deroin got to have 'some sympathy' for the Saint-Simonians, but sympathy it remained. Although she worked with many Saint-Simonian women in different fori, she remained distanced from and critical of the movement and particularly of its religious and mystic ideas and dogmas. Deroin was among the first women who wrote in *La Femme Libre*: her *Appeal to Women,* was published in the first issue of the newspaper in August 1832, was translated into English by Anna Wheeler and was reprinted in the Owenite newspaper *The Crisis* in June1833:

> When the whole of the people are roused in the name of Liberty, and the labouring class demand their freedom, shall we women remain passive and inert spectators of this great movement of social emancipation, which takes place under our eyes?[55]

Influential as her first article was on both sides of the channel, Deroin only wrote one more article, published in the fourth issue of the newspaper[56] and then she withdrew. As she explained in the letter she wrote to Auclert, she was indignant at the way some women in the Saint-Simonian circles understood the idea of free love.[57]

Little is known about Deroin's life between 1832 and 1848 apart from the fact that she gave birth to three children—two daughters and a son—and that caring for her family occupied a great deal of her time. But it was also during these years that after some failed attempts, she eventually became a qualified teacher and opened a school for children, which she ran until the 1848 revolution.

Having distanced herself from the Saint-Simonian gospel, Deroin was influenced by Fourier's ideas, but also by other socialist theorists of the period, including Pierre Leroux and Etienne Cabet.[58] Moreover, Flora Tristan's idea of *The Workers' Union* (1843) inspired Deroin's attempts to form a workers' association, a project that eventually led to her arrest and imprisonment in 1850. Deroin was indeed immersed in the events of the 1848 revolution from a range of politically agonistic positions: as a 'femme libre', a journalist and a *clubiste*,[59] a workers' delegate, as well as a candidate in the 1849 legislative election—the first woman to stand in a national election. To do this she closed the school, left her children to the care of their father and took back the name of her revolutionary youth. This is how she wrote about her political activity to Léon Richer,[60] founder of the French League for Women's Rights:

> When in 1848, I wrote and spoke in public, I did not do it because I thought I was talented, but because I was excited by a powerful impulsion, which surmounted my natural timidity through the conviction that I had to accomplish the mission that had inspired me since my youth. When M. Eugène Pelletan told me one day that I was acting as if I were firing a gun in the middle of the street to attract attention, he was right, but it was not to attract attention to myself but to the cause that I was devoted to. This is why I stood in the National Assembly, having previously asked Mme George Sand and Pauline Roland to do it; they refused and that is why I did it: I was convinced that I had to knock on all closed doors.[61]

Already from prison as well as after her release, Deroin continued her revolutionary activities mostly through writing. The first volume of her *Almanach des Femmes* was published in Paris in the beginning of 1852, but in August she took refuge in London in fear of more persecution and imprisonment. Her children joined her in 1853, but not her invalid husband who died from exhaustion and the anxieties of his family adventures. It was in London that she got involved in the socialist circles of the time: she published the second volume of the *Almanach* as a French/English bilingual edition in 1853, while its third volume in 1854 was Deroin's last extant publication. It was also in her struggle to survive that she took up the needle again and worked as an embroiderer, as well as a private tutor in French. Life was difficult for Deroin in the first decade of her exile. In 1861, she opened a school for the children of foreigners and exiles, but as she wrote to Richer, the school was a financial failure:

> These two years were a period of great distress for me and my children, because of the lack of fees payment from most of my pupils, whose parents were very poor. [...] I can't enter into more detail about the difficulty of our situation, aggravated by the illness of my son.[62]

Deroin outlived her son and her younger daughter and went through her old age with the support of a pension of six hundred francs that she eventually got from the French government in 1880. Her last extant thoughts for a different future are inscribed in the letter she wrote to Auclert in early January 1886:

Thanks for your nice letter and your good wishes to me for a long life, which I desire and I hope to be realized, not because I believe in a complete triumph of our aspirations in my present life but because I wish I could work a bit more, before passing to my following life, with all the ardour of my religious and social convictions and with more experience and intellectual power to manifest them.[63]

It is from the same letter that we know that she had been working on her autobiography, which she never finished: 'I have not gathered yet all the necessary notes for my biography, which I am preoccupied with in the hope of being useful and which will probably appear, after I have entered a different existence',[64] she wrote, but a full biography of hers has yet to be written. Deroin died forgotten by her contemporaries and has remained a riddle even in contemporary feminist debates. Throughout the book I will draw on a number of biographical sketches and references that have been written about her life and work,[65] particularly taking issue with Scott's (1996) argument that Deroin had 'only paradoxes to offer' in the debates around political rights.

NOTES

1. Minutes of the trial, cited in Serrière 1981, 20.
2. For an overview of the seamstresses' representation in socioeconomic and historical studies of the nineteenth and twentieth centuries, see Coffin 1996. See also, Walkley 1981; Rowbotham 1993; Green 1997; Crowston 2001.
3. I refer here to Thomas Hood 'Song of the Shirt', which was published in the popular magazine *Punch* in 1843 and had a lasting effect on sensitizing the public about the dreadful working and living conditions of the Victorian seamstress.
4. See Amireh 2000; Alexander 2003; Harris 2005 for a rich overview of cultural representations of the seamstress.
5. I refer here to the French opera *Louise* written in 1896 by Gustave Charpentier.
6. See among others: Voilquin 1866, 1869; Keckley 2006 [1868]; Bouvier 1983 [1936]; Pesotta 1987 [1944] and 1958.
7. The Rana Plaza disaster in April 2013, when 1,129 garment workers lost their lives after the collapse of an eight-storied garment factory building in the wider area of Dhaka in Bangladesh is a painful reminder of the need for histories of the present to inform current actions and policies in the garment industry and beyond.
8. Letter from Augustine, a young proletarian woman to the *Tribune des Femmes-La Femme Nouvelle* 1(17), 228, April/May 1833.
9. See Coffin 1996, particularly Chapter 1.
10. See among others: Scott 1988; Coffin 1996; DeGroat 1997; Green 1997; Rogers 1997; Crowston 2001.
11. There were a range of sewing machine technological developments in the late eighteenth century, but the first sewing machine that came was patented in 1829 by the

French artisan Barthélemy Thimonnier; it was fiercely opposed by tailors, becoming obsolete by 1845, but it was triumphantly revived by Singer in the 1860s and 1870s. See Coffin, 1996, particularly Chapters 2 and 3.

12. *Bon Marché* was the first Parisian department store to open in 1852, but the first generation of these stores was the *magasins de nouveautés,* of the 1820s and 1830s. For a history of Parisian department stores, see among others: Miller 1981.

13. Also known as the 'bourgeois monarchy', this is the period of the reign of Louis-Philippe (1830–1848) who was brought to the throne after the 1830 July revolution that led to the abdication of Charles X and the fall of the Bourbon monarchy. For historical studies about the July Monarchy 1830–1848, see among others: Pinkney 1973; Pilbeam 1983; Popkin 2010.

14. Roger Magraw has noted that 89 strikes broke out only in the period between 1830 and 1833 (1992, 53).

15. See among others: Bell and Offen 1983; Moses 1984; Cross and Gray 1992; Moses and Rabine 1993; Scott 1996; Gordon and Cross 1996; Draper 2011.

16. See Moses and Rabine 1993, particularly Chapter 2.

17. For an overview of the literature on the Saint-Simonian movement and ideas, see Pilbeam 2014.

18. Their *Exposition* included their religious principles as well that have been widely discussed in the Saint-Simonian literature, but go beyond the remits of this chapter.

19. I will further discuss these name changes and the overall history of the journal in Chapter 3.

20. *Apostolat des Femmes-La Femme Nouvelle* 1(7), 69, November 4, 1832. See also, Riot-Sarcey 1992, 1994.

21. BnF, Bibliothèque de l'Arsenal, Fonds Enfantin ou Fonds Saint-Simonien/ Ms7608/112 lettres/Correspondence du Globe (Dames), (BnF/BdA/FE/MS7608/ CdG/Deroin). Also transcribed and published by Riot-Sarcey (1992, 116–39).

22. See Ranvier 1897, 1908, 1909; Serrière 1981; Riot-Sarcey 1992 and 1994; Scott 1996; Draper 2011; Rancière 2012.

23. See the very last issue of the second volume of the *Tribune des Femmes-La Femme Nouvelle,* April 1834.

24. For an overview of this literature and of the Fourierist ideas, see Beecher 1986, 2001.

25. For the organization of these communities, see 'The Phalanstery' in Beecher and Bienvenu, 1971.

26. It has to be noted here that Bell and Offen (1983) and Moses and Rabine (1993) have translated and presented lengthy extracts of some important feminist writings of the July Monarchy. Apart from some very short introductions, however, these documents have not been further analysed.

27. See Tamboukou (2003a) for a discussion of technologies of the female self.

28. Désirée Véret, veuve Gay to Victor Considerant, letter dated, June 21, 1890. Archives Nationales 10AS 42(8), 59, 2, (AnF/10AS42/8/DVG/59/2).

29. Victor Considerant (1808–1893) was a follower of Charles Fourier's ideas and a significant historical figure in the movement of French Romantic Socialism. See Beecher 2001 for a rich intellectual biography.

30. See Beecher 1986, 2000, 2001.

31. Véret-Gay to Considerant, letter dated, June 21 1890, (AnF/10AS42/8/DVG/59/2).

32. Véret to Enfantin, letter dated September 11, 1831, 1. Bibliothèque de l'Arsenal, Fonds Enfantin, Ms7608/Correspondance du Globe (Dames)/Désirée (J.)/4 lettres/40(1) [in microform] (BnF/BdA/FE/Ms7608/CdG(D)/DJ/40,1). Also in Michèle Riot-Sarcey 1992, 69–70.

33. 'From my work you will know my name', *Apostolat des Femmes-La Femme Nouvelle,* 1(7), 69–70, November 4, 1832.

34. Véret to Charles Fourier, letter dated August 14, 1833, transcribed and published by Riot-Sarcey 1995, 6.

35. Véret-Gay to Considerant, letter dated, September 7, 1890, (AnF/10AS42/8/DVG/62/2).

36. Véret-Gay to Considerant, letter dated, October 2, 1890, (AnF/10AS42/8/DVG/64/2).

37. For Owen's educational ideas, see among others: Donnachie 2000.

38. See, letterhead of Gay's letter to Enfantin, dated May 28, 1856: '*Exposition Universelle 1855, Mention Honorable, Mme Gay, Modes, Rue de La Paix 19*', (BNF/BA/FE/CD/7728/163). See also Riot-Sarcey (1994, 281, 343).

39. Véret-Gay to Considerant, letter dated, September 17, 1890, (AnF/10AS42/8/DVG/63/2).

40. Désirée Véret, veuve Gay to Victor Considerant, letter dated, October 3, 1890, (AnF/10AS42/8/DVG/64/3).

41. Marie-Reine Guindorf, 'To our readers' in *La Femme Libre-Apostolat des Femmes,* 1(6), 41–43, October 1832.

42. Here, Guindorf refers to the first silk workers' uprising in Lyon, further discussed in Chapter 3.

43. Guindorf, 'Response' in the *Apostolat des Femmes-La Femme Nouvelle,* 1(6), 48–50, October 1832.

44. Ibid.

45. The *Loi Guizot* of 1833 reduced illiteracy through the establishment of state primary education, but it had many problems: primary education was not made compulsory and was only free for children of very poor families. Although every commune of more than 600 inhabitants was obliged to operate a boys' school as well as a training college for teachers, there was no provision for girls, whose education was dependent on whether there was space, a ridiculous condition that Guindorf wrote vehemently against. Yet, girls had to wait until the *Loi Duruy* of 1867 to have the same educational opportunities. For an overview of girls' education in France, see Anderson 1975.

46. Guindorf, 'Response' in the *Apostolat des Femmes-La Femme Nouvelle,* 1(12), 144–47, February, 1832.

47. Guindorf, 'Society for Educational Methods' in the *Tribune des Femmes-La Femme Nouvelle,* 2(6), 93–96, January 1834.

48. Suzanne Voilquin, *Tribune des Femmes-La Femme Nouvelle* 2(11), 182.

49. See Voilquin 1866, Chapitre XXXIX 'Suicide de Marie-Reine', 479–82.

50. Deroin, 'Profession of Faith', (BnF/BdA/FE/MS7608/CdG/Deroin/22). Also, in Riot-Sarcey 1992, 128.

51. According to Adrien Ranvier (1897, 198), Deroin was in the process of writing her *Souvenirs de 1848* in 1880, but this work was never completed and there were only fragments of her political writings among the papers that she gave to Ranvier, but which have now unfortunately disappeared. Some of these writings have been included in Ranvier's biographical sketches (1897, 1908, 1909), and most notably her *Testament*, which has been published in its entirety (Deroin 1909).

52. Jeanne Deroin, veuve Desroches to Hubertine Auclert, letter dated, January 10, 1886. Bibliothèque Historique De la Ville de Paris, Archives Marie-Louise Bouglé, Autographs, Jeanne Deroin, Carton 4247, 9 lettres, (BHVP/AMB/Au/CP4247/JD).

Also transcribed in la Bibliothèque Marguerite Durand, Recueil: Deroin, Jeanne. Dossier documentaire. (BMD/R/DJ/DD)

53. BnF/BdA/FE/MS7608/CdG/Deroin/23. Also, in Riot-Sarcey 1992, 128–29.

54. Ibid., 30–31 and 132–33.

55. Jeanne-Victoire [Deroin], *La Femme Libre-Apostolat des Femmes* 1 (1) 1–3, August 15, 1832. For different translations of this article, see Bell and Offen 1983, 146–47 and Moses and Rabine 1993, 282–84. I discuss the challenges of various translations in Chapter 2.

56. Jeanne-Victoire [Deroin]'Alliance of Science and Industry' in *Apostolat des Femmes-La Femme Nouvelle* 1(4), 1–2, September 19, 1832.

57. Deroin to Auclert, letter dated, January 10, 1886, (BHVP/AMLB/Au/CP4247/JD).

58. Pierre Leroux's *De La Ploutocratie*, published in 1848, had criticized the accumulation of the means of production in the hands of the few, while Etienne Cabet's *Voyage to Icaria*, first published in 1840, was propagating an egalitarian and harmonious communist society.

59. 'Clubistes' were the members of the many revolutionary clubs that erupted in Paris during the 1848 revolution. For a historical overview of these clubs and electoral committees, see Alphonse Luca's 1851 classical study, *Les Clubs et les Clubistes*.

60. For a discussion of Léon Richer's relations with nineteenth-century feminists and the politics of the French League for Women's Rights (1882–1891), see Bidelman 1976.

61. Deroin to Léon Richer, *Bibliothèque Historique de la Ville de Paris*, Archives Marie-Louise Bouglé, Autographs, Carton 4247, (BHVP/AMLB/Au/CP4247/JD).

62. Deroin to Richer, letter dated 1857, (BHVP/AMLB/Au/CP4247/JD).

63. Deroin to Auclert, letter dated, January 10, 1886, (BHVP/AMLB/Au/CP4247/JD).

64. Ibid.

65. See Ranvier 1897, 1908, 1909; Thomas 1948; Adler 1979; Serrière 1981; Zerilli 1982; Riot-Sarcey 1989 and 1994; Scott 1996; Pilbeam 2003; Draper 2011.

Chapter 1

Adventures in a Culture of Thought

Genealogies, Narratives, Process

'If a woman counts on making a living with her needle, she will either die of hunger or go into the street', Jules Simon gloomily predicted in his 1860 influential study *L'Ouvrière,* a publication that presented and indeed constructed women's labour as the nineteenth-century social problem par excellence (1860, 193). Although differently configured, women's work is still a problem, while the seamstress is a central figure in the assemblage of antagonistic power relations, discourses and material practices that have been interwoven around this problem during the last two centuries. It is thus genea-logical analytics in the study of the seamstress that I chart in this chapter. But how is the genealogical approach to be understood?

Questions of truth are at the heart of Foucauldian analytics, which have been motivated by the Nietzschean insight that truth cannot be separated from the procedures of its production. Consequently, genealogy is concerned with the processes, procedures and apparatuses, whereby truth and knowledge are produced, in the discursive regimes of modernity. Drawing on the Enlighten-ment suggestion of 'emancipation from self-imposed immaturity' (Rajchman 1985, 56), the Foucauldian genealogy writes the history of the present: it problematizes the multiple, complex and non-linear configurations of the sociopolitical and cultural formations of modernity. What are the conditions of the possibility for needlework to emerge as the feminine labour problem par excellence, how has the seamstress been marginalized in the social and political movements in modernity and why is women's work still a riddle even among feminist theorizations and debates?

In addressing the historicity of such present questions and problems, gene-alogy conceives subjectivities and social relations as an effect of the inter-weaving of discourses and practices, which it sets out to trace and explore. As Foucault has clearly put it, 'I set out from a problem expressed in the

terms current today and I try to work out its genealogy. Genealogy means that
I begin my analysis from a question posed in the present' (1988a, 262). But
instead of seeing history as a continuous development of an ideal schema,
genealogy is orientated to discontinuities. Throughout the genealogical
exploration there are frequent disruptions, uneven and haphazard processes of
dispersion, that call into question the supposed linear evolution of history. In
this context of reversal, our present is not theorized as the result of a meaningful development, but rather as an event, a random result of the interweaving
of relations of power and domination. Genealogy as a method of analysis
searches in the maze of dispersed events to trace discontinuities, recurrences
and play where traditional historiography sees continuous development,
progress and seriousness. Women's work in the garment industry is a paradigmatic case of uneven historical developments and its study seriously devi-
ates from the canon of analysing the industrial formations in modernity. As
Coffin has aptly pointed out, 'In many instances, concerns to preserve gender
hierarchies trumped economic rationality, technological efficiency or political self interest' in the economic histories of the garment industry (1996, 6).

In this light, Foucault's take on genealogy as 'eventalization' is particularly pertinent, not only to the study of needlework, but also to the relations
between labour and political activism, which is at the heart of this study.
Eventalization is a different approach to the ways in which traditional historians have dealt with the notion of the event. It begins with the interrogation of
certain evidences in our culture about how things should be: 'making visible
a singularity at places where there is a temptation to invoke a historical constant, an immediate anthropological trait, or an obviousness which imposes
itself uniformly on all' (Foucault 1991, 76). This breach of self-evidences
also requires a rethinking of the various power relations that at a certain
historical moment decisively influenced the way things were socially and
historically established. As Foucault notes, this rethinking reveals 'a sort of
multiplication or pluralisation of causes' (ibid.). This means that the genealogist does not regard singularity as simply an isolated piece of data to
be added to his/her documents. The event under scrutiny is to be analysed
within the matrix of discursive and material practices that have given rise to
its existence, but also in the light of its effects in the historical course and the
historical imagination.

Take for example 'the ephemeral newspapers' that the seamstresses
edited and published between 1830 and 1850 that I will further discuss in
Chapters 3 and 5. If considered simply as short-lived publication events, they
are stripped of their forceful and unprecedented intervention in the political
histories of nineteenth-century France, as well as the history of feminism
overall. 'Feminism failed in France [because] it came early [and] burned
itself out', historian Theodore Zeldin has argued (cited in Moses 1984, 230).

Feminist historians have successfully refuted such evaluations: 'It is now clear that feminism which indeed came early in France, was frustrated at the start and that its progress was slowed—not because it "burned itself out" but because repressive governments repeatedly burned feminism', Claire Moses has responded (1984, 230). But what does 'coming early' mean? It certainly presupposes a linear process where things happen when their conditions are mature—a Hegelian and Marxist understanding of the historical process par excellence.

But the event within the genealogical approach is not just something that happens. Rather it is something that makes new things happen, disturbing the order of what we do, the certainty of how we perceive the world and ourselves. Philosophers of the *event* have seen it as a glimpse into the unreachable, the yet to come (Nietzsche 1990), a transgression of the limitations of the possible (Foucault 1963), a flash in the greyness of the virtual worlds that surround us (Deleuze 2001). As Gilles Deleuze has poetically put it, 'The event is not what occurs (an accident), it is rather inside what occurs, the purely expressed. It signals and awaits us.... It is what must be understood, willed and represented in that which occurs' (2001,170). Departing from good sense, the *event* sticks out from the ordinary, marks historical discontinuities and opens up the future to a series of differentiations. But how are such ruptures and differentiations to be studied?

Taking eventalization as a mode of understanding, the genealogist does not look beyond or behind historical practices to find a simple unity of meaning or function. The aim is rather to look more closely at the workings of those practices in which norms and truths have been constructed. Instead of going deep, looking for origins and hidden meanings, the analyst is working on the surface, constructing 'a polygon or rather a polyhedron' (Foucault 1991, 77) of various minor processes that surround the emergence of the event. What is to be remembered is the fact that the more the analysis breaks down practices, the easier it becomes to find out more about their interrelation, while this process can never have a final end.

As the genealogical turn to the past can never reach an origin—it rather encounters numberless beginnings—an important task of the genealogist is to identify points of *emergence*, critical historical moments when 'dissonant' events erupt in the course [and discourse] of history. *Emergence* refers then to a particular historical moment when things appeared as events on the stage of history. It is in the context of intense power relations at play that Foucault stabilizes this 'moment of arising' (1986a, 83). In this light, *emergence* is not the effect of individual tactics, but *an event*, an episode in a non-linear historical process. The analysis of *emergence* is not about why, but about how things happened; it is about scrutinizing the complex and multifarious processes that surround the emergence of the event. The publication of the first feminist newspaper *La Femme Libre* in August 1832, is a genealogical *emergence* par excellence: it erupted in the middle of the young seamstresses' engagement in the material conditions and restraints of their needlework. It also emerged as an effect of their political involvement in the glorious July days[1] as well as their association with the Saint-Simonian circles, which took up 'the social question' that had been neglected by the 1830 bourgeois revolution.

In tracing and analysing this complex nexus of power relations, discourses and practices that surround the emergence of the event, the genealogist has taken up the methodological move of charting a *dispositif*. As Foucault sees it, a *dispositif* is a system of relations that can be established between hetero-geneous elements, discursive and non-discursive practices, 'the said as well as the unsaid' (1980, 194). As a diagram of power par excellence, the *dispositif* relates to certain types of knowledge, which derive from it, but also condition it and includes 'discourses, institutions, architectural arrangements, regula-tions, laws, administrative measures, scientific statements, philosophic propo-sitions, morality, philanthropy, etc.' (ibid.). Women's work in the garment industry in the beginning of the nineteenth century is thus configured as a genealogical *dispositif* par excellence: it includes antagonistic labour relations and fierce gendered discourses embedded in the old hierarchies and structures of the clothing trades, the new economic forces of the early industrial era, as well as the radical technological changes that took the trade by storm. Such economic changes are related to a series of uprisings and turmoils in the polit-ical arena of the July Monarchy; they further make powerful connections with the romantic socialist movements of the nineteenth century, which opened up paths for feminist ideas and practices to emerge and unfold. In charting lines of this powerful *dispositif* what has also emerged is an assemblage of forces of desire and imagination that have to be considered alongside restraining discourses and structures of domination. Here Gilles Deleuze's and Felix Guattari's intervention in the philosophies of the *dispositifs* has been crucial.

In reading Foucault, Deleuze has underlined two important consequences arising from the concept of the *dispositif*: the rejection of universals, and a drive away from the Eternal and towards the new. As he has written, 'The new is the current. The current is not what we are but rather what we are in the process of becoming—that is the Other, our becoming other' (1992, 163–64). He therefore concludes that in each *dispositif* it is necessary to distinguish the historical part, what we are (what we are already no longer) and the current part, what we are in the process of becoming. Deleuze has further described the *dispositif as* 'a tangle, a multilinear ensemble' (ibid., 159), composed of lines and zones that are difficult to determine and localize. These lines are usually deployed in unforeseen directions, while it is amidst crises that new lines are created, and new directions open (ibid., 160). As Deleuze sees it, in each *dispositif,* the analysis has 'to untangle the lines of the recent past and those of the near future: that which belongs to the archive and that which belongs to the present' (ibid., 164). But how can lines of an open, radical future be traced? It is here I argue that Deleuze and Guattari's notion of the assemblage[2]—a configuration that is more directed to future becomings—makes fruitful connections with the Foucauldian *dispositif,* a diagram of existing power relations, 'the stubborn fact of the present' for Alfred Whitehead (1958, 44) as I will further discuss.

Unlike closed organisms, structural systems and fixed identities, assemblages do not have any organizing centre; they can only function as they connect with other assemblages in a constant process of becoming. An assemblage is defined as a conjunction 'of bodies, of actions and passions, an intermingling of bodies reacting to one another' on the level of content, but also as a nexus 'of acts and statements, of incorporeal transformations attributed to bodies' on the level of enunciation (Deleuze and Guattari 1988, 88). The assemblage thus allows for the possibility of open configurations, continuous connections and intense relations, incessantly transforming life. Given their polyvalent form as conjunctions of heterogeneous elements and as sites for the interplay of intense forces, the *dispositif* and the *assemblage* create a plane where Foucault's and Deleuze and Guattari's analytics can make connections.

As I will further discuss throughout the book, desire as a social force producing the real was at the heart of how the seamstresses immersed themselves in the revolutionary events of the July Monarchy. In this light, the seamstresses' radical practices in the beginning of the nineteenth century can be seen as a plane for multiplicities to emerge and make connections, as a contested site for power relations and flows of desire to be enacted, in short as both a *dispositif* and an *assemblage,* on the grounds of which unknown landscapes emerge in a future that was open and in the process of 'becoming other'. But how are we to understand *process*?

PROCESS AND BECOMINGS

It is well-known that in writing about 'becomings' and 'events' Deleuze drew heavily on Whitehead's philosophy, wherein process and transformation are central ideas.[3] 'The actual world is a process and process is the becoming of actual entities', Whitehead has famously written in his major philosophical work *Process and Reality* (1985, 22). Process is constitutive of experience for Whitehead and 'involves the notion of a creative activity belonging to the very essence of each occasion' (1968, 151). Being at the heart of Whitehead's philosophy, process has to be conceptually differentiated from what we usually understand as 'the historical process'. As Whitehead has pointed out, process should not be taken as 'a procession of forms', but as 'forms of process' (ibid., 140). What he means by making this distinction is that process in his conceptual vocabulary is not about a series of transformations of pre-existing forms but actually a mode 'of eliciting into actual being factors in the universe which antecedently to that process exist only in the mode of unrealised potentialities' (ibid., 151).

Whitehead also differentiates his own approach to process from the long philosophical tradition of flows and fluxes that goes back to Heraclitus: 'All things flow [but] what sorts of things flow? [...] what is the meaning of the many things engaged in this common flux, and in what sense, if any, can the word "all" refer to a definitely indicated set of these many things'? Moreover, how does this state of flux relate to its antithesis, 'the permanences of things—the solid earth, the mountains, the stones, the Egyptian Pyramids', Whitehead has critically asked (1985, 208). In responding to such questions, Whitehead has noted that there are two kinds of fluency: the fluency of becoming a particular existent, which he calls 'concrescence' and the fluency whereby an entity that has already become enters a process of new becomings—what he calls 'transition' (ibid., 210). In marking concrescence and transition as two kinds of fluency in the constitution of reality, Whitehead keeps flux and permanence together in his philosophy of the organism: 'We are in the present; the present is always shifting; it is derived from the past; it is shaping the future; it is passing into the future' (1968, 53).

Moreover, there are two species of process for Whitehead: the macroscopic and the microscopic: 'The former . . . effects the transition from the actual to the merely real. . . . The latter effects the growth from the real to the actual' (1985, 215). In this sense, every actual entity for Whitehead is complete as a microscopic process, but it is always incomplete in terms of its participation in the macroscopic process of the universe. As Steven Shaviro has pithily pointed out, Whitehead's understanding of reality as process moves the analytical interest from the philosophical question of 'why is there something rather than nothing' to the more sociologically driven one of 'how is that there is always something new' (2012, x)?

It is this interest of understanding process in how things change that is crucial in the seamstresses' genealogy: many of their actions have been downplayed and dismissed as short-lived, insignificant and inconsequential in the master narratives of history. Should they be considered, however, in the twofold configuration of concrescence and transition on both the macroscopic and microscopic levels, a different evaluation of their involvement in the historical process emerges, as well as a need to scrutinize and understand the minutiae of change, as I will further discuss.

Whitehead's way of looking at the 'how' of becomings goes through the work of 'prehensions', a notion he uses to denote understanding not necessarily linked to cognition: 'I will use the word prehension for uncognitive apprehension: apprehension that may or may not be cognitive' (1967a, 69). Prehensions are used to configure how an 'actual entity'—his term for denoting 'sensible objects'[4] (1985, 73)—becomes through the awareness of its environment: 'I use the term "prehension" for the general way in which the occasion of experience can include, as part of its own essence, any other entity, whether another occasion of experience or an entity of another type' (Whitehead 1967b, 234). What is realized according to Whitehead is 'a gathering of things into the unity of a prehension [which] defines itself as a here and a now and the things so gathered into the grasped unity have essential references to other places and other times' (Whitehead 1967a, 69). The notion of 'prehensions' thus enables Whitehead to map the complexity of the relational process of becoming in his overall theory of feelings.[5]

Whitehead actually draws on the experience of listening to music to give a concrete example of how prehensions work: 'Consider the audition of sound', he writes, and 'to avoid unnecessary complexity, let the sound be one definite note. The audition of this note is a feeling' (1985, 234). We follow Whitehead's example to this point, often wondering about what is new in this exposition of listening to music as a feeling. But here comes the unexpected twist: although 'the feeling has first an auditor, who is the subject of the feeling', this subject only emerges through listening to this note, he or she is constituted through the experience of listening to this note of music and cannot be perceived independently of or outside this particular experience: 'The auditor would not be the auditor that he is apart from this feeling of his' (ibid.).

We already have two elements in Whitehead's schema of prehensions so far: (a) the subject who listens [becoming a subject through listening] and (b) the note of music that is being listened to, which also emerges from 'a complex environment composed of certain other actual entities, which however vaguely, is felt by reason of this audition [...] the datum of this feeling' (ibid.), in Whitehead's vocabulary. Although conscious in its elevated form of recognizing this particular note of music, the feeling as mapped by Whitehead presupposes, among other spatio/temporal conditions, a nexus of 'antecedent physiological functioning of the human body' (ibid.) in a way that 'the nature apprehended in awareness and the nature which is the cause of awareness' cannot be separated, Whitehead has argued in his famous thesis against the 'bifurcation of nature' (1964, 30). But there is also a third important part in the schema of prehensions as exemplified in the actual occasion of listening: 'an emotional sensory pattern, the subjective form' in short the conditions within which the note is being listened to, which include not only the qualitative pattern of the note, its 'pitch, quality and intensity', but also 'the qualitative and quantitative auditory contributions derived from various nerve routes of the body', as well as 'qualities of joy and distaste, of adversion and of aversion' or what Whitehead has configured as 'positive and negative prehensions' (1985, 234).

The example of listening to the note of music thus lucidly fleshes out Whitehead's eleventh category of explanation in his overall philosophy of organism: 'That every prehension consists of three factors: (a) the "subject" which is prehending, namely the actual entity in which that prehension is a concrete element; (b) the "datum" which is prehended; (c) the "subjective form" which is how that subject prehends that datum' (ibid.). It is within this schema of prehensions that the three factors cannot be considered separately or as pre-existent, irrespective of their relations and entanglements. In this light, there are no 'subjects' or 'objects' in Whitehead's philosophy of organism, which is what makes it distinctive in the philosophical tradition:

> The philosophies of substance presuppose a subject, which then encounters a datum, and then reacts to the datum. The philosophy of organism presupposes a datum, which is met with feelings, and progressively attains the unity of a subject. But with this doctrine, 'superject' would be a better term than 'subject'. (ibid., 155)

Whitehead's lucid example of listening to a note of music as a mode of feeling the world, but also as a process of becoming a subject within a particular occurrence opens up a plane of consistency for reading and understanding the seamstresses' radical practices as traced in the archive: instead of looking at them as 'short-lived' occurrences that 'came early' or ' were burned out', I rather focus on processes of actualizing virtual possibilities: a different world to come. In doing so, their material world comes into play not as the backdrop of actions, or even as their conditions of possibility, but as forces and elements entangled in the process or realization. As I will further argue throughout the book, the seamstresses' material entanglement in the labour of needlework initiated processes within which their political ideas and actions were radically differentiated from other Saint-Simonian or Fourierist middle-class women, as well as the male leaders of the romantic social movements they were both emotionally and politically attached to. But what is the role of narratives in the process of feeling the world then and now?

FEELING NARRATIVES

Deleuze has argued that the *event* cannot be reached, 'has no present' (2001, 73). The *event* is always elusive being the perpetual object of a double question: 'What is going to happen? What has just happened?' (ibid.). In this sense, narrative becomes a medium for the *event* as an elusive process to be expressed or rather leave its signs: 'The pure event is tale and novella, never an actuality' (ibid.). Deleuze's take on narratives as signs of events makes interesting connections with Arendt's theorization of narratives as the only tangible traces of actions. Indeed, Arendt conceptualizes narration as the medium through which the uniqueness of existence enters the social and the order of discourse:

> With word and deed we insert ourselves into the human world, and this inser-
> tion is like a second birth, in which we confirm and take upon ourselves the
> naked fact of our original physical appearance. This insertion is not forced upon
> us by necessity, like labour, and it is not prompted by utility like work. It may be
> stimulated by the presence of others whose company we may wish to join, but
> it is never conditioned by them; its impulse springs from the beginning which
> came into the world when we were born and to which we respond by beginning
> something new on our own initiative. (Arendt 1998, 176–77)

Narration then is a process of responding to the world and connecting to it. It is important to remember here, however, Julia Kristeva notes, that given that stories keep on unfolding, the revealed *who* is subsequently dismantled, 'dispersed into "strangenesses" within the infinity of narrations' (2001a, 27). Thus, the 'unique existent', the revealed *who* in Arendt's philosophical thought has nothing to do with the individuals of the dominant philosophical discourse. As Olivia Guaraldo succinctly puts it, '*Who I am* can be told only in the form of a narrative recount of my appearance in the world. To appear means to stand before somebody else, and to depend upon that somebody in order to receive in return a confirmation of my existence' (2012, 99).

By evading the abstraction of universal principles, qualities or categories, stories throw light on a wide range of historical, sociocultural and political structures; they ground abstractions, flesh out ideas and thus create a milieu of critical understanding: 'I have always believed that, no matter how abstract our theories may sound or how consistent our arguments appear, there are incidents and stories behind them, which, at least for ourselves, contain as in a nutshell the full meaning of whatever we have to say', Arendt has written (1960, 1). Thus stories for Arendt are not just good for understanding or feeling the world. There is a strong link between the cognitive and political aspects in the act of storytelling: 'Thought itself [...] arises out of the actual-ity of incident, and incidents of living experience must remain its guideposts by which it takes its bearing if it is not to lose itself' (ibid.). Moreover, sto-ries are open processes in Arendt's thought: they contribute to the search for meaning by revealing multiple perspectives and remaining open and attentive to the unexpected. It is precisely in their openness that their epistemological validity lies: knowledge emerges through new beginnings and unexpected

connections in the web of contingent relations that constitute reality. As
Guaraldo has aptly put it, 'The comprehension of reality cannot exclude the
plurality of its constitution' (2001, 35). But here also lies the inextricable connection between knowledge, ethics and the political, since in the Arendtian
horizon, 'the need for understanding is political' (ibid.).

Stories guide thought and give it a political orientation, Arendt argues,
but in order to think politically as well as philosophically, you need a position from where to speak, you need to acknowledge your involvement in the
human web of relations: you are always in-the-world-with-others. The world
that Arendt has in mind, however, is mostly a world of ideas, despite the
fact that she had read Whitehead and had commented on the importance of
his notion of *process*. 'In the place of the concept of Being we now find the
concept of Process', she noted in the *Human Condition*, highlighting the fact
that 'the shift from the "why" and "what" to the "how" implies that the actual
objects of knowledge can no longer be things or eternal motions but must be
processes' (Arendt 1998, 296).

Seen in this light, the seamstresses' stories create archives for historical
and sociological understanding. Their material involvement in the conditions
of their labour further shows that 'the social' and 'the political' is a false
dichotomy and raises important questions around the material limitations in
Arendt's thought.[6] As Lisa Disch has pithily noted, Arendt's configuration
of the political as appearance in the presence of others 'permits her to avoid
specifying the constitutional guarantees that are necessary to make "the
given" of human plurality a meaningful part of public institutions' (1994, 56).

In considering this gap in Arendt's argument, I have drawn on Whitehead's
critique of the bifurcation of nature, but also on feminist neo-materialist thinking, and more particularly on Karen Barad's insights about the importance of
considering entanglements of matter and meaning. Echoing Whitehead's
philosophy of process, reinforced by the advances of atomic physics in the
last eighty years since *Process and Reality* was first published, Barad has
introduced the neologism of 'intra-actions' as a theoretical juxtaposition to
the usual notion of interactions. In doing this, she denotes a significant difference: while interactions occur between already-established and separate entities, 'intra-actions' occur as relations between components. Entities—both
human and non-human—actually emerge as an effect of these intra-actions,
without having stable points or positions, an argument succinctly summarized
in the following:

> Existence is not an individual affair. Individuals do not preexist their interac-
> tions; rather individuals emerge through and as part of their entangled intra-
> relating. Which is not to say that emergence happens once and for all, as an
> event or as a process that takes place according to some external measures of

space and of time, but rather that time and space, like matter and meaning, come into existence, are iteratively reconfigured through each intra-action, thereby making it impossible to differentiate between creation and renewal, beginning and returning, continuity and discontinuity, here and there, past and future. (Barad 2007, ix)

It is within the dynamics of intra-activity that meaning is enacted and particular types of knowledge emerge, while matter is not static or just a condition; it is rather an active agent in the process of materialization. 'Matter(ing) is a dynamic articulation/configuration of the world', Barad has argued (ibid., 151). It is this dynamic process of materialization that Barad conceives as agential or rather as 'a congealing of agency' (ibid., 151). 'Intra-action' is actually a notion that according to Barad 'constitutes a reworking of the traditional notion of causality' (2003, 815). Why is that? Causality as a relation presupposes pre-existing entities that act upon each other being constituted as causes and/or effects. In the absence of separability among the components of the phenomena, intra-actions between them become agentic forces through which the components become determinate within the conditions of the phenomenon that they are part of. Thus, in drawing on Barad's proposition of 'agential realism' and the correlated notion of 'intra-activity', what I will argue throughout the book is that the material/spatial conditions of the seamstresses' labour cannot be disentangled from the formation of their ideas and their political actions. Such dynamic intra-actions have also significantly influenced processes of my own work within the archives of seamstresses' narratives that I will discuss in the next chapter.

NOTES

1. July 27–29, also known as the French Revolution of the 1830 or *Les Trois Glorieuses*, was when the people in the barricades overthrew the Bourbon Monarchy in favour of the House of Orléans, hoping for a better future, which never came for workers. See Pinkney 1973.

2. The notion of the assemblage is Brian Massumi's translation of what Deleuze and Guattari (1988) have theorized as *agencement*, a noun which comes from the verb *agencer* which means 'to put together, organize, order, lay out, arrange' (Deleuze 1997, 183); these notions are probably more complicated than just assemble and this is why some commentators have suggested that the term does not have a suitable English equivalent. However, as the term has further been used by Manuel DeLanda (2006) in his assemblage theory, that has been influential in my use of the concept, I will keep its English translation.

3. There is today a growing body of literature around Deleuze and Whitehead. Isabelle Stengers' *Thinking with Whitehead* is a major philosophical work in itself in

this field (2011) See also Shaviro 2012 for an excellent overview and critical discussion of Deleuze and Whitehead encounters.

4. As Whitehead explains, he had to replace the notion of *sensible object* with that of *actual entity* 'so as to free our notions from participation in an epistemological theory as to sense-perception' (1985, 73).

5. See Whitehead, 1985, Chapter 1 in part III.

6. I will further discuss Arendt's (1998) critique of the social in Chapters 3 and 5.

Chapter 2

Mapping the Archive

Mnemonic and Imaginary Technologies of the Self

Over the years that I have worked as a narrative researcher, I have persistently defended the idea that a story never 'is', but always 'becomes'. It is not that we have, listen to or think of a story and then we tell it or write it; the story becomes in the process of being narrated; it further 'becomes' as we perceive it, although what we narrate or feel can never be the same story. Following Whitehead's warning against 'the fallacy of the perfect dictionary' (1968, 173) what I therefore suggest is that narrative researchers should be aware of the incompleteness of any storyline or narrative mode and take this incompleteness, the becoming of the story, not as a defect but as its actuality, as what it is, a process. Here again, and given the centrality of the Aristotelian poetics in how we make sense of narratives, process should not be understood as a procession of forms—beginning, middle and end—but as forms of process, as I have already suggested in Chapter 1. Moreover, it is not simply 'us' who are telling, writing, reading or listening to a story: 'we' become subjects as situated writers/readers/tellers/listeners within the premises of a story and when we move away, we 'become other'. The story, of course, or rather our feeling of it, becomes part of the storyworlds we emerge from, a component of our historicity and endurance, a memory trace that the past carries with it. But apart from anchoring us in the past, the story is also a vector of force that throws us into the future, encompassed in the unity of how we remember and recognize ourselves in the present, which is always already in transition, or what Whitehead calls, 'a passage' (1985, 178).

So there is neither a person, a narrator who tells or writes a story, nor a listener or reader who follows it: the story is a component of an assemblage within which both 'the subject' either as narrator or narratee, as well as the plot and the meaning of the story are mutually constituted through their relation and never independent of or outside it. Many of these suggestions are not new of course: we have a rich tradition in post-narratology that has troubled and problematized the text/reader relation (see McQuillan 2000). However, what I suggest here is that we should move beyond a merely dialogic pattern, important as such interventions have been in narrative analytics (Riessman 2008). Even the much celebrated and indeed fruitful angle of the Bakhtinian dialogic imagination (Bakhtin 1981) stands on the premises of pre-existing entities, be they the listener and the interviewee, the writer and the reader, the story, its plot and its characters. In moving us away from this, what I suggest is the need to consider the actuality of 'prehensions'—modes of grasping the world for Whitehead, which I have already explicated in the previous chapter. This is an area that has yet to be explored although there have been some important interventions in theorizing the materiality of stories, particularly in terms of spatial relations as well as in their entanglement with objects.[1] Still, such approaches presuppose the autonomous pre-existence of subjects, objects and places and are deployed within the problematic area, which Whitehead has identified as 'the bifurcation of nature' (1964, 30).

It is on stories in/as becoming that I focus in this chapter drawing on Whitehead, whose philosophy of organism has offered insights in how we can interrogate long-held presumptions about the world and our modes of thinking about it beyond a range of dualisms, such as objects/subjects, facts/values, appearance/representation, individual/society, reason/experience and agency/structure that are still prevalent in social theory in general and narrative understanding in particular.[2] In doing so, I consider in particular the problem of serendipity, a phenomenon that has been discussed as a recurrent theme in archival research. Why is it I ask that serendipity has become a *sine qua non* of archival research? In juxtaposing serendipity with the Whiteheadian lens of imaginative freedom, I chart storylines in the archive of my research on a matrix of rhythmical vibrations. In further following trails of narrative sensibility within the archive, I raise the question of how we can conceptualize the researcher and the archive as an *assemblage* rather than as separate and independent entities.

In this light, the archive is taken not only as a laboratory of memory (and forgetting), but also as an experimental time–space continuum, where memory and imagination are brought together in the study and understanding of documents. Whitehead's lucid example of the feeling of listening to a note of music, as discussed in Chapter 1, can be very well transposed in what I want to call the plane of 'narrative as feeling'. Here let us start with an actual archival event: feeling a story, or to become even simpler, just a storyline from an article written by Joséphine Félicité in the sixth issue of the first feminist newspaper: 'Women alone will say what freedom they want'.[3] Taking this line from an article of a proletarian woman, about whom we know nothing apart from the fact that her real name was Milizet, I want to map it on the chart of Whitehead's schema of prehensions.

In seeking for meaning, which is what narrative analysis is about, what we have here is 'the subject/researcher' who reads or rather becomes a reader through her involvement with 'the datum'. But how, one can ask, is it the case that the subject becomes a reader through her encounter with the story? We know very well that the researcher is already 'a reader' studying and analysing French seamstresses' texts. But the point to consider here is not that there are no readers as actual entities: we are not interested in the abstract notions of the reader that has already become or the story that has already been written. The point of the schema of prehensions is to understand the process through which both the reader and the story emerge, as intra-actively constituted within the boundaries of the 'narrative phenomenon', a notion that I will further explicate in the next section.[4]

ENTANGLEMENTS IN THE ARCHIVE: THE QUESTION OF SERENDIPITY

In employing the notion of 'narrative phenomenon' I have followed Barad's reconfiguration of Niel Bohr's[5] thesis that 'things do not have inherently determinate boundaries or properties, and words do not have inherently determinate meanings' (2003, 813). It is only through the configuration of a particular 'phenomenon' that things can be bounded and acquire properties and words can take up meaning. As Barad explains, 'Bohr's epistemological framework rejected both the transparency of measurement as well as the transparency of language' (ibid.) and in this light the primary epistemological unit for Bohr was 'the phenomenon', marked by the inseparability of 'the observed object' and 'agencies of observation' (ibid., 814). While challenging the separation between subject and object and knower and known, Bohr's philosophy-physics maintained and defended the possibility of objective knowledge within the configurations of a particular phenomenon. What Barad's proposition has added to Bohr's thesis, however, is that phenomena are not only epistemological units, milieus within which things can be measured and meaning can be enacted; phenomena in Barad's theorization are ontological units, constitutive of reality. It is in this light that the reader emerges as an entity through her entanglement in the 'narrative phenomena' of her archival research. Henri Bergson's idea of 'trance reading' (1970) is particularly illuminating here. As Isabelle Stengers has pointed out, Bergson 'asks readers [...] to agree to slow down, to let oneself be penetrated by the words, to release the grip that makes us think we know what they mean' (2011, 62). It is in the process of slowing down that the reader 'becomes', by prehending elements in the storyline that she had not thought about before. In doing this, she re-emerges as a reader with new ideas about meanings that the storyline carries with it. In this case, it is not just the reader who becomes other, but also the story: they both become through their entanglement and 'intra-actions' (Barad 2007).

It is in this light that we can perhaps see why or rather how amidst the pile of newspaper articles that the researcher read, she was drawn to this line, having eliminated or disregarded many others. 'We experience more than we can analyse', Whitehead has written in discussing different forms of process within the historic world (1968, 89). Since Whitehead's image of the historic world includes among others, 'molecules, stones, lives of plants, lives of animals and lives of men' (ibid., 86), archives can safely been included and examined under this light. Thus, the reader's 'decision' to focus on one particular line, and therefore the newspaper article that it was part of, 'feeling' its value[6] and consequently being entangled in the nexus of its possible meanings, is a very good example of the constant interplay between negative and positive prehensions in Whitehead's analysis:

> There are two species of prehensions: (a) 'positive prehensions' which are termed 'feelings', and (b) negative prehensions, which are said to 'eliminate from feeling'. Negative prehensions also have subjective forms. A negative prehension holds its datum as inoperative in the progressive concrescence of prehensions constituting the unity of the subject. (1985, 23–24)

It is in the interplay of positive and negative prehensions that we 'feel narratives' I suggest, that is to say, we are drawn to certain storylines, topics, characters or themes and not to others. We thus become situated readers or listeners in a course where the force of the story emerges from a process wherein 'reading does not consist in concluding from the idea of a preceding state the idea of a following state, but in grasping the effort or the tendency by which the following state itself comes out of the preceding one by a natural force' (Deleuze 1993 cited in Stengers 2011, 467). Since we are considering the becoming of the reader and the story within the archive, this forceful process of 'feeling narratives' might also throw light on what Mike Featherstone has sketched as the archival flâneurie:

> Yet once in the archive, finding the right material which can be made to speak may itself be subject to a high degree of contingency—the process not of deliberate rational searching, but serendipity. In this context it is interesting to note the methods of innovatory historians such as Norbert Elias and Michel Foucault, who used the British and French national libraries in highly unorthodox ways by reading seemingly haphazardly 'on the diagonal', across the whole range of arts and sciences, centuries and civilizations, so that the unusual juxtapositions they arrived at summoned up new lines of thought and possibilities to radically

re-think and reclassify received wisdom. Here we think of the flâneur who wanders the archival textual city in a half-dreamlike state in order to be open to the half-formed possibilities of the material and sensitive to unusual juxtapositions and novel perceptions. (Featherstone 2006, 594)

Although I do not want to downplay, let alone disregard the role of serendipity, my point is that there is something more than pure serendipity in the methods of innovatory [male] historians that Featherstone refers to. It is, I suggest, the 'openness' of possibilities for conceptual novelties that the interplay of positive and negative prehensions can illuminate. According to Whitehead, this interplay corresponds to the two ways in which societies both sustain and renew themselves, namely, '(i) elimination of diversities of detail and (ii) origination of novelties of conceptual reaction' (1985, 102). In this light, 'innovatory historians' emerge from the world of the archives as Whiteheadian superjects: 'For Kant, the world emerges from the subject; for the philosophy of organism the subject emerges from the world—a "superject" rather than a "subject"', Whitehead has written (ibid., 88).

Let us then transpose the problem of serendipity to the reading of Milizet's article above: the reader has been drawn to one storyline at the same time of eliminating others. But it was not by mere chance that this happened: it is in this interplay of positive and negative prehensions that new conceptual ideas erupt. Although such processes are not necessarily conscious or cognitive they create a plane of consistency for narrative meaning to emerge and mobilize trains of thought that will be elaborated after 'the return from the archive' (Farge 1989,11). The latter is the analytical phase that researchers enter once they have returned to their desks away from the archive to immerse in the process of making sense of their data.

But before considering 'the return' let us still stay within 'the stubborn fact' of the archive, its fever and its dust, its pleasures and its seductions, 'things gone by, which lay their grip on our immediate selves' (Whitehead 1958, 44). Here I refer of course to the rich body of literature that has looked at the multifaceted layers of the archive as a symbol and repository of power/knowledge, an institution of governmentality, a heterotopic place of archaeological excavation, a site of genealogical deconstruction, and most importantly, a laboratory of memory [and forgetting] par excellence.[7] In this context, what is it that makes serendipity a symptom of the archive? Or is it more than a symptom or a chance 'coming when it comes, as a free gift or not at all' (James 1912, 154)? Moreover, how does serendipity relate to 'the archival sensitivity' (Valles et al. 2011)? I want to approach these questions by thinking with Whitehead about 'the stubborn fact' of the archive (1985, 129).

As already discussed in Chapter 1, Whitehead's philosophy configures reality on both a microscopic and a macroscopic level and highlights the fact that process should be understood as both flux and permanence. On the one hand, there is the problem of following the process wherein each individual unity of experience is realized and, on the other hand, comes the recognition that there is some actual world out there, already constituted, 'the stubborn fact which at once limits and provides' according to Whitehead (ibid.). In this light, 'the stubborn fact', which belongs to the past, inheres in the flowing present wherein actualities are being constituted. This coexistence of permanence and flux creates conditions of possibility for the future, which is anchored in the present but has not been actualized yet. Each actual entity is thus an organic process that 'repeats in microcosm what the universe is in macrocosm [and] although complete as far as concerns its microscopic process, is yet incomplete by reason of its objective inclusion of the macroscopic process'(ibid., 215).

Whitehead's dual conceptualization of process as microscopic and macroscopic is a useful configuration in terms of understanding process in narratives: a story may be complete in terms of its microscopic actualization as an Aristotelian beginning–middle–end, but incomplete in terms of the macroscopic process of being entangled in the web of stories that comprise 'the storybook of mankind, with many actors and speakers and yet without any tangible authors' (Arendt 1998, 184). In the same vein, a story may be incomplete in terms of its microscopic process—incomplete, fragmented or broken narratives—and yet contributing as a condition in the macroscopic process of narrative understanding.[8]

But, attentiveness to 'the stubborn fact' is the weak link of all modern philosophies, Whitehead has remarked, 'Philosophers have worried themselves about remote consequences, and the inductive formulations of science. They should confine attention to the rush of immediate transition', to the fact that 'we finish a sentence because we have begun it, we are governed by stubborn fact' (1985, 129). It is our adherence to 'the stubborn fact' that I have considered in thinking about serendipity and chance in the archive. My argument here is that we tend to perceive as serendipity, phenomena that are actually signs of an important process in Whitehead's analytics, what he has poetically described as 'the flight of experience': 'The true method of discovery is like the flight of an aeroplane. It starts from the ground of particular observation; it makes a flight in the thin air of imaginative generalisation; and it again lands for renewed observation rented acute by rational interpretation' (ibid., 5).

REMEMBERING/IMAGINING

Imagination plays a crucial role in Whitehead's experiential philosophy: he actually argues that the process of experience in its complex and advanced phases emerges as an effect of a 'joint operation between imaginative enjoyment and judgement' (ibid., 178). It is through their encounter, Whitehead argues, that the method of imaginative rationalization unfolds. But what we have in the above metaphor of the aeroplane flight is what Whitehead has also discussed as 'conscious imagination' and 'mutual sensitivity of feelings' (ibid., 275), the idea that imagination leaps from the situatedness of a concrete experience, although it keeps the element of 'surprise as an unexpected gift' (Casey 1976, 69). Stories are important in congealing this process of imaginative rationalization, I argue, as they facilitate the experience of landing, namely they ground abstractions, flesh out imaginative fabulations and carry traces of events. Whitehead has actually suggested that we should rethink the role of propositions as 'tales that might perhaps be told about particular actualities' (1985, 188). Although propositions are not actual entities in Whitehead's philosophy, they lure us into feeling such entities and thus become components of experience: 'A proposition is entertained when it is admitted into feeling. Horror, relief, purpose are primarily feelings involving the entertainment of propositions' (ibid.). It is in this context that Stengers has suggested that propositions are vectors of abstraction (2011, 415), a statement that inevitably brings into mind Arendt's take on narratives as stories that ground abstractions, flesh out ideas and thus create a milieu where thought can emerge from the actuality of the recounted incident, as already discussed in Chapter 1.

It is therefore the role of memory and imagination woven together through narrative in archival research that I will now consider. 'Imagining lies within our own power, when we wish', Aristotle[9] has famously suggested in a long line of philosophical thinking around imagining. Taking my starting point from the supposed link of imagination to a wishful self, I rather want to suggest the idea of the 'will to imagination'. In doing this, I see imagination as a force that initiates something new in the process of archival understanding. What is important here is to rethink via Whitehead the link between imagination and perception and particularly what Edward Casey discusses as 'the imaginative extension of perception' (1976, 140) as a process of prehending women workers' narratives in the exemplar I have chosen.

In this light, the storyline of Milizet's article, 'Women alone will say what freedom they want', has evoked for the reader particular feminist memories—the emergence of an autonomous feminist movement in the 70s. Memory provides here 'a ready stock of material on which we can draw in making an otherwise chaotic imaginative presentation more coherent', Casey has suggested (ibid., 193). While reading Milizet's article, I remember drifting into a state of mind that was taking me away from my desk. I was imaginatively transposed to those days of feminist activism back in the 1970s when we had to stop our comrades from coming to the women's meetings as women needed space to think for themselves and most importantly to speak for themselves. 'Everybody wants to advise us about our freedom but their opinions do not really matter', Milizet wrote. Freedom for her was not only an agonistic affair always emerging through opposition and conflict, but also something to work for:

> Whoever else may desire our freedom, I desire it; this is what matters most. I wanted it before I knew the Saint-Simonians. I wanted it before I knew M. Fourier; I want it in spite of those who deny our rights; and I am perhaps working for it outside the circles of those who want it. But I am free. We have had enough of men's advice, direction and domination. It is up to us now to march in the direction of progress without a tutor. It is up to us to work for our liberty, by ourselves, us alone, it is up to us to work for it without the support of our masters.[10]

It was therefore in the process of feeling Milizet's valuation of freedom that a conceptual novelty arose: 'In each concrescent occasion its subjective aim originates novelty [which] in the case of higher organisms amounts to *thinking* about the diverse experiences', Whitehead has written (1985, 102). In this process, imaginative extension enriches perception and therefore understanding through material enactments. This imaginative extension is both physical and mental; there is no such distinction in Whitehead's denial of the bifurcation of nature: 'It is a matter of pure convention as to which of our experiential activities we term mental and which physical', Whitehead has written (1958, 20). In thus seeking answers to my questions about the meaning of freedom among the editors of the first feminist newspaper, I have imagined their struggles, worries and agonies of publishing a newspaper written by women only, by remembering my own involvement in the feminist press, a century later. It is in this process that I have felt the author's desire 'to say what freedom they want'—the phrase that had 'accidentally' captivated me in the archive. While there was not enough time for ruminations while still in the reading room, something did happen in the rush of transition: Milizet's storyline created an event, opening up vistas in the reader's imagination, which would later become an element in her grasped unity of prehensions that 'have essential references to other places and other times' (Whitehead 1967b, 65).

The geography of the archive, very close to the places where the first feminist newspaper was written and published, has had a notable effect in creating conditions of possibility for the imagination of the reader to roam within and beyond the space/time extensive continuum of the archive.[11] As Whitehead has written, 'There are two elements of common structure, which can be shared in common by a percept derived from presentational immediacy and by another derived from causal efficacy [...] (1) sense-data, and (2) locality' (1958, 49). Indeed, spatial relationships ingress in our modes of knowledge and experience, but we are not always consciously aware of such activities. But hand in hand with geographical proximity, loneliness in the archive has also been identified as a *condition sine qua non* of archival imagination. As Casey has suggested, the autonomy of imagining 'consists in its strict independence from other mental acts, from its surroundings, and from all pressing human concerns' (1967, 191). Of course, this romantic image of the lonely researcher in the archive, beautifully narrated by Arlette Farge (1989) and Carolyn Steedman (2001) among others, radically changes when the archival space becomes your desk, your room and your computer, when working with digitized archives and documents.[12] Still I argue, there is an uncanny feeling of dizziness or frenziness when you feel you have pre-hended something in your 'data', which makes you forget your world and its concerns, whether around or far away from you.

By freezing a moment in the archival process for the sake of dissect-ing its concrescence, what I want to highlight is that it is in this process of remembering/imagining that a storyline from an archival document initiates for the reader a mode of understanding that is congealed as the beginning of a new research story that is about to unfold. In the case of Milizet's storyline, 'Women alone will say what freedom they want', what has flashed as an idea is the recurrence of the need for women's autonomy and freedom in the course of feminist histories. What we therefore have is a rhythmical repeti-tion of remembering/imagining and a vibration of contrasting feelings around autonomy and freedom as opposed to relational attachment and solidarity—affective and political tendencies in the nineteenth-century feminist move-ment that I will further discuss in Chapters 3 and 5. Following Whitehead, 'My unity [...] is my process of shaping this welter of [archival] material into a consistent pattern of feeling' (1968, 166).

In thus trying to make sense of serendipity and chance in 'the thin air of imaginative generalisation', Whitehead's notion of vibration and of the vibrant existence is, I suggest, illuminating. This is how Whitehead explicates his notion of vibration: 'Suppose we keep to the physical idea of energy: then each primordial element will be an organised system of vibratory streaming of energy. [...] This system, [...] is nothing at any instant. It requires its whole period in which to manifest itself [like] a note of music [...]' (1967b, 35). Here again, the analogy with the note of music is very succinct in mak-ing us understand this idea of vibration.[13] Ideas and knowledge emerging from archival research require a period in which to manifest themselves, and this is why considering and analysing rhythms within the space/time continuum of the archive is so important. But also the archival documents themselves, in my case the French seamstresses' writings, are traces of the vibratory exis-tence of their writers, who equally require a whole period in which to mani-fest themselves. As Deleuze has put it, 'A quality perceived by consciousness resembles the vibrations contracted through the organism' (1993, 97). The question is not about 'scientific materialism' anymore, Whitehead argues, but of energy in the concrete expression of the organism as an event in the process of becoming (1967, 36–37). This is why I have argued that archival documents should be conceptualized as events and the analytical interest should shift from structure to process and narrative force (Tamboukou 2008), which transposed in Whiteheadian terms could also be defined as narrative energy.

RHYTHMS, IMAGINATION AND *ŒUVRE À FAIRE*

As readers in the archive we are caught up in a rhythmical feeling of time/space vibrations, while novel ideas in our reading and understanding of documents emerge from what Casey has configured as the phenomenon of 'the imaginal ark' (1976, 88), a plane of possible actions constituted by the act of imagining. Here it is important to note that processes of imagination—in the archive and elsewhere—are short-lived and discontinuous, as they occur in the Whiteheadian 'rush of immediate transition' (ibid., 76). No wonder then that such novel ideas often feel as coming out of the blue, as the gift of a chance, an unexpected encounter, a serendipity. This is of course not to deny the possibility of pure chance, which is always, already there; it is just that sometimes when you read accounts of archival research, serendipity emerges as a refrain, a rhythmical repetition which emits signs that there must be something different, something more [or less] than pure chance.

'Each initial feeling is an "expressive sign", giving rise to the creative process that will make it come into being as the feeling of a subject', Stengers has beautifully written about Whitehead's understanding of human experience (2011, 427). So far in this section I have taken an instant from my archival research on the French seamstresses' narratives to illuminate the emergence of an initial feeling and then think around serendipity and chance in the creation of novelties among the grey bulk of documents of archival research. I have always been captivated by William James' famous scene of the always-evasive character of chance: 'It escapes and says, Hand off! Coming, when it comes, as a free gift, or not at all' (1912, 154). In problematizing serendipity, I did not want to erase or deny the beautiful gift of chance. What I wanted to highlight though is that we should not trivialize the rarity of chance, when thinking about moments in the archive that had a catalytic role in how we feel narratives amidst the bulk of accumulated dusty documents we are surrounded by. As researchers we are not always cognitively aware of how busily modes of perception function before we enter the phase of conceptual analysis, where of course conscious knowledge emerges.

My argument is then that we should not conflate the gift of the chance with the often-dim area of perceptive experience, although there are, of course, interplays between the two, since we constantly emerge from the world and not the world from us.

But no matter whether by the gift of chance or through uncognitive apprehension, once importance has emerged as a mode of thought that makes us concentrate, 'attend to matter-of-fact' (Whitehead 1968, 4), there is a problem to be solved, questions to be answered, tasks to be fulfilled, work to be done. It is this anticipation of work to be done that sets off the flight of imagination, Stengers (2011, 462) has commented drawing on Etienne Souriau's notion of the *œuvre à faire*, as an adventure of human experience:

> In fact, if the poet did not already love the poem a bit before writing it, if all those who think of a future world that is to be brought in life did not find, in their dreams on this subject, some amazed premonitions of the presence called for, if, in a word, the waiting for the work was amorphous, there would no doubt be no creation. (Souriau 2009, 206)

Despite its institutional constraints and limitations, archival research is a world enabling the flight of imaginative experience, giving form to 'work to be done', shaping new modes of thought and ultimately initiating creative processes in how we can understand the documents we are working with, as I will discuss next.

GREY DOCUMENTS, NARRATIVE PERSONAE

'Genealogy is grey, meticulous and patiently documentary', Foucault has famously written (1986a, 76). It is the colour of the bulk of documents that give genealogy its greyness. But how does the genealogist work with the bulk of documents that she encounters? As I have already noted in the Introduction, there is today a rich body of literature around the nineteenth-century French feminist movement in France that I delved in, while following the genealogical move of *descent*, excavating layers of the archive and encountering the 'grey dusty documents' of genealogical research. 'Genealogy requires patience and a knowledge of details, and it depends on a vast accumulation of source material', Foucault has further observed (ibid.). It is precisely the genealogical attention to details, many of them having remained unnoticed and unrecorded in the narratives of mainstream history, that historian Paul Veyne has highlighted:

> Foucault has only one thing to say to historians: 'You may continue to explain history as you have always done. But be careful: if you look very closely,

if you peel away the banalities, you will notice that there is more to explain than
you thought; there are crooked contours that you haven't spotted.' (1997, 156)

A genealogical analysis of *descent* does not attempt to reconstruct the past,
nor does it trace the effects of past events in the present. In the analysis of
descent, the genealogist makes the effort to look directly at what people do,
without taking anything for granted, without presupposing the existence of
any goal, material cause or ideology. The aim is to strip away the veils that
cover people's practices, by simply showing how they are, and where they
come from, describing its complicated forms and exploring its countless historical transformations. As Veyne has seen it, practice in Foucault's thought
'is not some mysterious agency, some substratum of history, some hidden
engine; it is what people do (the word says just what it means)' (ibid., 153).
But as I have already discussed in Chapter 1, human practices, or actions in
Arendt's thought, can only be traced in stories. It is thus in unveiling practices
through a narrative understanding of the grey genealogical documents of the
feminist archive that my analysis has focused on. It was while becoming
attentive to details that I encountered the gaps and omissions of the previous
historiographies in the existing body of literature.

As already suggested in the Introduction, what struck me as a significant
omission from the beginning is a lack of interest in the life /lives of the documents themselves. Take the first feminist newspaper, initially entitled as *La
Femme Libre*: this is an often-cited document in the existing bodies of both
French and English literature and historiographies and has been referred to
and analysed by a range of social, cultural and feminist historians as well as
political and cultural theorists.[14] Interestingly enough, however, it has never
been translated in English in its entirety, although a small range of extracts
from its articles have been included in Moses and Rabine (1993). But it gets
worse: having gone meticulously through the existing literature on and about
this first feminist newspaper, I have not found a single case where the document is considered in its entirety: it is only fragments of it that have been used
by researchers and although some of the existing analyses are truly rich and
inspirational they have left the document without a life of its own. What I
argue is that this neglect of the life of the document is problematic and raises
important questions around the epistemology and ethics of narrative research:
simply put, we cannot engage with documents of life while ignoring the life
of documents.

Engaging with documents such as *La Femme Libre* further implies a recognition that a sensibility to the texts people produce in trying to make sense
of themselves and their relation to the world 'has implications for the investigation of these texts' (Stanley 2013, 5). While there is now more or less a
consensus around the situated nature of knowledges and interpretations, the

question remains of how a researcher who draws on documents of life can invite others to become visitors in the archive of her work, thus opening up her analysis to other views, interpretations, approaches and critiques. Hiding or shadowing the life of a document not only obstructs the possibility of different ways of seeing, but is also problematic in terms of the responsibility of the researcher who engages with the life of others. Since subjects are always, already entangled with the world and others, what is at stake here is an 'ontological ethics', whose genealogy can be traced back to Simone de Beauvoir according to Stanley (ibid., 13), while it reaches our present through feminist neo-materialist thinking.[15] It is in this context that I have raised a question that has been central in my overall research of writing feminist genealogies: 'How is it possible to go on telling and writing the stories we were entrusted with, in ways that are both transparent and meaningful, not in terms of how they represent "reality" or reconstruct the past—which they can't—but of how they allow lives to 'be looked upon in the end, like a design that has a meaning, stories of the feminist imaginary' (Tamboukou 2010c, 179).

ARCHIVAL ASSEMBLAGES, NOMADIC DOCUMENTS

Having referred to the archives of the future, what I want to do in this section is to map the archive of this research. In doing this I also address a range of problems, questions and issues that emerged through my archival research with the seamstresses' documents. We usually perceive archives as the end of the active life of a document, a place where a document is reposited to be protected and preserved for the creation of future memories and histories. And yet archives are beginnings as much as they are ends: they give their documents a new life and particularly with the advent of digitization, new and diverse forms of life; but they can also deprive their documents of a future life, by hiding them through mysterious cataloguing structures, complex classification practices or simply impromptu spatial arrangements. Arnold Hunt's statement is here utterly revealing: 'As a curator myself, I'm intrigued by the ways that the physical organisation of archives can affect—and sometimes obstruct—their use by historians. As the old saying goes: where do you hide a leaf? In a forest. Where do you hide a document? In an archive'.[16]

But apart from curators and archivists who create and organize archives, often hiding documents in them, researchers also create archival assemblages when they bring together documents from diverse archives and sources around the world. *Olive Schreiner's letters*[17] and the *Emma Goldman Papers*[18] are lucid examples of such archival assemblages that have influenced my own approach to the feminist archive. These are of course archival assemblages that have developed as major research projects in themselves. What I want to remind us here, however, is that all research projects create archival assemblages, be they documents, oral interviews, transcriptions or other research data, and there has been a lot of interest recently in what Miguel Valles (2011) has called archival sensitivity in interdisciplinary research. But researchers, like archivists, often hide the archival strategies or sources of their research, through their immersion in the power relations of knowledge production that Foucault (1989) has influentially theorized in the *Archaeology of Knowledge*.

While recognizing my own inevitable involvement in the power/knowledge relations of the archive I have nevertheless attempted to unveil my practices: I have thus created a plane of consistency for the archive of my research by bringing together an assemblage of diverse political writings and personal documents. Not only have I analysed them, but I have also created an archival blog for them, so that they can be accessed, viewed and revisited by future researchers.[19] Conceived as an *agencement* in Deleuze and Guattari's configuration (1988), these documents continuously create new meanings through the connections they make: they develop internal relations between and among themselves, but also external ones with other discourses and documents. Although the latter have not been included in the archive of this research, they are nevertheless components of the archive of knowledges that chart the discursive situatedness and limitations of this research. But what does this archival assemblage comprise?

As already discussed in the Introduction, the historical period under scrutiny is the twenty years of the July Monarchy (1830–1850) in France: thus, all the political writings address issues and events within this period *and* they include five short-lived feminist newspapers and periodicals, as outlined below:

1. *La Femme Libre / Apostolat des Femmes / Tribune des Femme* was the first feminist newspaper, founded by Véret on August 15, 1832. Véret co-edited the newspaper with Guindorf, but withdrew from its editorial team after the third issue, which is when Suzanne Voilquin came on board and remained as one of its editors till the end. The newspaper went through a series of changes of titles and subtitles, as well as editors that I will discuss in Chapter 3. All thirty-one issues are housed in the Bibliothèque Nationale de France (BNF), but they have also been digitized and are available through Gallica, the BNF digital library. I will discuss this newspaper in Chapter 3, but I have decided to keep the nuances of the name changes in my citations as I think they carry alive its turbulent histories. In my view, these histories get obscured by citations that have decided to use either *La Femme Libre* or *Tribune des Femmes* as its overall title. Moses, for example (1984), has mostly used the title *Tribune des Femmes,* but also *La Femme Libre [Tribune des Femmes]* or *Apostolat des Femmes [Tribune*

des Femmes], which I have also found inaccurate and misleading in terms of the title/subtitle's interesting histories. Overall, there is no consistency in her citations, which is another reason of confusion. Moses and Rabine (1993) continue the confusions above, while Scott (1988) has also used the title of *Tribune des Femmes*.

2. *La Voix des Femmes* was a daily newspaper edited by Eugénie Niboyet (1796–1883), but was run by a committee, which included Désirée Véret-Gay and Jeanne Deroin.[20] It appeared after the Provisional Government of the Second Republic suspended the security bond, that is, a caution payment against possible future offences for newspaper publishers, as well as the tax stamp for subscribers in February 1848. The newspaper ran between March 20 and June 20, 1848, with a period of suspension between April 29 and May 28. There are overall forty-six issues, as the newspaper ran three times a week between thirty-nine and forty-six issues. All issues are housed at BNF, the *Bibliothèque Historique de la Ville de Paris* (BHVP) and the Musée de l'Histoire Vivante in Montreuil, in the *Fonds: Des Trois Glorieuses à la Seconde République, 1830–1851*. Microfilms of all issues are also available at the *Bibliothèque Marguerite Durand*, but the newspaper has not been digitized yet.

3. *La Politique des Femmes*, a weekly newspaper run by Désirée Véret-Gay as its director and Jeanne Deroin as its co-editor, only published two two-page issues on June 18 and August 4, 1848. It shut down because its editors were unable to raise the security bond that the new press laws reimposed for publishers, as a way of curtailing the freedom of political critique after the 'bloody June days' that I will discuss in Chapter 5.[21] Both issues are housed at BNF but are also available in microfilms at the *Bibliothèque de l'Hôtel de Ville* (BHV). The second issue is also digitized and is accessible through Gallica. *La Politique des Femmes* reclaimed women workers' voice in the political procedures initiated by the 1848 revolution.

4. *L' Opinion des Femmes* was a monthly newspaper published in two periods. Its first two-page issue, directed by Jeanne Deroin with Désirée Véret-Gay as a co-editor, appeared on August 21, 1848. It was a continuation of *La Politique des Femmes*, under a different name as the very possibility of immersing in politics was denied to women after the government put down the June 1848 revolt. The first issue of the second period, edited by Jeanne Deroin, appeared in January 1849 and six eight-page issues were run till August 1849. All seven issues are housed at BNF. They are also digitized and available through a different document in Gallica.[22]

5. *L'Almanach des Femmes* are three volumes of an annual journal first published by Jeanne Deroin in Paris in 1852, after her release from prison and then in London in 1853 and 1854. The 1853 volume was bilingual (French–English). All three volumes are housed in the

British Library (BL), the BNF and the BHVP. The three small volumes
are also in a number of libraries in the United States, Canada and Europe
in printed form and in microfilm, but they have not been digitized yet.

Apart from the ephemeral newspapers and periodicals that I have outlined
above, the seamstresses wrote, sent and published a number of pamphlets,
open letters, petitions, political brochures and appeals, following the political
tradition of pamphlets and pamphleteering. The pamphlet emerged as one of
the most persuasive and effective means of communication in early modern
Europe: because of its short format it could be quickly written and easily
published and distributed. As Hallvard Moe (2010) has noted, the act of pamphleteering overcame many obstacles in public participation as it drew on the
low cost, flexibility and speed of the printing press. The fact that its authors
could remain anonymous added to the democratization of the public sphere: it
facilitated the wider exchange of ideas and enabled political critique without
the immediate fear of censorship and oppression. The author of the pamphlet
thus became less important than the political discourse, and the force of
the argument and its immediacy in the public sphere created political communities and audiences. Moreover, the pamphlet was also an imaginative,
complex and polyvalent literary and political genre, as Joad Raymond (2003)
has argued. In this context, the archive of my research includes a number of
political pamphlets and open letters written by Désirée Véret-Gay and Jeanne
Deroin between 1832 and 1849, which will be discussed in Chapters 3 and 5.

What is interesting in considering the range of feminist newspapers, periodicals, pamphlets and open letters is the peculiar diversity of the archives,
locations and forms in which they have been preserved. It took a lot of effort
on my part to locate all these diverse types and locations of the documents,
despite the fact that some of them were cited in the relevant literature, but
often in very confusing ways, with the notable exception of the careful bibliographical details of Riot-Sarcey's *La democratie a l'epreuve des femmes*,
which I have updated by adding the online locations of those documents that
have now been digitized.

Indeed, the fragmentation of the documents in the existing literature has
been extended to the fragmentation of their citations, exacerbated by the fact
that the on-coming rush of digitization has not been yet incorporated in the
full citations of these documents, not even in libraries or archives such as the
Bibliothèque Nationale de France or the *Archives Nationales* that hold both
printed and digitized forms of these documents. One would expect that these
documents would have been gathered at least in a feminist library such as the
Bibliothèque Marguerite Durand, or a feminist archive such as the *Archives
de Marie-Louise Bouglé* at the *Bibliothèque Historique de la Ville de Paris,*
or on the website of the association *Archives du Feminisme.*[23] This is not the

case, however, and sometimes even the references in the existing literature were misleading since the catalogue system of the archives had changed and documents had been reshuffled and redistributed to the point that not even archivists responsible for the collections had been able to track them. There were, for example, two letters from Désirée Véret-Gay and nine from Jeanne Deroin that were supposed to be in 'Cartons 42 and 47' in the *Fonds Bouglé* of the BHVP, according to Riot-Sarcey's list of sources (1994, 346). The problem is that there is not even such a thing as *Fonds Bouglé* in the official BHVP catalogue anymore. Bouglé's papers have now been renamed as *Archives Marie-Louise Bouglé,* since they include 'fonds' of many feminists. Moreover, the whole system of 'cartons' has changed, and when I visited the library in September 2014 looking for these eleven letters, they were unable to find them. It actually took me seven months, many e-mail exchanges with the archivists and a second visit to the BHVP in April 2015, to eventually locate them, after following an obscure footnote in a draft of a conference proceedings paper on Deroin's years in exile that I unearthed in the *Bibliothèque Marguerite Durand* (Baker 1997, n.20, 15).

It is important to note here that the history of *Bouglé's* archive is very interesting in itself: Marie-Louise Bouglé (1883–1936) was an active feminist at the turn of the twentieth century. She worked as a secretary, but in 1921 she began an intense archival work, collecting materials about and around women, including books, journal articles, pamphlets, essays, studies, as well as personal correspondences. She thus founded a feminist library, which opened in 1923 and ran on a voluntary basis, open to readers twice a week. After her premature death in 1936, her husband André Mariani looked after the library, but it eventually became part of *La Bibliothèque historique de la ville* de Paris in 1946. However, the collection was divided: its books became part of the general collection of the library, while its manuscripts were unsurprisingly stored in the basement. They were unearthed in 1977 by a graduate student, Maïté Albistur, and were eventually catalogued as a separate collection. Although it was initially named as *Fonds Bouglé,* it was eventually renamed as *Archives Marie-Louise Bouglé,* but the two names of the collection are still in use, even in the continuously updated website of the *Archives du Feminisme.*[24] Thus, confusion still continue as my adventure with Gay's and Deroin's letters has shown.

Women have been hidden from history, Sheila Rowbotham (1973) famously declared some forty years ago, thus initiating the feminist project of unveiling the silenced female subjects of the historical discourse. What I mostly encountered in my research was not so much silences in the archives but silences in the catalogues, their hidden structures, the fact that catalogues often do not reveal what is not included in their descriptions. In many cases, even unravelling the mystery of the changing names of documents—such as the very first feminist newspaper that has yet to get a definitive name—was an adventure in itself. And yet once I had survived the frustration of finding a document and mapping its complex archival geographies, such nomadic documents would become points of entry for genealogical emergences, allowing new questions and intellectual problems to emerge. Perhaps the feminist project of the twenty-first century might be to unveil the hidden structures of the archives and create assemblages of diverse documents in the way Liz Stanley and her colleagues have done it in bringing together online Olive Schreiner's letters (Stanley et al. 2013a).

What was also interesting in terms of the politics of cataloguing is that influential as all these women have been in feminist history as well as the sociopolitical movements of the nineteenth century, collections of papers under their name, what the French call 'fonds', have yet to be created. It is in the *Fonds Enfantin* and *Fonds Considerant*—leading father figures of Saint-Simonianism and Fourierism—that Désirée Véret-Gay's letters have been archived, while a number of them have been dispersed in different collections, difficult to be located and traced. Thus, there is no such thing as *Fonds Véret-Gay* or *Fonds Deroin*, while for Marie-Reine Guindorf there are no personal documents preserved at all, apart from her articles in the newspaper that she founded and edited. 'No documents—No history', Mary Beard famously argued in 1935 when she set out to organize a world centre for women's archives (Voss-Hubbard 1995) and although many things have changed in the feminist archives since then, such a centre has yet to be created, even on a national level, as the dispersion of the French archives poignantly reveals.

The scarcity of personal writings and documents is further a striking feature of this research archive. It is as if seamstresses were realizing Foucault's project of how 'to write in order to have no face' (1989, 17). Indeed, from the very beginning of their campaign in 1832, they signed their articles with their first names only, as a mode of rebellion against the name of the father or of the husband that was imposed upon them, a radical practice that I will discuss in Chapter 3. In a similar way and despite the fact that the seamstresses were prolific writers, they did not leave any journals, diaries, memoirs or autobiographies. With the exception of Voilquin's *Souvenirs* (1866), we thus lack a coherent narrative about the seamstresses' lives. They rather emerge as elusive figures laughing at us as we are trying to pin them down, in the way Foucault had imagined the author playfully vanishing, changing places and reappearing out of the blue (1989, 17). If it were not for Désirée Véret-Gay's few letters to Enfantin, Fourier and Considerant, we would not have any trace of her passionate life. But in reading these letters we only become more aware of how little we can know about the passionate life she embraced and celebrated.

The archive of the seamstresses' autobiographical writings in this book thus includes twenty letters written by Désirée Véret-Gay: (a) four letters addressed to Enfantin between 1831 and 1832, (b) four letters to Fourier between 1833 and 1834 and (c) twelve letters to Considerant between 1890 and 1891. Riot-Sarcey has transcribed and published Désirée Véret-Gay's letters to Enfantin (1992) and Fourier (1995) but the letters to Considerant can only be accessed at the French National Archives, both as manuscripts and in microfilm.[25] Voilquin's memoir, *Souvenirs d'une fille du peuple ou La Saint-Simonienne en Égypte* (1866) alongside Marguerite Audoux's autobiographical novel, *L'Atelier de Marie-Claire* (1920) and Jeanne Bouvier's *Mes Mémoires* (1936) are the only 'coherent' narratives that are included in the autobiographical archive of this research. Since they are different in form, content and context from all the documents outlined above, they will be discussed in Chapter 6 as distinct genres of the seamstresses' contribution to the literary formations of the late nineteenth and early twentieth centuries.

FEMINISMS IN TRANSLATION

Having charted the map of the archival documents, I now want to consider questions around language and translation. The documents I have studied and analysed were all written in French with the exception of the second volume of Jeanne Deroin's *Almanache des Femmes* (1853), which is bilingual. Working in translation has never been an unproblematic process and there is a growing body of literature and scholarship activity addressing these issues.[26] Moreover, the problematics of translation go beyond the linguistic transfer of meaning and enter ontological questions of how the self is already, always in translation in her communication with the other. In the context of contemporary globalized reconfigurations of knowledges across geopolitical, cultural and disciplinary borders, translation poses problems of how we move between worlds, how concepts travel and what are the effects of epistemological and theoretical nomadism. Feminist theory has always been at the heart of such problematics: it has almost come of age through and in translation. Moreover, the heated debates between French and Anglo-Saxon feminisms have now opened up to wider post/decolonial encounters that have brought to the fore feminist voices and perspectives across the globe.

Having survived a series of mistranslations or bad translations that have created misunderstandings and confusions between and among theories and ways of understanding, feminism has now entered the age of becoming nomadic (Braidotti 2000); it is making connections not only within different languages and cultures, but also with a range of disciplinary areas within and beyond the social sciences and the humanities, such as science and mathematics. This does not mean of course that the politics of translation, and also circulation, publication, editorship and citation are not immersed in networks of power relations. In problematizing 'the author', Foucault (1989) has drawn our attention to the way the status of the author creates entanglements of power/knowledge relations that condition the circulation and reception of any literary or academic work. In looking at problems of translation, I have therefore extended the notion of what Foucault has called 'the author's function' (ibid.) to what I want to call 'the editor's function'. In borrowing this Foucauldian notion, what I suggest is that the translation and publication of the seamstresses' writings need to be considered in the light of the social, material and cultural conditions that underpin the international circulation of intellectual and academic outputs. In this context, Clare Hemmings (2011) has shown how feminist theory has created its own canons and imposed its own silences and rules of circulation. Interestingly enough, her sharp critique of the 'political grammar' of feminism inevitably carries the author's inclusions and exclusions.

But let us return to the French documents and look at Jeanne Deroin's 'Appeal to Women', which was published in the first issue of *La Femme Libre*. As I have already noted in the Introduction, Deroin only wrote one more article for *La Femme Libre*, so she can hardly be associated with this newspaper. And yet her 'Appeal' has become one of the most well-known articles of the French feminist press in nineteenth-century France: it was almost immediately translated into English and was published in *The Crisis* as early as in 1833. It has further been included to later edited volumes of feminist documents (Bell and Offen 1983, Moses and Rabine 1993) and thus Deroin has become a referent author for a newspaper that she had deliberately and explicitly distanced herself from. Ironically, none of her articles in the *Opinion des femmes,* the newspaper that she founded and run in 1848/1849 have been translated or published in English. Moreover, Bell and Offen's translation is different from the one of Moses and Rabine and they are both different from the initial one in *The Crisis*.

Some of these differences are on the linguistic level, offering different renditions of the French sentence structure and syntax, but others touch problems and questions around concepts, as well as contexts. Just think about the conceptual transpositions that are at play in the very opening sentence of this document: 'When the whole of the people are roused in the name of Liberty, and the labouring class demand their freedom, shall we women remain passive'?[27] It is 'the people' and 'the labouring class' that are emphasized in the translation of *The Crisis*: the collective noun of 'the labouring class' replaces the singular masculine proletarian [le prolétaire] in Deroin's political discourse and hence bypasses and downplays the romantic emphasis on the actions and possibilities of the individual, a notion that was central in the Saint-Simonian circles that Deroin was influenced by when she wrote this article. The 'labouring class' in the translation of *The Crisis* becomes 'the proletariat' in Bell and Offen's translation (1983, 146), but still remains a plural noun. It is only in Moses and Rabine's much later translation that 'the proletarian' (1983, 282) emerges as the translation of the initial French 'le prolétaire'.

'La liberté' is also a troubling and elusive notion in the different translations of this article and overall in the translation of the French documents: sometimes it is translated as 'liberty' and others as 'freedom'. But liberty and freedom are not exactly synonyms. Bracketing the philosophical complexities of the concept, freedom in everyday speech and understanding connotes a state of being able to act without external restrictions, while liberty is always related to some sort of agonistic relations with external restrictions. Yet, it is never clear why, how and in which context translators use 'liberty' or 'freedom' to render the meaning of 'la liberté', while freedom is frequently used to translate notions that relate to emancipation. To return to the opening sentence of Deroin's *Appeal*, the word 'affranchissement' is translated as 'freedom' in *The Crisis* and in Moses and Rabine (1983, 282), while it is 'emancipation' for Bell and Offen (1983, 146); finally all three translations use 'Liberty' to render 'La Liberté'—quite rightly in this context, it has to be noted.

In highlighting some translation issues in Deroin's much cited 'Appeal', I have not tried to deliver any type of philological analysis of the text and its translations. Given its multiple and different translations over a long period of time, this text lends itself to some reflection upon the challenges of translation, but also becomes an exemplar for thinking about the various discourses and practices that have had an impact on the circulation of these first feminist documents across the Channel, as well as across the Atlantic. The fact that many of these documents have never been translated into English has also greatly influenced the tensions between French and Anglo-Saxon feminisms, and has discursively shaped one of the greatest confusion in the history of feminist thought: understanding sexual difference and the difference/equality debate. As Francine Descarries has incisively put it, 'The problem, then, is not simply one of translation. It is also one of differing conceptual and contextual structures' (2014, 566). What are then the implications of being a feminist 'with an accent' (Braidotti 2014), while working and writing within the hegemony of the English language in what counts as knowledge? Throughout the book I will try to address this challenge by showing the effects, but also the limitations of becoming 'a polyglot, a transversal, a nomad theorist' in Braidotti's conceptualization (2000).

DIFFRACTIONS AND REFRACTIONS

There is a strong tendency in narrative research for self-reflexivity. As researchers, we are expected to reflect on our methods and situate ourselves in the research process by thinking about the effects of our methodologies and theories upon the 'research findings'. While positing the epistemological project of 'situated knowledges', Dona Haraway has criticized reflexivity, putting forward 'diffraction' as an alternative tool of meaning making:

> Reflexivity has been recommended as a critical practice, but my suspicion is that reflexivity, like reflection, only displaces the same elsewhere, setting up worries about copy and original and the search for the authentic and really real. [...] Diffraction is an optical metaphor for the effort to make a difference in the world. [...] Diffraction patterns record the history of interaction, interference, reinforcement, difference. Diffraction is about heterogeneous history, not about originals. [...] Diffraction is a narrative, graphic, psychological, spiritual and political technology for making consequential meanings. (Haraway 1997, 16)

The optical metaphor of diffraction that Haraway has proposed as a pattern of mapping 'where the effects of difference appear' (1992, 300) has been taken up by Barad 'as a methodological approach [...] of reading insights through one another in attending to and responding to the details and specificities of relations of difference and how they matter' (2007, 71). Being a physicist as well as a feminist theorist, Barad has scrutinized diffraction as an optical phenomenon in not just classical physics but also in quantum physics. As a quantum way of knowing, according to Barad, diffraction apparatuses not only 'measure the effects of difference [but] even more profoundly, they highlight, exhibit, and make evident the entangled structure of the changing and contingent ontology of the world, including the ontology of knowing' (ibid., 73).

Diffraction is thus a useful mode of bringing together the questions and problems that arise from working with documents of life in the archives of feminist history. What I have tried to show is that methodological approaches cannot be disentangled from theoretical understandings and epistemological concerns in making sense of how and what we do within the material and discursive constraints of our situatedness, the embodied politics of location that feminist epistemologies have engaged with and brought to the fore (see Haraway 1988). Having moved beyond the age of methodological or theoretical purity, as researchers we often find ourselves thrown in the messiness of the adventure of ideas, concepts, translations and interpretation 'the middle of the pack, where there is always pushing, shoving and mutual constraint' as Whitehead vividly put it in a lecture, borrowing his metaphor from the world of rugby (see Stengers 2011, 468). Working in the archives of feminist history with political writings and documents of life has therefore been perceived and conceptualized as an ongoing process, a becoming in an adventurous world of ideas and practices, charted across space/time/matter conditions that I have tried to map in this chapter.

NOTES

1. See De Certeau 1988b; Miller 2011; Bell 2013 among others.

2. For a discussion on Whitehead's relevance to social theory, see Halewood 2008 and 2013.

3. *Apostolat des Femmes-La Femme Nouvelle* 1(6), 45–47, October 1832. Also published in Moses and Rabine, 1993, 291–92.

4. I have used this notion elsewhere in my work with artists' narratives: see Tamboukou 2014b; Livholts and Tamboukou 2015.

5. The Nobel laureate physicist Niels Bohr (1885–1962) was one of the founders of quantum physics and also the most widely accepted interpretation of the quantum theory, which goes by the name of the Copenhagen interpretation. For a detailed discussion of Bohr's philosophy-physics, see Barad 2007.

6. Value in Whitehead 'is that which enables, or grounds, the differences between feelings (or prehensions) as developed by individuals' (Halewood 2013, 71).

7. See among others: Farge 1989; Derrida 1998; Steedman 2001; *History of the Human Sciences* 1998, 1999; Burton 2005; Kirsch and Rohan 2008; Stoler 2009; Valles et al. 2011; Stanley et al. 2013. See also Moore et al., 2016 for a critical discussion of these different approaches to archival research

8. See Tamboukou 2010b, for a discussion of 'broken narratives'.

9. *De Anima*, 427b, 16–17.

10. 'Women alone will say what freedom they want', *Apostolat des Femmes-La Femme Nouvelle* 1(6), 46, October, 1832.

11. All addresses were around the Sentier, the garment industry district in Paris and Le Marais, where I worked in the archives of *La Bibliothèque Historique de la ville de Paris* and *La Bibliothèque de l'Aresenal*. See the book archive, for links to these addresses: https://sites.google.com/site/mariatamboukou/the-book-archive/mapping-the-seamstress.

12. For a discussion of digitized archives and documents, see Moore et al. 2016.

13. Previously in my research I have drawn on music to show how my work has always been an ongoing process of finding the rhythm between genealogical and ethnographic approaches to research (see Tamboukou 2012a).

14. See among others: Moses 1984; Moses and Rabine 1993; Scott 1996; Riot-Sarcey 1994; Pilbeam 2014.

15. For a critical cartography of neo-materialism in feminist thought and beyond, see among others: Dolphijn and Van der Tuin 2012; Hughes and Lury 2013.

16. Arnold Hunt is a curator at the British Library; see his contribution in a discussion about the politics of archival practices at: http://www.cam.ac.uk/research/discussion/qa-how-archives-make-history [Accessed, 14-11-2014].

17. This rich archive assemblage is available online, see http://www.oliveschreiner. org/ [Accessed, 14-11-2014]. For a rich analysis and discussion of this work, see Stanley and Salter 2014, Stanley et al. 2013a, 2013b.

18. *Emma Goldman Papers Project,* http://sunsite.berkeley.edu/goldman/ (EGPP), is housed at the University of California, Berkeley. See Falk et al. 2003, 2008; Falk and Pateman 2012. For further discussion of this project, see Tamboukou 2013a.

19. See: https://sites.google.com/site/mariatamboukou/the-book-archive.

20. Niboyet was an author and journalist, whose work and contribution to the feminist and democratic politics in the French July Monarchy have been theorized by Riot-Sarcey 1994.

21. The June days began as a protest against the government's decision to close down the national workshops that women workers had fought hard to establish and soon became a violent rebellious event.

22. Les Révolutions du XIXe siècle.

23. See http://www.archivesdufeminisme.fr/ [Accessed, 14-11-2014].

24. See Albistur 1985; Scott 1987.

25. *Archives Nationales / Fonds Fourier et Considerant/10 AS 42/T-Z/Dossier 8/ Lettres de Desirée Véret, veuve Gay.* 1830–1891, Microfilm : 681 Mi/74–75.

26. See among others: Lather 2000; Hemmings 2011; Braidotti 2014; Descarries 2014.

27. 'Lorsque tous les peuples s'agitent au nom de liberté et que le prolétaire réclame son affranchissement, nous femmes, resterons-nous passive' Jeanne-Victoire [Deroin], *La Femme Libre-Apostolat des Femmes* 1(1) 1–3, August 15, 1832.

Chapter 3

'From my work you will know my name'

Materializing Utopias

> When in the last women's session, I said that I do not want the Saint-Simonian name it is not at all because I deny the good that Saint-Simonians have done, neither do I doubt the good that they will do. [...] If I wanted to place myself under a name it would be certainly theirs that I would take.
>
> But I feel that there is different *work to be done*. For me all social questions depend on women's liberation; they will resolve them all. It is therefore towards this aim that all my efforts tend. It is under the banner of the new women that I will relate everything I am doing for our emancipation. Women's cause is universal and it is no way only Saint-Simonian.[1]

With this article written on November 4, 1832, in the seventh issue of *La Femme Nouvelle* [Apostolat des Femmes], Jeanne-Désirée [Véret], publicly distanced herself from the Saint-Simonian movement she had so passionately embraced only two years earlier. It was her last article written in the newspaper that she had founded in August 1832: What had happened in the course of three months? To understand the conditions of possibility for this first feminist newspaper to emerge, we have to imagine Jeanne-Désirée in the days after the revolutionary events of June 5 and 6, 1832, when the Parisian proletarians took to the streets again to demand from King Louis-Philippe to honour his title of being the King of the French People[2] and do something about them:

> KING OF THE FRENCH PEOPLE,
> The voice of the People is the voice of God; The King must listen to it. Many grand sovereigns fell because they did not do it.
>
> A young daughter of the People dares tell you the truth, have the courage to listen to her.

Your victory over the people […] is a sad triumph. […] Already prisons are full. […] In vain you are surrounded by a war apparatus; the power of the force is in agony; it will collapse under its weight; it will lead you in the fall, if you do not hasten to realise a vast industrial organization. […] Do you remember that it was in the sole hope of a better future that the People laid down their arms and let you rise to the throne! It is two years that they have been waiting!

The Philanthropic relief is impotent. Charity demeans the People and it only prolongs their life to make it more horrible. What they need is what they want: work, joy, enlightenment, a secure future for their children, rest for the elderly.

The People have neither faith nor enthusiasm for you. […] But outside you, a regeneration movement is in operation, associations multiply, the sciences and the industry are searching for new developments. […] Get out from this route as soon as possible; it leads nowhere.

You may not understand or appreciate my audacity; whether it excites your wrath or pity, I am ready for everything. My faith in the future gives me the force to dare all and to support everything.

The voice of the People fails you as carefully composed and denatured. It is my duty to make it heard in all its truth: I have performed this duty and I will continue it.

JEAN-DÉSIRÉE, née Véret[3]

Having witnessed the bloody events of the June rebellion in Paris that have been famously recounted in Victor Hugo's historical novel *Les Misérables,* Jeanne-Désirée wrote and delivered the letter above to the king on June 10, 1832. In writing the letter she inscribed herself in the revolutionary events of her times and threw light not only in the marginalization of women's involvement but also in the dark times that followed the repression of the uprising. The letter was further printed as a pamphlet and was distributed through the Saint-Simonian circles. As a young proletarian seamstress, 'a daughter of the people', Jeanne-Désirée had the courage to step forward and confront Louis-Philippe in terms of his responsibilities as 'the Citizen-King'.[4] She was fully aware of the risk she was undertaking in addressing the sovereign power: but telling the truth was both her right and her duty towards her people. In this light, her bold letter to the king is a parrhesiastic act par excellence, an entanglement of moments, practices and speaking situations wherein truth is being sought, negotiated, granted or denied.

As a modality of truth-telling, parrhesia became a critical notion in Foucault's late work and has been meticulously studied, analysed and discussed in his 1982 lectures at the *College de France* (2010). There are four essential themes constitutive of the parrhesiastic act: (a) speaking the truth; (b) having the courage to speak the truth in situations where there is a risk or danger for the truth-teller; (c) truth becoming a form of criticism coming from below and (d) speaking the truth as a duty related to freedom. As Foucault has pithily summarized it,

Parrhesia is a kind of verbal activity where the speaker has a specific relation to truth through frankness, a certain relationship to his own life through danger, a certain type of relation to himself or other people through criticism (self-criticism or criticising of other people), and a specific relation to moral law through freedom and duty. (Foucault 2001,19)

Although Jeanne-Désirée wrote a letter instead of speaking, her epistolary act is configured as a relational mode of truth-telling: from the very beginning of the letter, she highlighted the fact that doing truth is a daring and risky act and she boldly asked the king to have the courage to listen to her. Writing and speaking were thus fused in her political rhetoric in the practice of telling and listening to the truth. What also powerfully emerges from her discourse is the idea of democratic politics in terms of rights and duties. She reminded the sovereign of his duty to care for the people who left the barricades after the July 1830 rebellion, hoping for a better future. While addressing the king as an 'I', she also identified herself as 'a young daughter of the people'. Her subject position as a letter-writer thus emerges from a political multitude, a body of proletarians who were already in the process of forming associations, wherein 'science and industry' were interrelated with politics. In raising the importance of work and knowledge in the politics of her times, Jeanne-Désirée differentiated herself from the abstract political discourses of her contemporaries as well as from the spiritual orientations of the Saint-Simonian movement that she had emerged from. Already in her 'Letter to the King' there were signs of the transformations that she was to announce in her November article that initiated this chapter: 'From my work you will know my name'. What was indeed the meaning and the role of 'work' in the feminist movement that sprang from the July Monarchy? This is what I want to discuss next by looking closely at the first issue of the feminist newspaper that Jeanne-Désirée founded in August 1832, in the aftermath of the June rebellion.

THE SEAMSTRESSES' IMAGE OF THOUGHT

In introducing their newly-founded newspaper to their readers, Jeanne-Désirée and Marie-Reine were very careful in flagging up its limitations: 'This little brochure written and published by women, appears many times per month but on undetermined days'.[5] *La Femme Libre* was just 'a little brochure' and the indeterminacy of its publication was due to the fact that both its founder and director were seamstresses, working hard to earn their bread:

Young daughters of the people without any other knowledge than our religion and without any other resources than those produced with our needlework, we have begun a work, still small and obscure, but which will rapidly expand and will raise high political questions.[6]

In making this statement Jeanne-Désirée was aware of the material restrictions that their needlework imposed on the time and resources they could use for their work, but she was also in the mood of leaping into radical futures. The notion of the importance of initiation, of making a new beginning was further flagged up in her article on the 'Improvement of the fate of women and of the people through a new organisation of the household'.[7] Thus, despite the fact that their work was small and obscure, the seamstresses had truly made a new beginning, a crucial concept in Arendt's theoretical configuration of the human condition:

> Men are equipped for the logically paradoxical task of making a new beginning because they themselves are new beginnings and hence beginners, the very capacity for beginning is rooted in natality, in the fact that human beings appear in the world by virtue of birth. (Arendt 1990, 211)

Existentially inherent in the human condition, the notion of beginning further shapes Arendt's understanding of the political, an arena where new beginnings are always possible: 'The essence of all, and in particular of political action is to make a new beginning' (1994a, 321). What I want to add here though is that we can draw interesting parallels between Arendt's notion of the beginning as eruption of the new, and the philosophical tradition of 'the event' that I have discussed in Chapter 2. Placed in the context of 'the event' the initiation of the first newspaper disrupted the old regime of gendered relations within and beyond the social movements of the July Monarchy and opened up a new space of radical politics. As Suzanne [Voilquin] pithily put it in the last issue of *La Tribune des Femmes* in April 1834, Jeanne-Désirée 'was not the first to think of creating a women's newspaper, but was certainly the first to have the courage to do it'.[8] The seamstresses' 'little brochure' demanded indeed a lot of courage and was dependent on the scarce free time they could find beyond work, as well as their limited funds composed mostly of the subscriptions of the Saint-Simonian women's circle. But despite its material and time limitations, their 'little brochure' written and published by women only was 'an event' that erupted in the summer of 1832 initiating a series of events that were to shape the history of Western feminism. It is the *dispositif*—the assemblage of power relations, forces of desire, discourses and institutional practices surrounding the emergence of this event that I now want to chart.

As already shown in the previous section, *La Femme Libre* was entangled in the events that followed the June 1832 uprising. But apart from being a component of a revolutionary assemblage 'the little brochure' was also an expression of the proletarian women's frustration with their exclusion from the hierarchy of the Saint-Simonian movement: 'It was a form of response to the silence imposed upon women from father Enfantin', Riot-Sarcey has noted (1994, 61). As an expression of women's desire for autonomy and freedom, *La Femme Libre* emerged after Enfantin's paradoxical decision towards the end of 1831 to proclaim a period of waiting for the Woman Messiah, while excluding real women from the spiritual leadership of the movement. This is how Enfantin articulated the new regime of gender relations within the movement on November 28, 1831, in a lecture published in the *Globe*: 'Our apostolate can only be exercised by men. The free woman has not spoken yet. [...] Equality will be the moral law of the future. [...] Up until the free woman has revealed herself, no woman can participate in our work' (cited in Riot-Sarcey 1994, 57). Women in the Saint-Simonian doctrine, but also in all romantic nineteenth-century socialist movement became 'of the future', they were imaginatively projected in a time to come, while their "now" was absorbed by the glory and moral order of a different future. As Denise Riley has aptly put it, 'If women can be credited with having a tense, then it is a future tense' (1988, 47). Unsurprisingly, Saint-Simonian women did not quite get the gist of how exactly their exclusion would become a precondition of their freedom. Jeanne-Victoire [Deroin] was particularly vocal against this new religious male hierarchy in her *Profession of Faith:*

> Saint-Simonianism offers us a religious bond, a priestly hierarchy, a theocratic government: these words awake bitter memories of fanaticism and oppression. Still quivering by the bloody wars that we have had to wage to escape feudal and priestly domination, we must not move back, entrusting our future and disposing our liberties to the hands of a new pontiff, to the feet of new altars.[9]

Jeanne-Désirée was initially more personal in registering her disagreement with Enfantin, her spiritual leader, but also one of her loves in her life, as I will further discuss in Chapter 4. Before breaking the ties with the Saint-Simonian circles, she sent a letter to Enfantin explaining the reasons of her detachment from the movement: 'I am of the people, as I always communicate with them when I see them gather in public squares',[10] she wrote. But despite her love for the people, which was immense and made her eyes 'fill with tears',[11] she could also understand that not all Saint-Simonian men were truly waiting for the Woman to come. It thus fell on women to organize for a better future: 'For us women, our work starts, to us women the duty to search for social love [...] our apostolate works [...] we have taken the purple colour of the Dahlia'.[12] Jeanne-Désirée was adamant that women should look elsewhere, that they should stop following men, since what they had to say was 'so different from the nature of men'.[13] In writing to Enfantin about the need for women's autonomous organization, Jeanne-Désirée was open and frank about the emotional difficulties of this decision. And yet her letter to Enfantin was a definitive adieu:

> It is something stronger than my will that makes me write to you [...] yet you are the only one with whom I can be free. [...] I am strong enough to endure your frankness and your advice and I am not afraid any more of the influence that can interfere with my work. [...] Farewell, I embrace you and all humanity![14]

But the seamstresses' reaction to their exclusion from the Saint-Simonian hierarchy went beyond individual responses—either public like Jeanne-Victoire's or private like Jeanne-Désirée's. Thinking and acting within the possibilities, limitations and constraints of the Saint-Simonian discourses and practices, they took up the challenge of 'participating in the law of equality among themselves' (cited in Moses 1984, 56). This was after all what Enfantin had suggested they should do in an attempt to sweeten the bitterness of his decision to exclude them. Since Enfantin's followers were configured as an apostolate of men waiting for the Free Woman to speak, the seamstresses created an apostolate of women, proclaimed their autonomy and spoke for themselves. The foundation of their newspaper was an act of initiation that eventually led to their disillusion with the Saint-Simonian movement altogether.

Against this backdrop, the first issue of the newspaper was symbolically entitled, *La Femme Libre*. As a material and discursive act of freedom, it carries signs of the proletarian women's double rebellion: against the hegemony of the bourgeois monarchy in solidarity with the people, as well as against their oppression as women in solidarity with the equally oppressed 'privileged women'. Realizing the importance of universal freedom and boldly declaring that 'all social questions depend on women's liberation'[15] was a turning point in the political and cultural formations of the first autonomous feminist movement. In May 1832, a month before her 'Letter to the King' was sent, Jeanne-Désirée had also written an appeal to 'the privileged women', asking them to join forces with the proletarians, the daughters of the people: 'Privileged women and daughters of the people, an era of enfranchisement and truth, opens up, it is for us to walk it together'.[16] In calling for unity and cross-class synergies among women, Désirée was deeply aware of the constraints and limitations that their social differences imposed upon them:

> Yes, she is ambitious this proletarian young girl, bringing an envious eye on you, people of the world, so polite, so brilliant; she is ambitious, since looking sadly at these young, beautiful and richly dressed women, she lets escape a sigh

of pain, and wonders why fortune made her born in dark misery. She would also love the joy of the ball, the sumptuous feasts, the glittering jewellery, the tributes, the admiration.[17]

It was the seductions of the bourgeois world that made many proletarian girls follow the path of pleasure, overpass moral constraints and become 'kept women'. Jeanne-Désirée's appeal actually addressed two kinds of 'privileged women': those who were born rich and those who inhabited 'the vast camp of pleasure'.[18] Her situated position as a seamstress was crucial in the way she looked at the intersection of social class and gender relations. As Rancière (2012) has argued in his analysis of the French workers' cultural worlds in nineteenth-century France, it was not only through open confrontation, but actually through their entanglement and conversations with bourgeois values, worlds and ideas that workers intervened in the sociopolitical and cultural formations of their times. This encounter with 'the bourgeois other' (Reid 2012, xxi) was a recurrent theme of the seamstresses' experience, since they were in constant contact with the bourgeois women whose dresses they were making. Crowston (2001) has particularly discussed the cross-cultural encounters that the seamstresses' guild had facilitated and the way such encounters became a route for a culture of femininity to be developed and transferred across class lines. Through intense archival work into women's personal documents, Crowston has shown that many seamstresses crossed gendered lines of work and family and many of them chose to remain single and live independent lives. The life story of Rose Bertin (1747–1813), a poor peasant girl who eventually became Marie Antoinette's couturière,[19] is the ultimate example of a bourgeois success story in the pre-revolutionary regime. Her realization of the importance of women's union notwithstanding, Jeanne-Désirée was conscious that it was the proletarian women who would lead the struggle for women's liberation: 'Space then! Rich and gracious women whom the fortune of birth has favoured with the gift of wealth, give space for the daughter of the people. She has conquered her freedom and has saved you from your very long slavery'.[20]

THE ASSEMBLAGE OF NAME-WARS

Consciously aware of their historical role in leading women's liberation, the editors and contributors of the 'little brochure' chose their own names to sign their articles: Jeanne-Désirée [Désirée Véret-Gay], Marie-Reine [Guindorf], Jeanne-Victoire [Deroin] and Suzanne [Voilquin]. In doing so, they refused to be called by their fathers' or husbands' names in a symbolic rebellion against patriarchal domination.[21] In defending her decision not to be called

'Saint-Simonian' in the article that introduced this chapter, Jeanne-Désirée wrote,

> Men give birth to doctrines and systems and baptise them in their name; but we give birth to people; we should give them our own name and take only the name of our mothers and of God. This is the law dictated to us by nature and if we continue to take the names of men and of doctrines we will be slaves.[22]

Jeanne-Victoire had used more dramatic metaphors in interrogating the marital name in her *Profession of Faith*: 'This habit that obliges women to take the name of their husband, is it not, like the branding iron that imprints on the forehead of the slaves the initials of their master, so that they can be recognized by everyone as his property'?[23] Being coherent to her principles, Jeanne-Victoire refused to take her husband's name, an illegal act that was to be included in the police records of her trial in 1851: 'The lady Desroches has abandoned the name of her husband and has kept her maiden name as a kind of protest against marriage' (Ranvier 1909, 425). As a matter of fact, at the time of *La Femme Libre,* Jeanne-Victoire had rejected both marital and paternal names and had used a name of her own choice to sign her articles.

It goes without saying that not all women agreed with this position and there were a number of articles or announcements signed by their contributors' full name. Interestingly enough, it was the bourgeois Saint-Simonian women who stuck to their marital names: Caroline Beranger, Angeline Pignot, Adèle Miguet, Louise Dauriat, Adèle de Saint-Amand, while women who only used their first names called themselves *les femmes prolétaires*. The camp of the name-wars was thus both classed and gendered. There were also cases when women struggled to keep their paternal name: after her father's death Flora Tristan (1803–1844) lost both her fortune and the legality of her name since her parents' marriage was never officially registered in France. Things became even worse when she had to abandon her abusing husband: her struggle to reclaim her father's name was strangely a bloody battle against patriarchal domination.[24] Although Tristan was not a contributor to 'the little brochure', her ideas about the importance of *The Worker's Union* (2007/1843) were critically influential in the development of the seamstresses' political project of association, a theme that I will take up again later on in the chapter.

Thus, the seamstresses' patronymic opposition was neither simple, nor just cultural or symbolic: it was a sociopolitical act of rebellion, embedded in the materiality of their working-class position. As a matter of fact, their decision to use names of their choice was ridiculed and criticized on the grounds of their proletarian background. This is how Suzanne, who joined the editorial group after Jeanne-Désirée's withdrawal, responded to a sarcastic article in

Figaro, scorning 'half a dozen of seamstresses' for refusing to sign by their paternal or marital surnames:

> Truly, gentlemen of the selfless *Figaro,* could I please ask you to tell me how you understand human dignity, and whether half a dozen of seamstresses as you call us, are not equally respectable in consolidating their independence through the work of their needle, like other employees. [...] No gentlemen, it is not because of fear or shame that we silence the name of our husbands or our fathers, but because we want to respond ourselves through our words and our actions.[25]

It was the first time that such a rejection of the patriarchal surname appeared in 'the gendered history of naming' (Eichner 2014, 661), and although it reappeared as a symbolic act in the 1848 events, it was not marked as significant as in the time of *La Femme Libre*. What is also particularly interesting in this complex network of antagonistic power relations and forces of desire at play—'the assemblage of the name-wars', as I want to call it—is that Suzanne, one of the most firm opponents of the marital name, was also an ardent Saint-Simonian and a follower of Père Enfantin, 'a father' she had chosen as her intellectual and spiritual mentor and leader. Her response was thus an expression of a wider double movement within nineteenth-century feminism: integration within the romantic socialist movements of the nineteenth century and autonomy as women. By following 'lines of flight' in this movement I will now look at the three articles that comprise the first and only issue entitled as *La Femme Libre*.

LA FEMME LIBRE: THE SEAMSTRESSES' VOICE

> Since all people have been agitated in the name of Freedom and the proletarian claims his liberation, shall we women stay passive before this great movement of social emancipation operating under our eyes?
>
> Is our fate so happy that we have nothing to claim? Up to the present woman has been exploited, tyrannised. This tyranny, this exploitation has to stop. We are born free, like men, and half of the human beings cannot be justifiably enslaved to the other.
>
> Let us then understand our rights, let us understand our power. We have the power of attraction, the power of our charms—an irresistible weapon; let us learn how to use it.
>
> Let us refuse as our husbands any men who are not generous enough to con-sent to share their power; we do not want any more this prescription: *Women be subjected to your husband!*
>
> We want equality in marriage.... Better celibacy than slavery![26]

Jeanne-Victoire's 'Appeal to Women', the article that initiated the seamstresses' 'little brochure' was particularly expressive of a dual position that
has eventually become a recurrent theme in the history of feminism: solidarity with the people, autonomy as women. Women's right to freedom is
embedded in the tradition of radical egalitarianism: they were born free, like
men, in a Rousseauesque universe of natural rights, where freedom is at the
root of being human. Mary Wollstonecraft's philosophical articulation of
women's rights on the grounds of universal reason and freedom is also dis-
cernible in the article's discourse. As Taylor has argued, the feminist ideas of
the nineteenth-century romantic socialist movements were deeply influenced
by Wollstonecraft; her *Vindication of the Rights of Woman* 'created a whirl-
pool of excitement and controversy, which lasted for decades, and was still
swirling around the early Owenites when they began to produce their own
feminist writings, a quarter century later' (1983, 1). It is not surprising that
Jeanne-Victoire's appeal was almost immediately picked up by the Owenite
circles in London, was translated in English by Anna Wheeler and was published in *The Crisis* as early as in 1833.

The discourse of naturalness was Wollstonecraft's debt to Rousseau,
Rowbotham has noted (2014, 43), particularly in terms of how she envisaged
women's education, but 'nature' as an abstract concept has become a thorny
issue in the histories of feminism: 'You cannot talk vaguely about nature',
Whitehead has warned us (1968, 127). Criticizing such a lifeless use of nature
in the discourses of the nineteenth and twentieth century around women,
Riley has persuasively shown how 'nature flourished, among other places
within the argument for "separate spheres" which so tormented the suffrage
debates [and how] women's natural differences contributed to their fixation
within the domestic realm' (1988, 46). The controversies around women's
vague nature have thus become a referential point for later interpretations,
discussions and evaluations of Jeanne-Victoire's feminism. It goes without saying that Jeanne-Victoire both essentialized and celebrated women's
nature: the inherent 'power of attraction' and 'of charms' was configured as
an irresistible weapon that women had to learn how to use. Although critical of the Saint-Simonian hierarchies, as well as the religious structures of
the movement, Jeanne-Victoire was also writing within the Saint-Simonian
discourse of a harmonious association of different classes and sexes. Within
the Saint-Simonian new order, the male nature represented reflection and was
attached to rationality, while the female nature represented sentiment and was
attached to emotions. But here also comes the interesting twist: it was not on
reason but on emotions that the new peaceful society would be founded and it
was on the bonds of social love that the future of the world depended. Thus,
apart from reminding women of their natural rights to freedom, the 'Appeal'
also urged them to see themselves as part of the workers' movement within a

universal struggle for liberation; it was from this situated position that proletarian women were called into action:

> We are free and equal to men. [...] Universal association begins: there will only be industrial, scientific and moral relations amongst nations and the future will be peaceful. No more wars, no more national antipathies, love for all. The reign of harmony and peace is established on earth and the moment has come for women to have their place.[27]

Different as it was configured, women's nature in Jeanne-Victoire's discourse was very far away from the Rousseauesque idea, of 'domesticated romanticism' (Rowbotham 2014, 38), the perception that women's nature should find its fulfilment within the private sphere. As a matter of fact, the public and the private were interconnected in Jeanne-Victoire's article: freedom and emancipation in the public sphere came hand in hand with a 'here and now' denial of conjugal subjugation. In this light, 'the private' created conditions of possibility for resistance and revolt. Moreover, Jeanne-Victoire's urge for rebellion was not deferred to some indefinite future, it was the *now* that counted in the seamstresses' political discourse: as they lived the *now*, through the revolutionary events of the July Monarchy, time was differently experienced. In this light, Jeanne-Victoire's belief in women's maternal responsibility for a new world order through love, was neither naïve (ibid., 54), nor paradoxical (Scott 1996), but simply consistent with the theoretical directions of the romantic socialist movements that she had emerged from. After all both her 'words' and her 'deeds' were grounded and throughout her life she came forward with many practical proposals on how to improve workers' and women's lives as I will further discuss in Chapter 5.

Women's double subordination in terms of gender and social class further became a dual position vis-à-vis slavery in Jeanne-Désirée's contribution to the first issue: 'Up to the present women have been slaves, either submitted or revolted, but they have never been free'.[28] Consistent with her analysis in the appeal to 'the privileged women' that was discussed above, the article went on to look at two modalities of living in slavery: submission within the family, as 'slaves of social prejudices' or submission to men's sexual pleasures, 'under the personal dependence on men'.[29] Women negotiating freedom under both regimes of slavery were acknowledged and celebrated: 'Glory to women, who [...] have sacrificed to a noble pride the beats of the heart. [...] But also, glory to women, who have followed the instinct of freedom inside them and have thus smoothed the route of our emancipation'.[30] As I will further discuss in Chapter 4, the sexual politics of the nineteenth-century feminist movement in France was radical and far ahead of its times. If some women had taken the route of using sex to survive, their action had to be understood within the material conditions of their lives and should not be judged on abstract moral grounds.

But this radical critique of bourgeois moral values and sexual hypocrisy did not emerge out of the blue: it was deeply embedded in the seamstresses' deplorable working conditions in nineteenth-century Paris and beyond. As Julie Daubié wrote in her influential study on the conditions of the poor women, 'Social injustice makes the majority of the daughters of the people fall in and stay within the cesspool of prostitution' (1869, 2). Nineteenth-century working-class poverty was particularly harsh for young seamstresses. Their meagre wages were barely enough to cover minimum living standards and there was no kind of social security to cover illnesses, periods of unemployment, which were embedded in the garment industry or retirement. Sex work thus became a survival route for poorly paid or unemployed young women, seamstresses among them, and although a system of legal prostitution was in operation, 'clandestine prostitutes accounted for two-thirds of the total estimated number—a number which, for the city of Paris, is said to have tripled in the first three decades of the [nineteenth] century' (Moses 1984, 29–30). Moses has also noted that there were differentiations in the sex work economy: 'The lowest class of prostitutes was usually recruited among women leaving prison or the maternity hospitals' (ibid., 30), while courtesans or 'kept women' were in a better position, but still slaves of men's sexual pleasures, as in Jeanne-Désirée's article above.

But here it has to be noted that going to prison had also become a survival tactic for unemployed and destitute young women: 'Theft and other crimes became the ordinary methods of survival and it should be no surprise that since 1830, the number of female beggars imprisoned has more than tripled' (ibid., 29). In thus addressing the problem of prostitution, Marie-Reine [Guindorf] would call Christian women to think about it as a symptom of poverty and patriarchal oppression combined; she also urged them to reflect on their own entanglement in its material conditions of possibility:

> Without doubt you have moaned for these young and beautiful women that have been thrown in the abyss of vices. How you must suffer when you think that these wretchedly unhappy women have been lost by your husbands, your brothers, your sons! That they were also pure, they had dreamed the joys of a virtuous love and of the pleasures of feasts. But they were poor, misery was there as a hidden figure that came to destroy all the dreams of happiness.[31]

Prostitution as a social problem had already been highlighted in Enfantin's lectures on women in December 1831, where he had drawn parallels between women's and the proletarians' subordination (see Gane 1993, 117). The new moral order as envisaged by Enfantin would thus 'provide both a liberation of the flesh and a liberation of women from prostitution' (ibid., 118). But while initially following the Saint-Simonian critique of prostitution, the seamstresses decisively bent its traits: a new moral order would be the effect of women's liberation from the material conditions of their enslavement and not its cause. 'In emancipating women one emancipates workers; their interests are tied and their liberty depends on the security of all classes',[32] Jeanne-Désiré wrote in October 1832.

It was thus from a material basis that prostitution was criticized and analysed, becoming a recurrent theme throughout the thirty-one issues of the first feminist newspaper. Most importantly the seamstresses' critique of prostitution was directed against patriarchy and rejected any trend to pathologize, victimize or shame women for having chosen sex work as a mode of survival: 'Regardless of the past lives of women who will rally under our banners, they have the right to be respected like us [...] the mud that they have tried in vain to cover them with, will fall on their accusers'.[33] Without disregarding women's different positions and situations, Jeanne-Désirée thus tried to find a way to unite them not on the grounds of a new moral order, but on the plane of a new feminist ethics: 'United by the same love, the same desire, the harmonisation of the individual interest with the social interest',[34] she wrote in August 1832 echoing the Saint-Simonian principles that she was still advocating at the time. Three months later, she had become much more specific about the political strategies of women's union: 'My goal is to form an association of women of all opinions [but] I want those women who would work with us to rid themselves of the overly great preoccupations of Saint-Simonism, which prevents them from having their own ideas',[35] she wrote to Enfantin in October, shortly before officially denouncing her Saint-Simonian affiliation on November 4, 1832.

Through their autonomous movement, women had understood by then that their male comrades were not just ignoring or downplaying gender equality issues, they were actively 'preventing' women from forming and developing their own ideas. It was thus only by distancing themselves from the male intellectual leaders that women would have a chance to fight against the gendered power relations that they were immersed in. Walking away from the men they had admired and loved was not an easy task, however. Despite her disagreement and her detachment from the Saint-Simonian movement, Jeanne-Désirée went on writing to Enfantin throughout the years that she lived in France—he died in 1864, the same year that she took the road of exile anyway. Having profoundly felt his influence upon her life, she also asked him to become a mentor to her son: 'I am sending you my son, who very much desires to be welcomed by you, in the way you welcomed me, when I was his age',[36] she wrote on May 28, 1856. Women's decision to distance themselves from the leaders was thus taken in full awareness of its difficulties and its consequences, but it was also a critical response to the rigidity of the movements and its masters: 'Allow me to tell you, dear Victor: that the disciples of Fourier also had rigidities like their master. [...] And you, yourself, my dear old friend, are you not suffering from this rigidity? Haven't you suffered from it'?[37] Jeanne-Désirée wrote to Considerant on October 9, 1890. We will never know his answer.

The third and final article of this first issue of *La Femme Libre* was Marie-Reine's contribution on the importance of association: 'Association is our purpose. Women up until now have had no organisation that would permit them to liberate themselves [...] they have only been preoccupied with individual things that have left them in isolation'.[38] Despite her belief in the power of association, Marie-Reine was also very much aware of the differences among women as well as of the difference that these differences made. She did not expect that all women would agree with them or follow swiftly. Women needed time to articulate their ideas before they could converge; it was equally important that they could form their own groups and clubs before they could find a common platform for their cause:

> We have faith that many will rally with us and that others will imitate us by forming many agitating groups, each one following the ideas of their founders, until the moment when women, having accomplished the work that is proper to them, will reunite in forming one and only association. This publication then is only a means to reach the aim that we are putting forward. This is why we make an appeal to all women, whatever their rank, their religion or their opinion; provided they feel the pains of women and of the people, they should come and join us, associate with our work and participate.[39]

Marie-Reine had indeed quite a distinctive attitude to difference. It is no wonder that unlike Jeanne-Victoire and Jeanne-Désirée, who withdrew early, she stayed on in the editorial group of the newspaper till April 1833 and even when she stepped down as a director she continued to write articles till the end. For Marie-Reine then, the aim of the 'little brochure' was to facilitate women's multiple associations. Her idea about the possibility of women forming groups where they could develop their own ideas through the organization of political discussions, actually flourished during the July Monarchy culminating to the historical phenomenon of the Paris club movement particularly after the February 1848 uprising. As Peter Amann (1975) has noted, workers played a leading role in this movement as the clubs opened up a political space for deliberation and radical democratic politics from which they were previously excluded. Marie-Reine did not live to experience the Parisian club movement, but her co-editors and co-writers including Jeanne-Désirée, Jeanne-Victoire and Suzanne all participated in the club *Société de*

La Voix des femmes, which was connected to the daily newspaper *Voix des femmes,* as I will further discuss in Chapter 5.

Marie-Reine's article also highlighted the importance of education and culture in moulding women's position in life as well as their possibilities for change: 'Being immersed in a work of regeneration [...] we are aware of the position that women find themselves through education; we know that it has only given them narrow and disjointed ideas'.[40] While acknowledging women's weaknesses, Marie-Reine was also fully aware that she was the director of a newly-founded newspaper and that her editorial should shape and mould its future directions: 'We will talk of morality, politics, industry and literature not only according to established opinions and received norms, but also from our heart', she wrote.[41] It was this last twist—the route of the heart—that would make all the difference in the way the seamstresses rewrote the cultural scripts of their times. Throughout the thirty-one issues of the first feminist newspaper, they actively intervened in the cultural formations of the July Monarchy: they presented and reviewed books, both historical and literary, they discussed and criticized theatrical plays and musical productions, they published conference proceedings on women's education and, last but not least, they wrote poetry themselves. But while some of their political articles have been re-read, studied and analysed, their cultural work has been downplayed and silenced. It is this grey area of the seamstresses' intervention in the cultural politics of their times that I will consider later on in this chapter and will further discuss in Chapter 5, by focusing on Suzanne's autobiography, Jeanne Bouvier's memoirs and Marguerite Audoux's autobiographical novel.

The three articles that comprise the first issue of *La Femme Libre,* by Jeanne-Victoire, Jeanne-Désirée and Marie-Reine grapple with the proletarian women's double oppression from a range of angles and perspectives, but the common thread that unites all three of them is that they were written by seamstresses. The materiality of the work that the authors were embedded in had thus created a plane of consistency for their writings to be articulated, read and understood and for their ideas to unfold. *La Femme Libre* was thus a unique first issue: never again in its subsequent thirty issues would the first feminist newspaper be so harmonious and materialistic in the way women's oppression was studied and analysed. It is thus the effect of work and its embodied entanglements in shaping the materiality of their ideas that I want to consider in the next section.

WORK TO BE DONE, *ŒUVRE À FAIRE*

In trying to understand the importance of the first feminist newspaper, we have to perceive it as a process, a passage between virtual and concrete existence, what Etienne Souriau (2009) has theorized as *œuvre à faire*, work to be done. What is the existential mode of this important concept that has already been noted in Chapter 2? There are three characteristics of the *œuvre à faire* in Souriau's analysis: liberty, efficacy and fallibility (2009, 202). Let us see how these traits illuminate the initiation of *La Femme Libre*. The decision to found a 'little brochure, written and published by women only' was an agonistic act of establishing freedom. In initiating it, the two seamstresses materialized the idea of the importance of women's liberty and expressed their conviction that freedom would only come from women and not from any enlightened male leaders. This realization of the need for autonomy and freedom emerged through their involvement in the Saint-Simonian movement: it was not an act of anger or revenge, but the effect of a process of political maturity, a 'politicogenetic phenomenon' as I will further discuss in Chapter 5.

Being politically involved in the romantic socialist movements of their times, the seamstresses also knew that pamphleteering was an effective way of propagating their ideas. As already discussed in Chapter 2, the pamphlet emerged as a flexible means of political action and communication within the public sphere of the July Monarchy and beyond. There was a well-established publishing network among the Saint-Simonian circles and the seamstresses used it to advance their movement. But they also knew of the perils and risks of the work that they had undertaken: their movement was 'like climbing a mountain at night, always uncertain of the abyss that you might encounter' (Souriau 2009, 205).

Most importantly, the 'little brochure' was not a project, in terms of concrete plans to be performed, managed or mastered. It was rather 'a dramatic exploration, a spontaneous adventure' (ibid.); it was the waiting for the work that mattered, the process of making it, the ideas that animated it, the vectors of its forces, not its final form. Souriau rejects both the idea of finality and futurity for the *œuvre à faire*, as these configurations exclude the experience felt in the process of making. 'If you consider the *œuvre à faire* as a project', he writes, 'You miss, the delights of discovery, of exploration, in short the experiential input in the historical route of the advancement of the work' (ibid., 207). The trajectory of the work includes the experience of all encounters in the process of realization: the efforts of fidelity, painful acceptances, onerous refusals. The important element here is the process of 'instauration' of establishing something new and innovative—the Arendtian idea of making a new beginning as discussed above.

As creators of a new brochure, the seamstresses had to subsume themselves to the force of the work, to enable and facilitate its autonomous realization and they did that by inviting all women to express their will, their fears and their dreams: 'What we mostly want is that women outgrow the condition of their spirit and the constraints that society keeps them in and that they dare speak with all the sincerity of their heart about what they think of and want for the future',[42] Marie-Reine wrote in her editorial. Speaking the truth and speaking from the heart was what the seamstresses wanted women to accomplish, but here also lay the perils of the adventure. Saint-Simonian women, as well as other proletarian women who joined their movement, wanted many different and often contradictory things and they expressed them through their articles and letters in the newspaper. Although its editors tried to keep the newspaper open to all opinions, they did not succeed in containing their disagreements. Jeanne-Désirée withdrew from the editorial group after the first issue, while her last article appeared in the seventh issue. Jeanne-Victoire wrote a second article on the 'Alliance of Science and Indus-try' in the fourth issue and then she also withdrew: 'The Saint-Simonians committed serious errors', she wrote to Hubertine Auclert shortly before she died, but this was because the most intelligent men among them had not accomplished a moral progress, while women remained under their influence and did not learn how to think for themselves.[43] But despite its problems and shortcomings, 'the work waits for us', Souriau notes, 'If we make mistakes, it will return, always there, always questioning us: "what are you going to do"' (ibid., 209)?

There are thus three situations to be considered in relation to the *œuvre à faire*: (a) questioning—'what are you going to do'? the oeuvre keeps asking the creator; (b) exploitation—'by calling me, the work exploits me', Souriau notes (ibid., 211); and (c) the necessary existential reference of the actualized work to the *œuvre à faire*, the distance between 'work done' and 'work to be done'—what Souriau calls 'the diastematic relation' (ibid., 212). There is always *œuvre à faire*, work to be done for the world we are responsible for, Souriau concludes (ibid., 215). It was precisely this sense of responsibility for women's world that animated the seamstresses and kept them going even when their work seemed to be failing vis-à-vis the disagreements or opposi-tions they confronted. Ultimately, it is not work that can ever fail but the world without work, without activity: if there is no work, there is no being: nothing is given in advance, everything is being constituted in the process of the *œuvre à faire*.

Considering the three situations of the *œuvre à faire* as outlined above, we thus come to the conclusion that when we create we are not alone. We are always in dialogue with the work which interrogates us, calls us, guides us and steers us; side by side with work, we are not alone; when we explore the paths that lead to the work's final actualization, we are never alone. It is some of these paths to the seamstresses' *œuvre à faire* that I now want to retrace.

WORK, LABOUR AND THE MATERIALITY OF IDEAS

> For several days the newspapers are filled with details of the movements that
> have taken place among the workers in Lyon. Whatever their opinions they have
> talked about them and have evaluated according to their views. In the presence
> of all these opinions, we cannot stay mute. It is more than a political question
> that is at stake in Lyon, it is about a social question that we cannot overpass
> because our future depends on its solution.[44]

The uprisings of the silk workers in Lyon between 1831 and 1834 have been
theorized and discussed from many angles and perspectives in the histories
of the labour movement in France.[45] Already in the first year of the newspaper, Marie-Reine had drawn on the events in Lyon to castigate the bourgeois
intellectuals' indifference to the plight of the proletarians. In doing so, she
had highlighted people's material needs for bread, work and education, but
she was also careful to note that not everything should be about material happiness: 'There is no doubt that life is not wholly about material enjoyments,
apart from riches, people should have intellectual and moral joys, but we
should not start with the latter'.[46] Important as intellectual life was, its material conditions of possibility should not be downplayed or ignored, but it was
for workers to raise 'the social question' and it was on its solution that the
political question was dependent.

The centrality of the social question in Marie-Reine's article significantly
challenges the critique of 'the social' in a body of political and feminist
analytics that I now want to revisit. In doing so, I will first discuss whether
Arendt's (1998) tripartite configuration of labour–work–action is a useful
lens through which we can look into the particulars of the social question
in workers' lives and then I will consider how the seamstresses' writings
respond to Riley's (1988) problematization of 'the social' vis-à-vis women.

In theorizing the human condition, Arendt (1998) has identified and
configured two major planes of difference: (a) the difference between *vita
activa*—the life of action and *vita contemplative*—the life of the mind and
(b) different levels and relationships within them. While challenging the hierarchically inferior position of the *vita activa* in the philosophical and political
tradition, Arendt has examined hierarchies within the *vita activa* that have been
blurred and obscured by the supremacy of the *vita contemplativa*. This is how
she has configured the tripartite relationship between work, labour and action:
labour for Arendt is what we incessantly and repetitively do to renew life,
'the activity which corresponds to the biological process of the human body'
(ibid., 7); work is about intervening in the make-up of the natural world and
creating objects that will constitute the traces of civilization, 'the activity which
corresponds to the unnaturalness of the human existence' (ibid.); finally action
is what we do or what we say, 'words and deeds' (ibid., 19) through which

we appear in the world and we connect with others, 'the activity that goes on directly between [men] without the intermediary of things or matter [and] corresponds to the human condition of plurality' (ibid.). Unlike work, actions do not produce objects: their only tangible traces are the stories that have been told and written about them, an approach that I have already discussed in Chapter 2.

In the context of her tripartite configuration then, what Arendt identifies as a problem in our understanding of the human condition is the conflation of labour and work, as well as two important historical reversals in the labour–work–action schema: (a) the reversal of the primacy of work vis-à-vis action and (b) the ultimate 'victory' of labour over both work and action. 'We live in a labourers' society', she has famously lamented (ibid., 126), where our life is directed in the pursuit of material happiness. What is problematic in the history of these two reversals for Arendt is that we have lost faith in the constitutive power of action in initiating new beginnings and thus founding freedom.

In further analysing the socio-historical and political conditions that have made these two reversals possible, Arendt has carefully considered the time-consuming nature of labour—as identified by the Greeks, theorized by Plato and Aristotle, and revolutionized by Marx—as well as the means–end direction of work, juxtaposing both with the open, unpredictable and irreversible mode of action, wherein the means–end distinction is dissolved, as the end actually becomes the means. What historically emerges as a crisis for Arendt is not the Marxist alienation of (man) from (his) labour, but the human alienation from the world. We live in a world that does not feel any more as a home to us, she has repeatedly argued throughout her work, since our involvement in the web of human relations and therefore in action is the only way we can feel again 'at home in this world' (ibid., 135).

In the light of Arendt's analysis of work and labour, what I therefore suggest is that the publication of the first feminist newspaper has cultivated and nurtured the need of feeling at home in this world through political action, which was embedded in the social conditions of the workers' lived experiences. The seamstresses' articles and letters have indeed shown that their involvement in the Saint-Simonian circles radically intervened in their home–work continuum, opened up new ways of seeing the world and made them start thinking what they were doing. As Jeanne-Désirée wrote in her epistolary *Profession of Faith:*

Since I have been transformed, I feel a happiness that I had ignored till now. [...] I went there looking for a bit of droll amusement and I have returned filled with admiration and astonishment for the grandeur of the ideas and the unselfishness of the apostles.[47]

In writing this letter to the *Globe*, Jeanne-Désirée was referring to the impact that the Saint-Simonian concern about the social questions had upon the disillusioned workers in the aftermath of the July 1830 revolution. But what emerges from the archives of the seamstresses' writings is that far from being an obstacle for the appearance of action, both labour and work became conditions of possibility for it, through the political spaces that their involvement in the socialist movements of their era opened up for them. In this light, rather than being hierarchically ordered and historically reversed, the activities corresponding to labour, work and action should be reconfigured as an assemblage: they do not just interact, but are actually constituted through their entangled 'intra-actions' (Barad 2007).

What I suggest then is that the historical reversals that Arendt has examined in her tripartite configuration of labour–work–action should be revisited in the light of two important components that were neglected in her analysis: (a) how matter matters and (b) the gendered experience of work and labour. As Whitehead has incisively put it, stressing the importance of our entanglement in the material world: 'It is never bare thought or bare existence that we are aware of. I find myself as essentially a unity of emotions, enjoyments, hopes, fears, regrets, valuations of alternatives, decisions—all of them subjective reactions to the environment' (1968, 166).

It is also within the assemblage of the material and gendered entanglements within the *vita activa* and the *vita contemplativa* that the social question and its separation from the political also needs to be revisited. In looking at the socialist 'utopias' of nineteenth-century France, Riot-Sarcey has pointed out that the notion of the political has historically rested on a constructed distinction between the political domain referring to the representation of the nation and the social domain referring to individual and collective relations (1998, 16). Following this false dichotomy, Arendt has vehemently criticized 'the social' as having thrown its shadow upon the political, particularly drawing on the French revolutions of the nineteenth century, a theme that I will further discuss and analyse in Chapter 5. Riley has also problematized 'the social' as an intermezzo space, within which nineteenth-century women's vague nature and spiritual qualities were harnessed, while their desire for political action was both contained and constrained:

> The nineteenth-century 'social' is the reiterated sum of progressive philanthropies, theories of class, of poverty, of degeneration; studies of the domestic lives of workers, their housing, hygiene, morality, mortality; of their exploitation, of their need for protection. [...] It is a blurred ground between the old public and private, voiced as a field or intervention, love, and reform by socialists, conservatives, radicals, liberals, and feminists in their different and conjoined ways. (Riley 1988, 49)

In the same line of thought with Riot-Sarcey, Riley has particularly commented on how the social was conceptualized as dislocated from the political, taking the striking example of how poverty was constructed as a social rather than a political problem in the work of French political economists (ibid., 51). It is precisely this dislocation of the social from the political that the seamstresses writings attacked on its head as it was happening. What emerges from their work is that the social and the political should be taken as an assemblage of discourses, institutions and practices: 'words and deeds' historically entangled together. Marie-Reine was convinced that not only was the social question a precondition of any political development, but that they both unfolded together and they were actually constituted through their intra-action. Matter mattered in the seamstresses' political discourse, since political subjects emerge from the world and not the world from the subjects in Whitehead's process philosophy. As Marie-Reine forcefully put it in her writings,

> I have touched the question of coalitions and I have said that in my view they could not in themselves advance the solution of the great problem that preoccupies us. I should therefore explain my thoughts; say what I desire and what I think for the future of workers and of women. Because it is only when the problem of the organisation of work and the redistribution of benefits have been resolved that the freedom of the people and of women will have been truly conquered.[48]

It was not the first time that Marie-Reine was foregrounding materiality in her articles. Already in April 1833 she had written about the importance of struggling for both 'material' and 'social emancipation', which were interrelated and co-dependent: 'I am far from believing that *material emancipation* is *everything* that *the people and women need.* I know that they also need *social emancipation,* but I repeat, one cannot be established without the other, for they are essentially linked and cannot be'.[49] It is obvious that by 'social' Marie-Reine meant 'political', or maybe a fusion of the social and the political, which as Riot-Sarcey above has argued had been discursively separated in the nineteenth-century playfields of power. But how would the freedom of the people and the freedom of women be conquered? This is how we are led to the next path of the *œuvre à faire*: the importance of associations.

IN THE SPIRIT OF ASSOCIATIONS: WOMEN AND THE WORKERS' UNION

> For those who examine today the state of society, one fact must seem remarkable, it is the tendency of all spirits to bring themselves towards association: this fact is even more remarkable as we live in an era of dissolution, when everything goes, but everything will also be reconstructed, because as they say most often, *nothing dies, but everything is transformed;* this is a proof that *the order of the future will be to draw upon association*. At this moment human

beings of all parts associate to make their opinions prevail; we women should
also spread our ideas to make people understand that our EQUALITY with the
man, far from lowering them, as some seem to believe, will be on the contrary
a pledge of happiness for all.[50]

As already discussed in the Introduction, association was at the heart of the
nineteenth-century romantic socialist movements; it became particularly
crucial in informing concrete political, economic and social projects and
although it formed the basis of their doctrines and programmes there were
some notable differences among them. But associations were also a politically dangerous project when it came to workers' associations: they were
first forbidden under the 1791 *Chapelier Law,* which remained in power
till 1894, while this general ban was reinforced several times as a result of
the governments' repression of the workers' insurgences throughout the
July Monarchy. What is therefore beautifully articulated in Marie-Reine's
article above is the power of association in congealing moments of change
in the flow of 'concrescence' and 'transition', a configuration that is at the
heart of Whitehead's process philosophy (1985, 210), as already seen in
Chapters 1 and 2.

It is precisely the dual play between 'concrescence' and 'transition' that
Marie-Reine highlighted in her statement that *'nothing dies, but everything is
transformed'*. Moreover, it is the reality of matter that stays on while passing
through flows and transformations that founds the importance of association
in her discourse—the 'stubborn fact' of the past for Whitehead (1985, 129).
Whitehead was indeed very much interested in how groups of entities—be
they microscopic like atoms or macroscopic, like humans—manage to
cohere and endure, thus forming some kind of unity or association. On this
plane of thought, association is inherent in the constitution of the real: 'Every
actual entity is in its nature essentially social' (ibid., 203). Association is
also linked to the idea of novelty since what comes to exist always combines
components, which were previously dispersed. In this sense, the thorny relation of the individual to society, which has attracted so much ink in social
theory, is not about relations of interiority, exteriority or even integration.
Individuals and societies are assemblages that are constituted through their
entanglement and intra-action, and so are associations. It is no wonder that
Bruno Latour (2005) has drawn on Whitehead in configuring his sociology
of associations.

It is thus in a Whiteheadian context that the importance of associations
has to be understood in the seamstresses' discourse. As we have already seen
in Marie-Reine's editorial above, her call to women was not simply about
unity, but about association: she had urged them to form their own groups and
propagate their ideas, enter processes that would be transformative and would

eventually bring them together as an assemblage of new women and new ideas. In this light, *La Femme Nouvelle*, the newspaper's subtitle, was interestingly accompanied by two words: 'Truth and Union'. But apart from situating themselves as women claiming their freedom against patriarchy through associations, the seamstresses also strongly identified themselves as *femmes prolétaires* and daughters of the people and it was from their working-class background that their ideas and practices derived. The formation of women's and workers' associations was thus at the heart of their project. Their ideas and writings would actually largely influence Tristan's well-known project of *The Workers' Union* and their entanglement would eventually become one of the main theoretical influences that shaped women workers' associations in the 1848 revolutionary events.

Written in 1843, ten years after the publication of the seamstresses' 'little brochure', *The Workers' Union*, which Tristan tenderly referred to as 'my little book' (2007, 23) included many of the issues and themes that had originally been articulated in the seamstresses' writings: the importance of autonomy, the urgency of action, the insufficiency of welfare and philanthropic societies, the historical role of progress, the urgent need for the elimination of poverty, the power of education, the right to work, a rational, fair and harmonious reorganization of the industry and the household and, last but not least, the salience of culture:

> Workers, what can be said now in defence of your cause? In the last twenty-five years, hasn't everything been said and repeated in every form? There is nothing more to be said, nothing more to be written, for your wretched position is well known by all. [...] Now the day has come when one must *act,* and it is up to you and *only* you to act in the interest of your own cause. [...] So leave your isolation: unite! *Unity gives strength.* (ibid., 37–39)

Tristan was very specific about the practicalities of the *Workers' Union,* which would rely on a capital accumulated by the workers' dues to their union. This financial project echoed the way the seamstresses had managed to fund their 'little brochure' through their members' subscriptions: 'Readers before suppressing your feelings and imagination with the icy words, "it is impossible," remember that France has between 7 and 8 million workers and with a membership of two francs each, that makes 14 million in a year', Tristan wrote in an attempt to persuade workers about the material grounding of her project (ibid., 52). Influenced by Fourierist ideas about the importance of work, as well as the project of the *phalansteries*, Tristan proposed the construction of the Workers' Union Palaces, co-operative educational and welfare institutions which could further offer opportunities to the workers to engage in meaningful industrial and agricultural work and training:

I come to you to propose a general union among working men and women, regardless of trade, who reside in the same region—a union which would have as its goal THE CONSOLIDATION OF THE WORKING CLASS and the construction of several establishments (Workers' Union palaces), distributed evenly throughout France. Children of both sexes six to eighteen would be raised there; and sick or disabled workers as well as the elderly would be admitted. (ibid., 2007, 39, emphasis in the original)

In putting forward the idea of 'the Workers' palaces' Tristan had also been influenced by the 'national workshops' that had emerged in Paris and throughout France in the 1830s, as an attempt to set up co-operatives that would later evolve in trade associations and unions (see Cross and Gray 1992, 80). Since such self-help organizations did not accept women or the poorer unskilled workers, Tristan was critical of their sectarian operation, which in her view could temporarily comfort suffering, but could not radically solve the great social problem of poverty: 'Alleviating misery does not *destroy* it; mitigating the evil is not the same as *eradicating* it. If one really wants to attack the root of the evil, one needs something other than private societies', she wrote (Tristan 2007, 49). We see here in Tristan's project 'a curious blend of materialistic perceptions and idealistic visions', Beverly Livingston has pithily commented (1983, xviii).

Materialism was indeed an issue for Tristan: although she had lived experiences of harshness and poverty, she did not write from the seamstresses' situated position, but from that of a journalist, orator and political activist. Her ideas about the possibility of workers uniting, despite the differences and rivalries between and within their trades, reveals how little she was aware of what, for example, it meant to be a *lingère* and not a dressmaker, a tailor or a seamstress—some notable differences in the garment industry that I have already discussed in the Introduction.[51] In short, Tristan did not have any direct experience of the effects of hierarchies within the labour force as well as the role of gender in shaping its internal relations, antagonisms and politics. Being herself a seamstress in the contested field of the Parisian garment industry, Marie-Reine Guindorf knew only too well about its internal battles and conflicts and although she was also advocating unity among women, she saw it emerging through passages between and among differences—an effect of a process of multiple associations:

There are many [men] who deny that women will ever become their equals; we cannot make them change their ideas, but we will be able to present to them accomplished acts, when we form a united body, where everybody will have the same desire, the same purpose. Women, understand this well, it is by association that we will be able to reach this purpose; let's unite then, leaving aside all small rivalries that so often divide us, let's form a single body only wherein each member will act following its own ideas, by reporting them to a united centre. Without doubt we have not yet arrived at this desired moment. [...] But we can hasten this moment by uniting.[52]

Marie-Reine's ideas about the possibility of women's unity through autonomous political action were very different from Tristan's ideas about the workers' union. Despite her personal and political connections with the seamstresses, Tristan held some significantly different ideas vis-à-vis women's position. She thought that forming a women's movement was a much more difficult project than organizing a workers' association, since workers had a proletarian platform to stand on while women were separated by so many lines of difference. Her project was to transform women's position from that of 'a pariah' to a central figure: 'Woman is everything in the life of the worker', she repeatedly argued (Tristan 2007, 79, 82). But although she demanded rights for women, she did not envisage them as political figures; it was the role of the workers to politically defend women's rights: 'I invite you to appeal for women's rights, and meanwhile at least to recognise them in principle', she wrote (ibid., 87). Tristan wrote appeals to bourgeois men and women asking them to assist the project of the workers' union, she wrote appeals to workers, but she did not write appeals to women. Hers was a peculiar feminism that has been read and interpreted from diverse positions, disciplinary fields and angles, ultimately vacillating between liberalism and socialism, Máire Cross and Tim Gray (1992) have argued.

And yet Tristan has become the most well-known figure of nineteenth-century French feminism; she has been credited 'as the first political analyst to call for an international union of workers (even before Marx) and as the first to link socialism and feminism' (Tristan 2007, backcover). My contention is that while her 'little book' was certainly the first to call for workers' international unity, the origins of its ideas should be traced back to the seamstresses' 'little brochure' that has received little or no recognition on this front, having been subsumed by the Saint-Simonian utopianism of some of its articles and contributors. In the light of the above, the seamstresses' 'little brochure' and Tristan's 'little book' cannot be considered in terms of relations between previously constituted entities, but as intra-acting components and relations of the assemblage of the July Monarchy feminist discourses and practices. Although Tristan did not contribute to the 'little brochure', she was part of the Saint-Simonian, Fourierist and Owenite circles of her time.[53] She was also a very good friend with some of the militant journalists and seamstresses, including Deroin and Roland, who took care of her daughter Aline after her premature death in November 1844 (see Pilbeam 2014, 64). The ideas that were eventually articulated in *The Workers' Union* were thus formed and crystallized in dialogue and conversation with the seamstresses' movement and publications and they sprang from a plane of consistency that had been created around the importance of work: 'So to work! To work, my brothers. The work will be rough, the difficulties numerous, but think of the greatness of the goal! The greatness of the reward! *Through you,* the unification of human kind' (Tristan 2007, 130).

Tristan's writings were widely circulated among French workers at the time of its publication and beyond. As Doris and Paul Beik have noted, 'While writing *Workers' Union* Flora was able through her contacts with workers intellectuals to read several chapters to groups of their friends' (1993, xix). It was the time when French workers having realized the importance of education had started attending night classes and engaging with a range of cultural activities, influentially analysed and discussed in Rancière's *Proletarian Nights* (2012). In looking at the history of proletarian literature, Michel Ragon has noted that there was a 52 percent increase in male literacy between 1828 and 1846 (1974, 82). Journals, newspapers and pamphlets attracted increasing audiences, while cultural events became inspirational sites in workers' lives. Workers, seamstresses among them, immersed themselves in the cultural formations of the July Monarchy, but most importantly contributed to them. It is signs of the proletarian's intellectual lives and interests that we can trace in the seamstresses' 'little brochure', a theme that has remained neglected in the otherwise rich body of feminist literature around this first feminist newspaper.

THE POWER OF WORKERS' EDUCATION,
THE CULTURE OF LABOUR

> Like the rest of the people we are deprived of education or we receive it with restraints and within very narrow limits. [...] But it is mostly with regard to women that the draft law is so behind, having made no reference to them at all. The only thing that they have added in the end is that there will be schools for women if there is space. IF THERE IS SPACE? How? Isn't it that everywhere women need education? Do you therefore want to leave them ignorant for ever?[54]

In February 1833, Marie-Reine wrote a fervent article 'On Public Education' in the twelfth issue of what had by that time become *La Femme Nouvelle.* As already noted in the Introduction, the article addressed some of the problems of public education in the context of the debates that were held before the *Loi Guizot* on primary education was finally voted for on June 28, 1833. There were two issues that Marie-Reine particularly addressed: the need for girls' education to be recognized, as highlighted above, but also the importance of free public education:

It is easy to prove how little it has been understood: 'In every community there will be a school where children will be admitted in exchange of a small fee; the parents who won't be able to pay will have to be given by the Mayor a certificate of poverty, after which their children will be admitted.' Here are therefore the children for whom education will be a charity. Do you think it will be gentle for the parents to have to talk about their misery to people who used to consider them with disdain and more often with pity, which is more painful than to be the object of contempt? [...] There is only one way to remedy this and it is to open schools to all, those who can pay and those who don't without parents having to be obliged to have to use such painful formalities.[55]

In highlighting the importance of educating workers in general and women workers in particular, Marie-Reine asked for specific cross-class collaboration. She thus urged women of the privileged classes to come forward as teachers of the people and not only as charity ladies: 'It is therefore you, women who are privileged through education and wealth that I address. [...] Let's unite, let's form courses, where you will come to teach those of your sisters that have been deprived of the benefits of education'.[56] She further highlighted the important work of the *Free Association for the Free Education of the people,* an educational organization, which was initially founded in July 1830 as *The Polytechnic Association for the Education of Workers* and was subsequently reorganized and renamed in May 1831 (see Christen 2013). As it was the first educational association to admit women in its courses, Marie-Reine was adamant that all women should wholeheartedly support it. As a matter of fact, Marie-Reine herself eventually left the editorial team of the *Tribune des Femmes* to devote her scarce free time to the project of educating women workers.

Marie-Reine's article above is thus a lucid articulation of the problems of women workers' education in the July Monarchy and beyond. Among other ideas it highlighted the need for women's direct intervention in the politics and policy making in education, concretely linking social questions to political claims and demands. It further configured education as the ground for specific material and political connections between women and the people to be made, in what we would recognize today as class/gender intersections. Finally Marie-Reine took a holistic approach to the aims of workers' education, configuring it as a movement for changing the self, as well as for changing the world. What is further particularly striking about this early nineteenth-century article is the contemporaneity of some of the questions it raises around education, poverty and gender. The improvement of women workers' education was thus at the forefront of the seamstresses' discourse and eventually became the force that mobilized the proletarian's encounter with and contribution to the cultural formations of modernity, an intellectual movement, which has left its traces in the pages of 'the little brochure':

Yes, I repeat it, the press will be silent and icy about us for much longer; it is at
the theatre that we will find our most powerful allies. It is the theatre [...] that
responds with dignity to the discourse of emancipation. [...] Since the ideas of
liberty and equality have agitated all hearts, certain authors have felt and recognized the immense influence that we have exercised. [...]When then will they
talk about us? When are they going to stop identifying us with feelings that are
not our own?[57]

By highlighting the role of art in raising consciousness about the women's
condition, Suzanne initiated and sustained a series of book and play reviews
throughout the thirty-first issues of the seamstresses' 'little brochure'. Taking the view that literature and drama should reflect the social reality of their
world, she scrutinized authors about the way they depicted, psychographed
or silenced women in their work: 'Oh Béranger! With your forceful voice,
demand our emancipation, moral, intellectual and material! [...] Create new
songs for us! Your muse is a woman',[58] she wrote to the famous poet and
song-writer Pierre-Jean de Béranger (1780–1857) in an epistolary appeal to
include women in his verses for his beloved people.

Suzanne's critical interventions were swift and timely, as she tried to keep
pace with the busy cultural and intellectual life of Paris.[59] Her review of
Reine, Cardinal et Page, by François Ancelot, published in Paris in 1832,
appeared in the tenth issue of *La Femme Nouvelle,* on December 5, 1832,
a few days after the one act vaudeville had its premiere at the *Théâtre de
Vaudeville* in Paris. Suzanne was enthusiastic about the author's insights in
women's world:

The character of the queen in M. Ancelot's play is superbly traced. He expresses
better than me, what I expect from women. [...] At last then, an author who
understands us! The rest that he has shown in this nice vaudeville and in his
other works are excellent paintings! He touches the intimate feelings of the heart
with a feminine truth and delicacy! The intrigue is based upon a true fact; the
play is written with elegance; the characters are truthfully historical and staged
very well through the effect of contrasts.[60]

Her review did not come out of the blue. Already from the fourth issue,
shortly after she took over as a co-editor, Suzanne had initiated 'Variétés',
a cultural column where the seamstresses busily engaged with the Parisian
cultural production. Their cultural articles were well informed, beautifully
written and cogently argued. Rey-Dussueil's *Le Monde Nouveau*, published
in 1831 was severely criticized in terms of the way the author presented his
four female characters in an erudite four-page article.[61] The sixth issue had
a celebratory announcement of the 1832 publication of *L'Ami du prolétaire*,
which was warmly recommended to the readers for its 'high questions of

morality, politics, industry and general history, treated from a Saint-Simonian philosophical point of view'.[62] In the eleventh issue published in January 1833, Suzanne reviewed the book 'La femme selon mon cœur' by Eugène L'Héritier, which had just been published.[63] She praised the author for the way he had represented women in his romance: in the midst of the stereo-types and conventions of the genre that romances draw on, this author has succeeded in creating something new, Suzanne argued, 'new in relation to feelings and characters',[64] as he has written about 'the intellectual and moral emancipation of women'.[65] What is particularly fascinating is that in the end of the review, Suzanne opened a dialogue with Marie, a character from this romance, responding to some of her comments about Saint-Simonian women: 'We are mystics, you say; you don't believe it Marie [...] who have come to realise on earth the paradise that they have only glimpsed spiritually'.[66]

Fictional beings are modes of existence for Souriau; they may be fragile and inconsistent, but they do have an existential status: 'One cannot charac-terise them essentially by the fact that, by way of representation, they do not correspond to objects or to bodies. [...] They exist in their own way only if they have a positive reason to exist. And they do' (2009, 131–32). Marie's 'positive reason to exist' is the way her fictional figure concentrates on other possibilities of being a woman. By reading the novel, its diverse readers find in Marie a referential mode of existence. These fictional beings depend on the reception that they get from their readers/audiences and the latter connect and communicate through their relation to them: many of us share Mrs Dalloway, Mme Butterfly or les Demoiselles d'Avignon; they are fictional beings and yet they exist. Marie is just that positive existence that Suzanne felt she could share with others.

But the seamstresses' interest was not only confined within French drama and literature. In the eighth issue of the newspaper,[67] there was a lengthy review of James Lawrence' highly controversial books, L'enfants de dieu ou la religion de Jésus réconciliée avec la philosophie, published in French in August 1831 and L'empire de Nairs ou le paradis de l'amour, a utopian romance in twelve books, translated into French in 1803, but first published in German in 1801 as Das Reich der Nairen. Lawrence was English but he wrote in German; eminent reviews at the time of The Empire's publication had commented that this was a book that followed Wollstonecraft's ideas, criticizing marriage and propagating freedom in gender relations, on a plane of love and human happiness (see Graham 1925). Enthusiastic as she was about the work, Suzanne did not seem to share the author's opinions about marriage declaring eight years of happiness in her own, which alas was to end very soon, as I will further discuss in Chapter 5.

What is also worth noting is that Suzanne's engagement with the literary creation of her times would make connections with her overall political and social analyses. Thus, in the fifteenth issue of the newspaper in her article, 'Thoughts on the Religious Ideas of the Century',[68] which was a critical overview and appreciation of the Saint-Simonian religious ideas, Suzanne would draw on Lawrence's *God's Children* and particularly his ideas about freedom in love and the supremacy of maternity. Moreover, her review article of Lawrence's work in the eighth issue of the newspaper actually followed her response to an article in *La Revue des deux mondes*, which had ridiculed the editors of *La Femme Nouvelle* on the basis of their needlework: 'The new women have conquered their independence on the needle tip; they have been emancipated from men's domination by making him his shirts', said the article.[69] As we have already seen, the seamstresses had been repeatedly ridiculed by the French press on the grounds of their social class. As a matter of fact, Suzanne's response to the *Figaro* article that I have discussed above was included in the same eighth issue with her response to *La Revue;* in confronting its derisory article, Suzanne actually made connections between the two: 'Believe me, savant gentlemen of *La Revue*, joking is not your weapon. In your hands, it does not make us laugh; it hurts and is repugnant'.[70]

It is not accidental that Suzanne's bitter response to the press' scorn of the seamstresses' intellectual abilities was accompanied by a forceful demonstration of their critical engagement with literature and drama. Apart from her reflection on Lawrence's books as discussed above, Suzanne also wrote a beautiful review of *Aoust 1572 ou, Charles IX a Orleans,* a historical drama by Jean Lesguillon that she had seen performed at the Théâtre du Panthéon. The play was first published in 1833, but Suzanne offered her readers the first visceral impressions of the drama performance in early December 1832: 'Before I can articulate any thought, it has to pass from my heart, I can only talk of my impressions', she wrote,[71] leaving the task of analysis to 'a more exercised and knowledgeable pen'.[72] The importance of feelings notwithstanding, some reflections and evaluations were unavoidable: although the historical facts of the drama referred to the massacre of St Bartholomew's night, the sentiments were almost contemporary, Suzanne suggested, making allusions to the turbulent politics of the July Monarchy. She further commented on the charming scenes of love and her overall feeling was that there was a lot of hope among young French intellectuals, a generation that the playwright was emerging from.

What we therefore have in Suzanne's review which 'passes from her heart', but still reaches the life of her mind, is the interplay between the three modes of experience in Whitehead's philosophy that I have already discussed in Chapter 2: presentational immediacy, causal efficacy and conceptual analysis (1958, 19). While Suzanne had thrown herself in the immediacy of feeling the play, her enjoyment of 'the drama moment' carried along memories and past formations, 'the hand of the settled past' in Whitehead's analytics (ibid., 50). Her aesthetic experiences—anchored in the past, dragged into the present and ultimately thrown into the future—have inevitably brought conceptual analysis in the playfield of the three modes of perception. In this process, aesthetic experience has got entangled with the unrealized potentiality of its future and has become political. Moreover, Suzanne has been constituted as a subject through this experience: her work identity as a seamstress does not necessarily confine her—let alone determine her, as the 'selfless gentlemen of the *Figaro* would have it. It is through doing and feeling that the Whiteheadian superject emerges in the social milieu of work, culture and politics. Since an intense experience is an aesthetic fact, and all aesthetic experiences are feelings arising from contrasts for Whitehead (ibid., 280), it is the politics of aesthetics as expressed in the seamstresses' 'little brochure' that I now want to consider, drawing on Rancière's (2004) influential work in this field.

THE POLITICS OF AESTHETICS

Unlike common perceptions, art is not an abstract universal for Rancière but rather a discursive regime, historically, socially, culturally and politically specific. Rancière has identified three such regimes, which, although overlapping, have specific rules of classification and taxonomy underpinning what is recognized and understood as art: the ethical regime, the representational regime and the aesthetics regime. Within the discursive limitations of the ethical regime, art is linked to the notion of originality and truth as exemplary theorized and discussed in Plato. Although derived from and related to the Platonic ideal, the representational regime has historically imposed strict taxonomy rules and classificatory principles encompassed in what Rancière has famously theorized as 'the distribution of the sensible', *le partage du sensible*:

> I call the distribution of the sensible the system of self-evident facts of sense perception that simultaneously discloses the existence of something in common and the delimitations that define the respective parts and positions within it. The distribution of the sensible reveals who can have a share in what is common to the community based on what they do and on the time and space in which this activity is performed. (2004, 12–13)

In Rancière's analysis then, 'the distribution of the sensible', configures the boundaries between what is visible and invisible, sayable and unsayable, audible and inaudible, in short, distribution denotes both inclusion and exclusion. Drawing on Aristotle, Rancière gives a good example of the distribution of the sensible in politics, flagging up how inclusion and exclusion are simultaneously at work:

Aristotle states that a citizen is someone who *has a part* in the act of governing
and being governed. However another form of distribution precedes this act of
partaking in government: the distribution that determines those who have a part
in the community of citizens. (ibid., 12)

We know of course that women and slaves were by default excluded from
the community of citizens from classical antiquity well into the twentieth
century. What is more interesting, however, is the way Plato before Aristotle
had justified the exclusion of the artisans from the government of the community on the simple basis that 'they *do not have time* to devote themselves
to anything other than their work' (ibid., 12, my emphasis). It is only in
the aesthetic regime according to Rancière that art is not conceptualized
in terms of hierarchies, divisible spaces and times, but as an open plane of
playful appearances, always fusing into ways of doing and modes of being,
life and art being inextricably interwoven. But this fusion of life and art
opens up a battlefield of forces and there is always a tension between art as
autonomously standing and art as/in life. In this context, Rancière has further
delimited two interrelated planes in the politics of aesthetics: 'The politics of
the becoming life of art' (Berrebi 2008, 2), where diffusion is at work and
'the resistant form' (ibid.), whereby art resists its entanglement into other
forms of life, and it is from this separation that the politics of the aesthetic
experience emerges.

In this light, aesthetic practices for Rancière are 'forms of visibility
that disclose artistic practices', while artistic practices are 'ways of doing
and making' that intervene in the general distribution of ways of doing and
making as well as in the relationships they maintain to modes of being and
forms of visibility (2004, 13). Although not artistic per se, the seamstresses'
'aesthetic practices' as inscribed in their journal create a powerful exemplar
for Rancière's analysis and particularly for the way he links aesthetics and
politics in the distribution of the sensible. His specific reference to 'the properties of spaces and possibilities of times' (ibid.) in delimiting who could
be included in the community of artists, intellectuals and thinkers has been
fleshed out in the heated debates that we have already seen unravel in the
pages of their 'little brochure'.

Although scorned and ridiculed, the seamstresses were nevertheless heard.
In the thirteenth issue of their newspaper published sometime in March 1833,
Suzanne critically discussed Charles Nodier's[73] article about *La Femme
Libre,* which appeared in the second issue of *L' Europe Littéraire.*[74] Nodier
was against the idea of freedom for women: he thought it was premature but
he could see it as a possibility in some distant future. Should they become
free, women would lose their protection and their love, the author feared. It is

around the fact that the author was afraid of women's freedom that Suzanne's response was structured: 'We must be very powerful to have caused you such fright, truly I am very proud of this. All we ask for is equality and you are afraid to see society fall down',[75] she wrote. Suzanne's immediate intervention in the cultural production of her days is particularly striking here. But Nodier's article on the idea of women's freedom, published in the second issue of a prestigious literary journal, is also a sign of the influence that the seamstresses' 'little brochure' had in the cultural and literary circles of its time, as well as the effect of its agonistic encounter with 'the bourgeois other' (Reid 2012, xxi).

Having intervened in the aesthetics of the 'distribution of the sensible', the seamstresses' aesthetic practices have thus sided with what Rancière (2004, 29–30) has identified as the crucial link between 'the aesthetic avant-garde and the political avant-garde: the invention of sensible forms and material structures for a life to come', a kind of 'aesthetic anticipation of the future'. In this context, Rancière (2012) has most persuasively argued that the division between the intellectual as thinker and the worker as doer cannot be grasped or contested by historical interpretations framed within the analytics of workers' resistance: 'The worker, who without having learnt to spell, tried his hands at making verses to the taste of the day, was perhaps more dangerous for the existing ideological order than the one who sang revolutionary songs', Rancière has boldly suggested (2011, 181). For Rancière, politics essentially involves opposition to 'the police order' that underpins and sustains the distribution of the sensible; politics emerges as a challenge to the 'distribution of the sensible' by those who are excluded, 'the part which has no part' (2004, 29–30). Thus 'the distribution of the sensible' has a double sense in Rancière's work: it is both a form of symbolic violence, but also a form of resistance, in the sense of the possibility for redistribution, which is inherent in the very notion of distribution. But how does Rancière conceive the notion of redistribution?

In his reading of the nineteenth-century workers' poetry, prose, as well as letters and diaries, Rancière has actually highlighted 'the thinking of those not "destined" to think' (2012), as a historical exemplar of 'redistribution of knowledge and truth'. Rancière has particularly written about the surprises and unexpected finding he encountered while doing archival research with workers' writings:

> I set out looking for wild expressions of revolt, but I came across politely written texts, requesting that workers be treated as equals. [...] I came across letters [...] about a Sunday in May when [a carpenter] set out with two companions to enjoy the sunrise on the river, discuss metaphysics at an inn, and spend the rest

of the day converting the diners at the next table to their own humanitarian and
social gospel. (ibid., ix)

Rancière has further commented on the workers' yearning for education
and culture, citing at length Deroin's frustration for not having received formal education in her *Profession of Faith*: 'Weary of searching without understanding, I compared and related what was said to me or what was taught me
by books to fairy tales' (Deroin, cited in ibid., 50). Thus, against the dominant
idea within the social and historical sciences that 'the vocation of workers is
to work [...] and to struggle and that they have no time to waste playing at
flâneurs, writers or thinkers' (ibid., viii), what workers needed, Rancière has
argued, was time and space away from labour obligations, so as to be able
to think, read and write, activities that since Plato's *Republic* were only the
privilege of citizens who relied on slaves, women and artisans to look after the
material necessities of life. It was thus conditions of possibility for such intellectual and existential needs that the seamstresses' cultural column created.

Such possibilities, enacted and facilitated within the structures of the nineteenth-century romantic socialist movements, were particularly important
for women workers, seamstresses among them: unlike Rancière's carpenters
and his friends, women workers would never have the leisure of strolling
on a Sunday since their home/labour shift was even more difficult to resist,
challenge or escape. Women workers' lack of time was structured on the
intersection of both waged and domestic labour, and in this light, a Sunday
stroll was barely an option at least for those women workers who had a family to attend to. It is no wonder that all editors of the 'little brochure' were
very young and either single—like Jeanne-Désirée and Marie-Reine—or in
'unconventional' marriages and open relationships, like Suzanne. Moreover,
the fact that they were seamstresses also meant that during the slack periods
in the garment trade they had more time on their hands to engage in cultural
and political activities. The fact that *La Femme Libre* was founded in the
middle of August, at the heart of the low season, was not accidental: it followed the ebbs and flows of the garment industry that the seamstresses were
organically embedded in.

Suzanne's initiative to run a cultural column opened up a forum for cultural discussions and exchanges in the seamstresses newspaper' and has thus
inserted anti-rhythms in the distribution of the sensible. In introducing the
notion of anti-rhythms in the distribution of the sensible here but also elsewhere in my work (see Tamboukou 2015a), I have problematized Rancière's
argument that the politics of aesthetics should be about the democratic project
of redistribution: 'Democracy, in fact, cannot be merely defined as a political
system, one among many, characterised simply by another division of power.
It is more profoundly defined as a certain sharing of the perceptible, a certain

redistribution of its sites' (Rancière 2004, 104). Although I am in agreement with the democratic project of redistribution within the Foucauldian conceptualization of power that my analysis draws upon, any mode of redistribution will necessarily involve a new regime of the distribution of the sensible. As Ross Birrel has aptly noted, although Rancière's notion of the 'distribution of the sensible' is largely influenced by Foucault's and Deleuze's thought, the idea of the possibility of redistribution marks the point where they part company (2008, 3).

Differences in the conceptualization of domination and resistance notwithstanding, I still think that should Rancière's notion of the redistribution be reconfigured as a 'cut' in processes of becoming, it could open up alternative ways of conceptualizing resistance; this is why I have suggested the idea of 'anti-rhythms' as a mode of disruption of the distribution of the sensible rather than its redistribution (Tamboukou 2015a). In making this proposition I have drawn on the theories of assemblages that I have already discussed in Chapter 2. Seen as a component of the July Monarchy *artpolitics assemblage*, the seamstresses' cultural practices have inserted anti-rhythms in the distribution of the sensible and have created interstices, ruptures and lacunae—heterotopic spaces, as I will discuss in the next section, wherein new beginnings and new sensorial modes have emerged, or as Rancière has put it, 'new passages toward new forms of political subjectivisation' (2008, 14). As Isabelle beautifully expressed it in the utopian verses of her poem, 'The Bohemian Woman', published in the twelfth issue of *La Femme Nouvelle* in February 1833:

Live and have nothing to fear
Here is the secret of destiny:
Mortals with sensitive hearts,
Humans breaking their shackles,
[...]
In embracing a new system
The charmed universe will say
'Happiness is not a problem any more'
And the crime will finally cease.[76]

THE FORCE OF THE EPISTOLARY FORM:
HETEROTOPIAS REVISITED

'We will only include articles written by women. [...] We will also receive letters particularly relevant to the questions that we deal with in our publications',[77] Marie-Reine wrote in the postscript that concludes the first issue of

La Femme Libre. Her invitation was more than welcome among her readers: during the two years of its publication, the newspaper received many letters from a range of situated positions, opinions and angles. The editors also wrote letters in response to their correspondents, but they also reprinted letters they had written for other newspapers and publications. What was the role of epistolarity in shaping the form of the first feminist newspaper? This is what I want to look at in this section.

> Barely twenty-two-years old, I have naively told you all my thoughts: if I have not understood well, if I have spoken badly, it is my fault and I submit to your critique; if on the contrary I have told the truth, if there is some merit in what I have just written, it is to you Ladies that I owe it, because it was your words that made my heart vibrate and have warmed up my imagination. You can use these lines in whatever way seems suitable for you.[78]

By concluding her letter to the editors of the *Tribune des Femmes*, declaring her gratitude to the 'Ladies' words that moved her feelings and ignited her imagination, the young proletarian woman who signed as L. B., vividly expressed the importance of the newspaper in opening up relational and dialogic spaces between and among its contributors and its readers. Her letter was published in the fourteenth issue of the newspaper, the same that announced the change of its name from *Apostolat des Femmes* to *Tribune des Femmes*, keeping the subtitle of *La Femme Nouvelle* as the newspaper's symbolic continuity. In the editorial of this fourteenth issue, Suzanne explained the reasons for this name change, the last in the newspaper's two years' publication history: 'Several ladies have refused to write in this newspaper because this title of the *Apostolat* signified a kind of solidarity that they could not accept. And since we have never wanted to hold back the development of social ideas, we have decided that in the future the little paper will be entitled *Tribune des femmes*'.[79] It was of course the Saint-Simonian signification of 'The Apostolate of Women' that several ladies could not identify with and thus the editors' decision to redefine the ideological platform of 'their little paper', a reference that echoes the very first editorial of *La Femme Libre* as the seamstresses' 'little brochure'. There is not much difference in the French language between a *feuille* and a *brochure,* or is there? A *feuille* certainly emits signs of a draft, as well as of fragments, much more so than a *brochure,* but here again there are language slippages as the perception of their publication changes from a *journal* in the first line of the editorial to a *feuille,* three lines later.[80] Ambivalence, indecisiveness and openness marked the seamstresses' discourse and have left their signs both in the content as well as the linguistic expression of their ideas, including the series of changes in the titles and the subtitles of their newspaper that I will further discuss in the final section of this chapter. It is here that the epistolary mode of the seamstresses' 'little paper' becomes important. But why?

In exploring 'the content of the form' of narrative discourse in historical thought, Hayden White has suggested that 'narrative, far from being merely a form of discourse that can be filled with different contents, real or imaginary as the case may be, already possesses a content prior to any given actualisation of it in speech or writing' (1987, xi). In her influential work on epistolarity as a form, Janet Altman, has particularly stressed the fact that although the audience is crucial in all literary works, reading is actively shaping the epistolary form and 'in no other genre do readers figure so prominently within the world of the narrative and in the generation of the text' (1982, 88).

It is thus the I/you relationship that the seamstresses' 'little brochure' has particularly emphasized and nurtured. What is important here is the centrality of confidence and trust that underpins the epistolary relationship: 'You can use these lines in whatever way seems suitable for you', L. B. wrote to the editors in signing her letter.[81] There is actually an interesting link between epistolary and dramatic scenes in the theatre, Altman has pointed out: 'In both epistolary narrative and the theatre, the confidant's voice constantly relieves that of the hero; [he] "asks questions, fills in parts of the exposition, gives advice"' (ibid., 51). Moreover, the confidant, 'not only listens to, comments upon, and relates part of the hero's story, but actually influences it', Altman has further noted (ibid.). The epistolary experience is thus a reciprocal one: through the epistolary act, the reader is actively invited to contribute to the story by responding to it, but since they can always get a new response from their addressee, correspondence as a relation is inherently open. In this light, the epistolary story is always, already incomplete and this openness is its sine-qua-non condition and not a defect, in the Aristotelian narrative configuration of beginning–middle–end. If epistolary stories are always relational, then the subject positions that their characters can occupy either as readers, or writers, or both, are always, already relational as well as vulnerable and therefore political in the Arendtian sense: they depend on each other for their mere survival and they exist through their immersion in the epistolary relationship and from it into the web of human relations.

The seamstresses' epistolary articles, as well as letters thus create a forceful assemblage enacting what Adriana Cavarero has theorized as the neglected I/you relationship and particularly the marginalization of the singular you: 'The *you* is a term that is not at home in modern and contemporary developments of ethics and politics', she has written (2000, 90). Judith Butler has also been interested in the dyadic encounter of the narrative scene and the ethical responsibilities that arise from it, despite the fact that the stories emerging from this encounter will always be incomplete and constrained by prior discursive limitations: 'The narrative authority of the *I* must give way to the perspective and temporality of a set of norms that contest the singularity of my story', Butler has noted (2005, 37). But despite the institutional, discursive, sociopolitical and cultural limitations that charted the *dispositif* of the seamstresses' 'little paper' other spaces still opened up in between interstices, ruptures and gaps. Although it was initially the Saint-Simonian doctrine that created conditions of possibility for this first feminist newspaper to appear, its epistolary form both created and sustained heterotopic spaces wherein feminist positions and ideas were eventually congealed. In thinking about how the Saint-Simonian utopian doctrine was eventually transposed into a heterotopic feminism, Foucault's elegant juxtaposition between *utopias* and *heterotopias* in language creates a plane of consistency for meaning and understanding:

> *Utopias* afford consolation: although they have no real locality there is nevertheless a fantastic, untroubled region in which they are able to unfold; they open up cities with vast avenues, superbly planted gardens, countries where life is easy, even though the road to them is chimerical. (2000, xviii, emphasis in the original)

Saint-Simonianism offered the seamstresses imaginary fields of messianic futurity: the Woman to come, communities where children would grow up in happiness, the elderly would get some rest at the end of their hard-working lives and men and women would live together in love and harmony. As we have seen from their letters to the *Globe,* the seamstresses were initially seduced by such promises and they were willing and brave enough to work for them; they soon realized, however, that the consolation these utopias offered was short-lived, while the material harshness of their present life dragged them into immediate action: founding a newspaper was an initiating act of having a voice of their own, making their way into feminist heterotopias, but ...

> *Heterotopias* are disturbing, probably because they secretly undermine language, because they make it impossible to name this *and* that, because they shatter or tangle common names, because they destroy 'syntax' in advance, and not only the syntax with which we construct sentences, but also that less apparent syntax which causes words and things [...] to 'hold together'. (ibid., emphasis in the original)

Following some trails of the seamstresses' 'little brochure' we have indeed witnessed how 'disturbing' heterotopias can be: we have grasped and lost our patience at the struggle and impossibility of finding a name—both for them-selves, as well as for their newspaper; we have agonized alongside them in the process of charting the complexities of their world, of maintaining a plane of coexistence between disparate components, subjects, voices and relations, of 'holding things together'. The seamstresses' 'little brochure' ultimately became an ambiguous space, a fluid process bursting with uncertainties, contradictions and paradoxes: it was untimely; this is why it failed and disap-peared, some historians—feminists among them—were quick to comment, as we have seen in the Introduction. But if we try to read it as an *œuvre à faire*, an event, 'the experience of the outside',[82] then a different space of understanding opens:

> This is why utopias permit fables and discourse: they run with the very grain of language and are part of the fundamental dimension of the *fabula*; heteroto-pias [...] desiccate speech, stop words in their tracks, contest the very possibility of grammar at its source; they dissolve our myths and sterilize the lyricism of our sentences. (ibid., emphasis in the original)

It is thus with a desiccated, non-lyrical, but yet rhythmical mode of reading and rewriting that I will now conclude this chapter.

REWRITING THE 'LITTLE BROCHURE': RHYTHMS AND MAPS

'What we live are rhythms, rhythms experienced subjectively', Lefebvre wrote in his major work, *The Production of Space* (1991, 206), but it was only at the end of his academic life, when perhaps he had more time to indulge in his love for music—being a pianist as well as an intellectual and activist—that he wrote the small book on *Rhythmanalysis*. Lefebvre's rhythmanalysis looks at the rhythms of social spaces and their effects on the subject, includ-ing the researcher: 'Everywhere where there is interaction between a place, a time and an expenditure of energy, there is *rhythm*' (2004, 15). In this light, rhythm in his work is configured as repetition of movements, gestures, action, situations and differences, as interferences of linear and cyclical processes, but also as 'birth, growth, peak, then decline and end' (ibid.).

Rhythms for Lefebvre are of the world and in the world, they are con-figured as cyclical repetitions entangled with linear processes, but they are never identical—there is always something new and unforeseen emerging from their repetition. Lefebvre also warns us against confusing rhythms with movement or sequence of movements, speed, or machines (ibid., 5). The meaning of rhythm is obscure, he argues (ibid.); we thus need to learn how to discern them, how to listen to the rhythms of a house, a street, a neighbourhood, an archive. But what does it mean to think and live rhythm? 'Rhythmanalysis could change our *perspective* on surroundings', Lefebvre emphatically notes; it makes us aware that there are no sensible objects out there to be discovered or known: 'nothing inert in the world, *no things*: very diverse rhythms' (ibid., 17, emphasis in the text).

In making my way in the turbulent literary world of the seamstresses' 'little brochure' I have found Lefebvre's rhythmanalysis a useful way of reading and understanding the first feminist newspaper. As I have already discussed in the Introduction, what had deeply troubled me in reading the rich body of feminist literature around and about this newspaper was the fragmented way that it has been read, presented and used. In my attempt to engage with this newspaper from the standpoint of process philosophy, I allowed myself an extended period of reading, transcribing and translating. In doing this, I had to slow down and throw myself in the force of the seamstresses' words, re-imagining and feeling their ideas and inspiration.

It was in this process of 'trance reading'—Bergson's (1970, 14) idea that I have discussed in Chapter 2—that I finally succeeded in listening to the newspaper's rhythms. But how much of these readings can be rendered into writing? Norman Denzin has incisively written about the difficulty of turning evidence into data, pointing to how little attention this process has attracted (2009, 146). Even less has been written about how extended research with archival documents is turned into academic outputs, be them books or articles: how much have we read and thought about, but how little can we write—so many words, so many stories, so little space and time!

In the previous sections of this chapter I have tried to create simulations of the newspaper's rhythms through rewriting. As Stanley has luminously suggested, transcribing is about rewriting any archival document, which is never the same after its transcription. Drawing on Michel de Certeau's ideas of 'historiographical operation' (1988a), as a process of writing and rewriting, Stanley has coined the notion of 'archigraphics'—technologies of writing the archive—which encompass a range of practices, including transcriptions, annotations, notes and citations.[83] Writing and rewriting are thus at the heart of how History is being made and drawing maps has certainly been among the practices of historiography. Moreover, the act of drawing maps has been theorized by Deleuze as Foucault's way of writing genealogies: 'To write is to struggle and resist, to write is to become, to write is to draw a map' (1988, 44). Deleuze's commentary actually draws on a self-description that Foucault made in an interview in *Nouvelles Litteraires,* on March 17, 1975: 'I am a cartographer'. It is thus Foucault's line of drawing cartographies that I will now follow below, but there are also a range of mapping technologies presented in the blog I have created as the book's online archive.[84]

MAKING CARTOGRAPHIES

I have always been fascinated by maps, perceiving them as the magic of visually ordering the immensity and chaos of our world. Maps transcend and complete interpretations and stories, they chart topographies of themes, topics, subjects and lines of thought; they create visual images enabling leaps of imagination, but they also invite their viewers to become visitors of the worlds that they simulate and represent. It is actually my desire to invite you readers in the seamstresses' literary world that my attempt to map their newspaper is all about.

The seamstresses' 'little brochure' ran 31 issues in two periods: 20 issues in the first period—August 1832–August/September 1833 and 11 issues in the second—October 1833–April 1834. The first 5 issues were 8 pages long, but the size of the newspaper doubled and remained 16 pages till the end, with the exception of the sixth issue in the second period that had a 3-page 'supplement'. Overall then, it ran in 280 pages in the first period and 184 in the second, its two volumes comprising 464 pages. Its initial print run was 1,000 and the Saint-Simonian extensive network, which included printers, libraries, reading rooms and bookstores, facilitated its circulation. The printing size of the newspaper was thus a constant pattern, a form that emitted signs of its coherence and professionalism in the French socialist press. Another constant of the newspaper was its frequency: although it did not appear on fixed dates—given that its editors were also full-time seamstresses—it more or less had two issues per month, with the exception of a three months' gap in the first period between the seventeenth issue in April/May 1833 and the eighteenth issue in July 1833; there was also only one issue in October 1833 and January and March 1834 in the second period. Unlike the second period's issues that were all dated in the cover—although only giving the month of the publication—most of the issues in the first period were not dated—with the exception of the second and fifth issues—but all dates can be inferred by their content and sometimes the dates in the signatures of their contributors.

The seamstresses' initial indifference in calendar time is quite striking: it shows how totally immersed they were in the revolutionary durée, the moment and events of their incalculable present. Time was not experienced as a linear, measurable entity to be used [and abused]. Here it is also important to remember that the seamstresses were young women: time or the passing of it did not really matter; eternity was their time. More importantly, they seemed somehow to prehend the untimely nature of their movement and its newspaper: having ignored Enfantin's urge to wait for the *Woman*, they were becoming this Woman, they were leaping into radical and unforeseeable futures, beyond the constraints of dates, conditions and 'real' possibilities. In this light, the lived moments of the seamstresses' *now* were actualized

singularities surrounded by a multiplicity of virtualities in the temporal fluid-
ity of 'women's time' as influentially theorized by Julia Kristeva (1981). Far
from being constrained by any sort of calendar time their 'little brochure'
was their way of writing for a future that their 'present could not recognize'
(Grosz 2004, 117), it was about imagining 'the out-of place and the out-of
step' (ibid.).

Unlike dates, which did not seem to matter, at least in the first year,
names *did matter*. I have already given an overview of these name changes
in Chapter 2, but here I want to look closely at the symbolic significations
of such changes. The first issue was entitled as *La Femme Libre* with *Apostolat des Femmes* as a subtitle. The second issue appeared as *Apostolat
des Femmes* with *La Femme Libre* as a small print heading; this subtitle
became *La Femme de l'Avenir* in the third issue and *La Femme Nouvelle*
till the twelfth issue. The thirteenth issue was the only issue published as
Affranchissement des Femmes, still with *La Femme Nouvelle* as its subtitle.
Finally, it was renamed *Tribune des Femmes* carrying *La Femme Nouvelle* as
a subtitle till the end of its second period. Carrying connotations of provoking
moral values, *La Femme Libre* disappeared from the newspaper in the third
issue; the latter was published just after the Saint-Simonian trial that took
place in Paris on August 28 and 29, 1832, resulting in Enfantin's and two of
his followers conviction for offending public morals.[85]

Although the title *Apostolat des Femmes* was the feminist response to Enfantin's decision that the Saint-Simonian apostles would only be men until the
arrival of the Woman Messiah, its subtitle, *La Femme de l'Avenir* seemed to be
in line with the Saint-Simonian dogma of 'waiting for the Woman'. This is why
La Femme Nouvelle, a subtitle implying that the 'new woman' did not have
to wait for her future realization, almost immediately replaced it. It was with
the final titles, *Affranchissement des Femmes* and *Tribune des Femmes* that the
religious elements in the name of the newspaper were dropped and it was actually with this name that the majority of the issues—eighteen out of thirty-one—
were published. In introducing the posthumous publication of Claire Démar's
Ma Loi d'Avenir, Suzanne actually wrote that it was because she was trying to
solicit articles from Démar that she decided to change the title, so that it could
allow her space to express her thoughts (Démar 1834, 14). Interestingly, dates
actually emerged as a constant after the dust of the name-wars had been settled.

Apart from the title/subtitle changes, there was also an ebb and flow with
slogans and epigraphs. The first front-page slogan appeared in the third issue:
'With the emancipation of the woman will come the emancipation of the
worker', both nouns in the singular to denote the Saint-Simonian importance
on the individual. In connecting women's emancipation with that of the workers', the editors sought to clarify their position vis-à-vis the controversies that
the title *La Femme Libre* had initially caused in the Parisian bourgeois circles

in general and the Saint-Simonian community in particular. But as internal differences had not stopped, this turmoil was transferred to the changes in epigraphs and slogans: the fifth issue came with a new slogan: 'Liberty for women, liberty for the people through a new organisation of the household and industry'. The link between women and the people of the first slogan was kept, but the importance of the reorganization of the household was flagged up. The sixth issue, which initiated Suzanne's editorship, interestingly added two words, 'Truth and Union', below its main title and before the epigraph, thus highlighting the importance for women to be united despite their differences. But as the final change to the front epigraph in the tenth issue signifies, internal conflicts went on and thus the need to invoke Jean d'Arc's religious heroicism: 'Equality among us of rights and duties; Since our banner is to pain, It is just that it be to honour (Jean d'Arc)', which remained till the end with just a small reordering in the eleventh issue: 'Since our banner is to pain, It is just that it be to honour (Jean d'Arc); Equality among us of rights and duties'.

All these changes in names, titles, subtitles, slogans and epigraphs forcefully express the fact that there never was such a thing as a 'Saint-Simonian feminism' given the so many differences that we have seen staged in the name-wars, but also in the contents and discourses of their articles. As I have already argued in the Introduction, it is ideas and trends that we should explore in the archive of the seamstresses' documents. Indeed, the archive of their newspaper does not reveal any kind of linear or coherent 'ism', simply because there wasn't any, not only among authors or even in the corpus of writings of one author only, but even in the textual space of single sentences. The seamstresses' newspaper carries signs of what it means to write difference, but it is also a tangible trace of ideas and social movements in becoming.

THE BECOMING OF A FEMINIST NEWSPAPER

Although the names of the newspaper changed many times during the two years of its publication, the editorial team did not see any dramatic changes after Jeanne-Désirée's withdrawal. Suzanne's editorship gave a sense of continuity to the newspaper; in the last issue of April 1834, she was able to look back at the newspaper's past editors and pay tribute to their contribution: she devoted several thoughts to Jeanne-Désirée, 'who founded our little paper under the title *Apostolat des Femmes,* without any material means to start this work, jointly with *Marie-Reine* and me, who only joined them towards the second issue'.[86] In Suzanne's view, 'Jeanne-Désirée's thought was too artistic to allow her to stay with a work for long',[87] but even when she withdrew, she asked for her title as the founder of the newspaper to be kept. Jeanne-Désirée's desire for her legacy to be kept is indeed striking:

it seems that the seamstresses were fully aware of the historical importance of their actions, as well as of the need for these actions to find their way in the discourse of history.

Unlike Jeanne-Désirée, whose 'artistic soul' was not fit for perseverance, Marie-Reine only left to serve the people: 'Her days are devoted to work and her evenings are employed in educating women and the daughters of the people',[88] Suzanne wrote in the last issue. Suzanne was able to stay on as editor till the end, since by the time she joined the newspaper she no longer needed to work as an embroiderer: her husband was an architect, they lived in a flat rented from a Saint-Simonian sympathizer at a very low price and even when they separated she was supported by the Saint-Simonian community in a way that allowed her to work part-time and keep four days per week at the newspaper only (see Moses and Rabine 1993, 48). When Marie-Reine withdrew after the thirteenth issue in March 1833, Suzanne co-edited the newspaper first with Angélique [surname unknown] from the fourteenth till the nineteenth issues and then with Célestine [Montagny] for the twentieth issue of the first period, as well as the nine issues of the second period. It was only for the two last issues that Suzanne signed as the only editor.

The newspaper had several contributors during the two years of its publication. Around thirty women wrote articles, literary and drama reviews, poems as well as lengthy letters. Apart from the founder and the two co-editors, the names of the contributors include Jeanne-Victoire, Isabelle [Gobert], Joséphine-Félicite, Gertrude, Juliette B**, Angélique, Sophie-Caroline, Célestine [Montagny], M. F., Francoise Rosalie, Emilie, Pauline, Amanda, Mademoiselle E., Augustine, Armantine, Concordia, Marie Camille de G. as well as those who signed with their full name: Angelique Pignot, Adèle Miguet, Louise Dauriat, Caroline Valchere, Jenny Durand, F. Dazur and Adèle de Saint-Amand. There were finally six contributors who remained totally anonymous; interestingly enough, one of them wrote an article about the emancipation of the colonies, which was presented as an issue of universal importance, while the second, who was a reader from New Orleans, wrote about the terrible situation of black slaves.[89] Anonymous as they remained, these are the only two articles that bring race in the discussion of emancipation.

Overall then, the newspaper comprises ninety articles, fifteen cultural reviews and responses, fourteen letters, four poems, two reprints and translations and fourteen small announcements and pieces of news. Half of these articles, cultural reviews and letters were written by the editors: Suzanne wrote twenty-four articles, nine cultural reviews, eight letters and eight smaller pieces of news and announcements; Marie-Reine wrote sixteen articles, two lengthy epistolary responses and one literary review and Jeanne-Désirée wrote six articles and perhaps two letters from England under a pseudonym. The majority of the contributors did not write more than two articles, reviews or letters, although there were some women who contributed more: Isabelle [Gobert] wrote six articles and two poems; Joséphine-Félicite wrote five articles and Gertrude wrote three articles and one review. There were thus no 'regular contributors' as Moses (1985, 65) has suggested[90]; it was the founder and the two editors who shaped the content and theoretical directions of the newspaper.

Earlier in this chapter, I have discussed in detail the themes of the first issue, highlighting its uniqueness in terms of how it addressed the sociopolitical and economic conditions of women's oppression and subordination. These themes were examined from different angles and perspectives throughout the thirty-one issues of the newspaper, while women workers' education became a recurrent topic. As a matter of fact, the second period of the *Tribune des Femmes* was almost dominated by the discussions of a series of seminars organized by the *Society for Educational Methods*, where the question of how to develop the intellectual movement among women was addressed, albeit not solved according to Marie-Reine, who wrote in January 1834:

> Here we have arrived at the sixth conference on the same question, and is the solution more advanced than in the first day? I don't think so. On the contrary, the question has shifted: instead of searching ways to use women's intelligence, we now search for ways to develop it. This constitutes the fact that the question was badly posed.[91]

Interestingly enough, Marie-Reine's approach to this question was quite different from Suzanne's article on the same issue, where the question of how to improve and develop women's intelligence was validated; in following it Suzanne looked back at a genealogy of important men who had written about women's education.[92] It was not the first time that the two co-editors had expressed different views about women's position. Among the many themes that were discussed in the pages of the first feminist newspaper, two basic trends emerged: a material, grounded and sociopolitical approach to women's condition, mostly expressed by Marie-Reine's heterotopic positionality and a spiritual trend mostly expressed by Suzanne, which was abstract, mystically driven and utopian in nature. The fact that Marie-Reine worked as a seamstress throughout, while Suzanne had abandoned the garment trades was not accidental in how differences in their ideas were shaped and expressed. Their differences notwithstanding, the two co-editors remained good friends till the end; when Suzanne came back from Egypt at the end of 1836, it was at Marie-Reine's flat that she stayed, until she could find a way to support herself. Suzanne wrote tenderly about how kind Marie-Reine and her husband had been to her: 'Come stay with us, they told me, some calm days will give you the opportunity to redirect your life. [...] I did not hesitate and stayed with the young couple till January 8, 1837' (Voilquin 1866, 479).

It was thus in the spirit of friendship and association among differences that the seamstresses' 'little brochure' was written and published. Its themes included topics that were both constant, about women's subordination, and also emergent from particular events and situations, which were not necessarily specific to women. For example, the Saint-Simonian trial in August 1832 was discussed at length early on in the newspaper as a response to the unfolding events.[93] Marie-Reine wrote a fervent article, raising 'the weak voice of a woman, who dared ask for the abolition of the death penalty in the fifth issue of the second period',[94] while Armantine joined her voice in the anti-duel debates that followed the death of François-Charles Dulong in January 1834.[95]

Apart from a range of calls to women to unite despite their differences and to men to recognize women's rights and support their struggle, constant topics and recurrent themes included: the problem of prostitution, motherhood as women's advantaged position in society, projects around young women's protection, articles on religious ideas and standpoints, debates around morality, emotions and feelings, questions around the oppressive institution of marriage and the necessity for divorce to be legalized again. There were also letters and responses to other newspaper articles and debates, reprints of brochures and speeches from the activities of Saint-Simonian communities, as well as women's organizations around France. In the second period, there were finally a number of articles about England and the United States and towards the end of the second period, news about the Saint-Simonians, who had already left for Egypt.[96]

All articles were individually signed with the exception of the 'Response to G***', the only collective article in the two years of the newspaper, which appeared in the thirteenth issue of the first period and was signed by *Les Femmes Nouvelles*. As its title indicates, the article was a response to Gertrude who had written about the Christian origins of women's emancipation but had also vehemently attacked and criticized Saint-Simonianism and its ideas about women's emancipation:

> What has Saint-Simonianism done? It has come to proclaim women's emancipation in the middle of such immoral and absurd ideas that the first task of a woman who wants to write in this journal is to protest, so that emancipation be separated from all the theories and writings that have been associated with the *Globe*.[97]

It is here interesting to note that as a collective response to Gertrude, the article starts and signs with a 'we', but 'I' crept into its discourse: 'As we want to prove our impartiality and tolerance vis-à-vis all opinions we have decided to publish your article [but] before we go any further I think you must listen to what is moral or immoral for us'.[98] Oscillating between the 'I' and the 'we' and despite its overall religious spirit, the article deployed a persuasive argument: morality was materially redefined; it was further linked to happiness and was mapped on the act and not on the mind: 'Morality for us is in the act [...] the spirit and the flesh are equally holy', the *Femmes Nouvelles* wrote.[99] The seamstresses' quest for happiness, both individual and social, was indeed at the heart of how they re-imagined their future, viscerally engaging with what I want to call 'the right to love', the theme of Chapter 4, which I will now turn to.

NOTES

1. *Apostolat des Femmes—La Femme Nouvelle* 1(7), 69, November 4, 1832 (my emphasis). For a full [different] translation of the article, see Moses and Rabine 1993, 296–97.

2. In the beginning of the July Monarchy, King Louis-Philippe proclaimed himself as the 'King of the French' instead of 'King of France', thus denoting his difference from the Bourbon monarchy that the July revolution had overthrown.

3. *Lettre au Roi* [Letter to the King], 1.

4. This is how Louis-Philippe was called because of his bourgeois ideas, beliefs and attitude. See Howarth 1961.

5. *La Femme Libre-Apostolat des Femmes* 1(1), preamble. August 15, 1832.

6. *Apostolat des Femmes-La Femme Nouvelle* 1(5), 36, October 8, 1832.

7. 'Amélioration du sort des femmes et du peuple par une nouvelle organisation du menage', in ibid., 36–39. For a translation of an extended extract from this article, see Moses and Rabine 1993, 289–91.

8. *Tribune des Femmes* 11(2), 181. April, 1834.

9. BnF/BdA/FE/MS7608/CdG/Deroin, 17 and in Riot-Sarcey 1992, 126.

10. Jeanne-Désirée to Enfantin, letter dated, October 20, 1832, BnF/BdA/FE/Ms7608/CdG(D)/DJ/43, 1. Also, Riot-Sarcey 1992, 77–79.

11. Ibid.

12. Ibid., 2.

13. Ibid., 3.

14. Ibid., 3–4.

15. Jeanne-Désirée, 'From my work you will know my name', *Apostolat des Femmes—La Femme Nouvelle* 1(7), 69, November 4, 1832.

16. Jeanne-Désirée, *Aux Femmes Privilégiées* [To the Privileged Women], 3.

17. Ibid, 2.

18. Ibid.

19. For more details of Bertin's life, see Sapori 2010.

20. *Aux Femmes Privilégiées*, 2.

21. Following the politics of 'her name', in this chapter I have referred to the seamstresses with the names they chose to sign their articles or letters.

22. *Apostolat des Femmes-La Femme Nouvelle* 1(7), 70, November 4, 1832.

23. BnF/BdA/FE/MS7608/CdG/Deroin, 36 and in Riot-Sarcey 1992, 135.

24. For a discussion of Tristan's relation to the 'name of the father', see Moses and Rabine 1993, pp. 124–42. There is a rich body of literature around Tristan. See Cross and Gray 1992; Grogan 2000; Cross 2004.

25. *Apostolat des Femmes-La Femme Nouvelle,* 1(8), 86–87, December 1832.

26. *La Femme Libre-Apostolat des Femmes* 1(1), 1–2, August 15, 1832.

27. 'Appeal to Women', *La Femme Libre-Apostolat des Femmes* 1(1), 2, August 15, 1832.

28. Ibid., 3.

29. Ibid.

30. Ibid., 4–5.

31. *Apostolat des Femmes-La Femme Libre,* 1(2), 3, August 25, 1832.

32. 'Improvement of the fate of women and of the people through a new organisation of the household', Ibid. 1(5), 37, October 8, 1832.

33. Ibid., 1(2), 5, August 25, 1832.

34. Ibid.

35. Jeanne-Désirée to Enfantin, letter dated, October 20, 1832, BnF/BdA/FE/Ms7608/CdG(D)/DJ/43, 2–3. Also, Riot-Sarcey 1992, 78.

36. Gay to Enfantin, letter dated, May 28, 1856. (BnF/BdA/FE/CD/7728/163, 1)

37. Véret-Gay to Considerant, letter dated, October 9, 1890. (AnF/10AS42/8/DVG/65/4)

38. *La Femme Libre-Apostolat des Femmes* 1(1), 7, August 15, 1832.

39. Ibid.

40. Ibid.

41. Ibid., 8.

42. Ibid.

43. Deroin to Auclert, letter dated, January 10, 1886, in BHVP/AMB/Au/CP4247/JD, 2–3, also in BMD/R/DJ/DD/42–43.

44. *Tribune des Femmes-La Femme Nouvelle* 2(9), 146, March, 1834.

45. Collectively known as *La Révolte des Canuts*, these uprisings were among the first in the French Industrial Revolution. Following a general wage decrease in October 1831, the silk workers asked for a minimum wage to be set, but the government turned them down and further banned all workers' associations. See Bezucha 1974.

46. *Apostolat des Femmes-La Femme Nouvelle,* 1(6), 49, October 1832.

47. Letter to the *Globe,* dated September 11, 1831. BnF/BdA/FE/Ms7608/CdG(D)/DJ/40, 1. Also, in Riot-Sarcey 1992, 69.

48. *Tribune des Femmes-La Femme Nouvelle* 2 (10), 165, April, 1834.

49. Ibid., 1(16), 205, April 1833, emphasis in the original.

50. Ibid., 1(15), 198–99, April, 1833 [all emphases in the original].

51. For a more detailed exposition of trade differences within the garment industry, see Coffin 1996, particularly Chapter 1, pp. 19–45.

52. Marie-Reine, 'In the Spirit of Association', *Tribune des Femmes-La femme Nouvelle* 1(15), 199–200, April, 1833.

53. At the time *La Femme Libre* was founded, Tristan was obliged to stay away from Paris to avoid her abusing husband to take custody of their daughter Aline.

In April 1833, she travelled to Peru and she only came back to Paris in early 1835, when the newspaper's short life had already come to its end. See Beik and Paul 1993, xiv.

54. Marie-Reine [Guindorf], 'On Public Education', *Apostolat des Femmes-La Femme Nouvelle,* 1(12), 146, February, 1833.

55. Ibid., 145.

56. Ibid., 146.

57. Voilquin, 'Reine, Cardinal et Page', Comedy in One Act de M. Anselot' *Apostolat des Femmes-La Femme Nouvelle* 1(10), 118, December, 1832.

58. Voilquin, 'Letter to Béranger', ibid., 1(12), 150, February, 1833.

59. For an overview of the cultural world of the seamstresses and links to them, see the book archive at https://sites.google.com/site/mariatamboukou/the-book-archive/references-and-sources/cultural-worlds [Accessed, 17-5-2015].

60. Ibid., 119–20.

61. *Apostolat des Femmes-La Femme Nouvelle* 1(4), 4–8, September 19, 1832.

62. Ibid., 1(6), 56, October 1832.

63. Ibid., 1(11), 134–36, January, 1833.

64. Ibid., 134.

65. Ibid.

66. Ibid., 136.

67. Ibid., 1(8), 83–86, December, 1832.

68. Ibid., 1(15), 185–95, April 1833. For a translation of lengthy extracts from this article, see also Moses and Rabine 1993, 311–13.

69. Ibid., 1(8), 80–81, December 1832.

70. Ibid., 81.

71. Ibid.

72. Ibid., 82.

73. Charles Nodier (1780–1844) was a French romantic author. See Richard 1964 for an overview of the author and his work.

74. This was a literary journal, which was only established in 1833, but with great literary names as contributors, including Balzac and Nodier among others.

75. *Affranchissement des Femmes-La Femme Nouvelle* 1(13), 166, March 1833.

76. *Apostolat des Femmes-La Femme Nouvelle* 1(12), 152, February 1833.

77. *La Femme Libre-Apostolat des Femmes* 1(1), 8, August 15, 1832.

78. *Tribune des Femmes-La Femme Nouvelle* 1(14), 180, April 1833.

79. Ibid., 169–70.

80. Ibid.

81. Ibid.,180, April 1833.

82. This is how Foucault read Blanchot's work. See Blanchot and Foucault 1990.

83. For a detailed discussion of 'archigraphics', see Stanley forthcoming, 2016.

84. See https://sites.google.com/site/mariatamboukou/the-book-archive.

85. Duveyrier and Chevalier were the two Saint-Simonians convicted alongside Enfantin to a year in prison, while Rodrigues and Barrault were each fined 50 francs. See Pilbeam 2014 for more details about the trial, particularly Chapter 3, 44–69.

86. *Tribune des Femmes,* 2(11), 181, April, 1834.

87. Ibid.

88. Ibid., 182.

89. Both articles were published in *Tribune des Femmes,* 2(4), 57–58, December 1833. The fact that they came from New Orleans is not accidental. There were many Saint-Simonians who had emigrated to New Orleans at the time in a way to find lands to create co-operative communities, Voilquin's estranged husband and her sister among them.

90. Moses (1984, 65) has mistakenly included Jeanne Deroin, Pauline and Caroline Beranger among 'the regular contributors' of the newspaper. As I have already shown, Deroin only wrote 2 articles in the beginning of the first period, Pauline only 3 reviews and Beranger only 2 short announcements about her project of raising funds to pay back Enfantin's debt.

91. *Tribune des Femmes,* 2(6), 93–94.

92. Ibid., 90–93.

93. *Apostolat des Femmes/La Femme de l'Avenir,* 1(3), 1–8.

94. *Tribune des Femmes,* 2(5), 84.

95. 'A word about Duel', ibid., 2(7), 117–18. See also Nye 1998, 138.

96. See Pilbeam 2014 for a discussion of the colonial conditions and effects of the Saint Simonian projects in Egypt and Algeria.

97. *Affranchissement des Femmes/ La Femme Nouvelle,* 1(13), 154.

98. Ibid., 157.

99. Ibid., 160

Chapter 4

Feeling the World

Love, Gender and Agonistic Politics

To Father in Melinmontant
31-8-1932
Finally, here is the immortal judgment. Like Jesus you appeared before the judges of a law that falls into disuse; you were convicted and were crucified in the mind as he was in the flesh. But you will see your law established, as your reign is of this world.

Enfantin, the time has come for me to speak to you frankly. I have detached myself from the ties of the old family and while your arrest seemed to annihilate the apostolate of men, the old society was admitting my birth father in one of its retreat houses and by removing the fear of seeing him without bread in his old years, a free road opened for my impatient ardour for freedom and it seemed to promote in this way the apostolate of women. Thus I can speak to you freely today because my actions are consistent with my words and soon the world will know me as you yourself first came to know me.

But I still want mystery even a little of it. I enter a totally new path; there is a side in my life, which was compressed by my will and my pride and I came very close to be almost completely destroyed; I want to talk about feelings, I have always feared love because I did not have faith in the morality of men. This was the cause of the dryness, or rather of the apparent hardness of my heart; I only felt deaf concussions, an internal fire was devouring me and my tears were flowing inside me like a burning lava. Never did anybody guess this tenderness inside me. Never did a man find the secret to make my soul flourish and spread on everything around me. I am not this beauty, this indefinable charm, which unites and binds everything, because I have not been linked to anybody. However, there is a whole world inside me. This world makes me if not happy, less and less unhappy than the one around me. I had a strong contempt for the human race, I was tranquil in my indifference, I was self-sufficient, I was not linked to any individuals, but only to the infinity of my egoism, and by persuading myself not to want anything more, I had stopped searching for anything (or so I had thought); I was in such a state when I saw you and you have upset and destroyed my dreams, you have not given me enough to satisfy me but you have given me enough to make me desire more. Your caresses, your kisses revived me, you brought me to life, but you have caused in me a real anarchy, the living image of society; there is good inside me, but it is harmful; all my feelings are scattered, divided, conflicting. I lack a bond, which will unify them and make of me a new woman. This bond is love.

Prosper you started it ... finish your work, the world is against us but it will change, it is because of you that I can love this world, which keeps throwing us mud: you have made me not to detest it, make it now that I love it, that I do not stiffen any more against such attacks and that I embrace them with my love.

The heart of the daughter of the people is still brute; the love that we imposed upon men did not have the power to soften her; she had another love that she only found in god. It is up to you to make her find love amongst men. It is of you that she was dreaming and the distance that she first kept from you, was it because you were not any more who you are now? The trouble, the uncertainty that she has for you now, is it because you are not any more who you will be later on, or maybe who you will become? Or even, because you are not him?

Make this uncertainty that preoccupies me stop soon, it has served its purpose, I intended to accomplish this, but now it hurts. I have not yet asked you to respond to my letters. I am content to read them in your eyes; now I need more than a glance, I won't see you any more until after I have received a letter from you, I won't see you any more without having a long meeting with you on a day, time and place that you will indicate.

I am conscious of what I am doing at this moment. It is not passion or weakness that makes me write this letter, but the faith that I am performing a religious act. I am speaking to you with the feeling of freedom, dignity and love that a woman ought to have for a man who describes himself as waiting for the word. I owe it to the cause of women and I would act selfishly if I listened to the love of a woman, who has very often been wounded by men's pride, for I could abandon myself to the love that your lofty virtues inspired in me; your pride did not wound me enough so that I can dislike you.

Nobody knows the content of this letter, today begins the mystery for me, from today I demand of you...

Adieu, ... I wait

I embrace you, Jeanne-Désirée.[1]

Three days after his trial for offending public morality and after Enfantin had been sentenced to a year's imprisonment and to a high fine, Jeanne-Désirée sent him a letter *de profundis* that has become one of the most well-known in her correspondence (see Riot-Sarcey 1994, 61). It is not difficult to see why: the letter is a beautiful assemblage of political and amorous epistolary writing bringing together thoughts, feelings and expectations; it talks of the heart and of the mind, it embraces flesh and the body, it remembers and it imagines, it articulates decisions and it raises demands. And yet, despite its richness in content and in form, as well as the many angles and ways it has been cited, discussed and analysed, this letter has never been translated in English before in its entirety. If it were not for Riot-Sarcey's thin volume, *De la liberté des femmes: 'Lettres de Dames' au Globe (1831–1832)*, Jeanne-Désirée's most well-known letter would have never been accessible to wider audiences, even in French.[2]

I was deeply moved by the force of this letter, but I was also intrigued and puzzled by it; I kept returning to it many times throughout this study, always with new insights and angles of understanding that unfolded as my research was excavating more and more layers in the archaeological site of nineteenth-century feminist thought. Love is, of course, the central theme of the letter. But what are love's different modes of existence within nineteenth-century feminism in general and the epistolary discourse of personal letters in particular? Moreover, how is love related to feminist politics? It is around these questions that this chapter will revolve by tracing Arendtian insights on love, while making rhizomatic connections with an assemblage of lines of thought that have explored love as Eros—a force rather than a passion.

LOVE AND/IN THE WORLD

Love was at the heart of Arendt's theoretical interests: her doctoral thesis was on love in St Augustine, while in writing Rahel Varnhagen's life, she particularly considered and discussed a Jewish woman's failure in 'matters of love' (Arendt 2000). Love is further extensively discussed in the chapter on 'Action' of the *Human Condition,* particularly in relation to forgiveness. Love, 'one of the rarest occurrences in human lives, indeed possesses an unequalled power of self-revelation and an unequalled clarity of vision for the disclosure of *who'*, Arendt wrote (1998, 242). Love is thus configured as an existential force through which human beings appear to each other and to the world. We can discern Jeanne-Désirée's appearance to the world in her letter to Enfantin above: it is by revealing, almost confessing her love to him that she emerges as an Arendtian 'who'—unique and unrepeatable. She actually seems to be very conscious of this appearance: 'Soon the world will know me as you yourself first came to know me',[3] she wrote, implicitly referring to her public appearance through the *Femme Libre*, the newspaper she had founded and which had already run its second issue.

But while facilitating the emergence of the uniqueness of the *who*, love is not concerned with the worldly character, 'the whatness' (Guaraldo 2001, 27) of humans or things: 'By reason of its passion, [love] destroys the in-between which relates us to and separates us from others', Arendt wrote (1998, 242). In short, love moves us away from the world, it is 'unworldly [...] not only apolitical but antipolitical, perhaps the most antipolitical of all antipolitical human forces' (ibid.). Arendt's ambivalence in relation to the worldly character of love is stark in the above often-cited extracts of the *Human Condition*. Removed from the political, love still remained important for Arendt; it actually became a *conditio sine qua non* for life, shaping as Kristeva has noted, the themes and directions of her later work (2001b, 31). But how can love as 'an antipolitical' force par excellence affect the configuration of the political?

Leaving aside Arendt's personal grounds and ties in considering this riddle, I want to focus on love as an existential notion in her political thought.[4] Here I draw on the argument that 'Arendt's categories and methods of theorising are not fully intelligible unless read against the background of German existentialism' (Hinchman and Hinchman 1994, 143) and particularly in relation to Karl Jasper's influence, who was the supervisor of her doctoral thesis on love. As Lewis and Sandra Hinchman have argued, Jaspers and Arendt attempted to bridge the gap between solitude and contemplation—so important for the 'authentic individual' of existentialist thought—and the worldliness of being, 'whether through "communication" (Jaspers) or action in the political arena (Arendt)' (ibid.). In this context, what I have elsewhere suggested is that love for Arendt is configured as a fort-da movement, through which the solitary individual flies away from the world, but then returns to it: an 'antipolitical' force that ultimately creates conditions of possibility for the constitution of the political (see Tamboukou 2013b, 44). It is 'this rebellious return, this desire for rupture, renewal or renaissance' that animates Arendt's writings on the world revolutions, Kristeva has noted (2001b, 34).

We can trace some signs of this impossibility in Jeanne-Désirée's troubling amorous relation with Enfantin: her love was anti-political in the Arendtian sense: she was in love with the man, who had excluded women from the Saint-Simonian hierarchy. To his suggestion that the Saint-Simonian Apostolate of Men should wait for the Woman, Jeanne-Désirée had responded by founding the Apostolate of Women and she had initiated a newspaper, which was literally composed and written in her own home, 17 Rue du Caire (see Adler 1979, 43). Since the Arendtian love is linked to forgiveness, Jeanne-Désirée had moved on with her feminist political project while still waiting for Enfantin to send her signs of love.

Jeanne-Désirée's contradictions and divided feelings show with clarity that Arendt's configuration of love as a force of life and change should not to be conflated with 'the inherent wordlessness of love' (Arendt 1998, 52). As Arendt poignantly points out, 'Love in distinction from friendship, is killed or rather extinguished, the moment it is displayed in public' (ibid., 50). Jeanne-Désirée seems to be sensitive to love's vulnerability to public exposure: 'Nobody knows the content of this letter, today begins the mystery for me',[5] she wrote to Enfantin at the end of her letter. She also seems to share Arendt's fear that 'love can only become false and perverted when it is used for political purposes such as the change or salvation of the world' (ibid., 52). Jeanne-Désirée's love for Enfantin was an inspiration for her political will to change the world and women's lives within it, but she would not 'use it' as a tool for her politics; quite the opposite: she loved Enfantin despite her feminist politics. Love is then a *conditio sine qua non*, but not the *conditio per quam* of the political: it can inspire revolutionary acts, but it cannot be used to justify or ground them; it certainly 'paves the way for a conceptualisation of life as mobility, alterity and alteration', Kristeva has aptly commented (2001b, 34). Love is thus a multi-levelled assemblage in Arendt's thought encompassing subtle reconfigurations of Augustine's notion that I now want to map and unravel.

Remembering (in) Love

Arendt's thesis 'Love and St Augustine' was defended in 1928, but while it was her first work to be published in German in 1929, it would become her last book-length manuscript to be published in English in 1996—twenty-one years after her death—although a synopsis of the dissertation in English was included as an appendix of Young-Bruehl's intellectual biography, *Hannah Arendt, For Love of the World* in 1982. There is a gap of almost seventy years, which has greatly shaped the ways in which Arendtian notions have been read, operationalized, defended or disputed in political theory in general and its feminist strands in particular.[6] My reading of Arendt's notion of love and the connections I draw with the political is thus situated in a field of scholarship that has followed the publication of her Augustinian thesis.[7] It has to be noted, however, that this connection has become controversial; as Joanna Scott and Judith Stark, the editors of this publication have noted, it 'will continue to be so until the whole corpus of her work in Germany and America, is evaluated and incorporated into the "orthodox" rendering of Arendt's political thought' (1996: viii).

Controversies notwithstanding, Arendt had started working on the thesis in 1960 with a publication in mind.[8] As she wrote to Jaspers in 1966, 'I am doing something odd on the side. [...] I am rewriting my *Augustine* in English. [...] It's strange—this work is so far in the past, on the one hand; but on the other, I can still recognise myself as it were; I know exactly what I wanted to say'.[9] The publication was never realized during her lifetime, but as a range of Arendtian scholars have argued, her thesis on Augustine remained central in the political writings of her maturity: 'The return to Augustine directly infused her revisions of *Origins of Totalitarianism*, her new study *On Revolution*, the essays collected in *Between Past and Future* and *Eichman in Jerusalem* with explicit and implicit Augustinian references' (Scott and Stark 1996, x).

Moreover, Augustine's thought was critical in how Arendt developed her section on 'the faculty of the Will and by implication to the problem of Freedom' (1981, 3) in her posthumously published work *The Life of the Mind*. As Young-Bruehl has noted, the notion of love binds together the three faculties in the *Life of the Mind,* namely Thinking, Willing and Judging (1994, 356). In this light, we *think* since we love meaning and the search for truth, we *will* the pleasure that the continuation of things can offer and we *judge* within the disinterested love that the image of the beautiful[10] can offer us: 'an image of judging as a disinterested love . . . put together with the image of thinking as an eros for meaning and the image of willing, transformed into love, willing objects to continue *being*' (Young-Bruehl 1994, 356, emphasis in the original). We can trace entanglements of Thinking, Willing and Judging in Jeanne-Désirée's love letter to Enfantin above: it starts with an acknowledgement of the unfairness of his trial, written as it was three days after his conviction, but it soon moves into its central theme, her will to understand the state of their relationship, as well as the nature and possibilities of her love: 'The time has come for me to speak to you frankly',[11] she wrote. The rest of the letter unfolds the tripartite function of Jeanne-Désirée's mind, which revolves around her intense and passionate love for Enfantin. But this recurrence of love as a concept binding the three faculties of the mind derives from the emergence of love as an effect of the Augustinian journey of memory, which creates conditions of possibility for the three functions of the mind to hold together.

In the quest of meaning for ourselves and our relationship to the world, the future cannot offer us any hope since it is directed to death, a certain point that defines the temporality of human existence, as influentially theorized by Heidegger (2003). In seeking fearlessness through love,[12] Augustine's philosophy offers a different image of time that comes from the future and is directed towards the past, the moment of the beginning of the world, as well as our own beginning, namely our birth. This image of time can be humanly conceptualized through memory: 'Time exists only insofar as it can be measured, and the yardstick by which we measure it is space' (Arendt 1996, 15). For Augustine then, memory is the space wherein we measure time, but what we can measure is only what remains fixed in memory from the 'no more' and what exists as expectation from the 'not yet'. As Arendt eloquently puts it, 'It is only by calling past and future into the presence of remembrance and expectation that time exists at all' (ibid.). Although timeless, the present does become 'the only valid tense', the *Now* 'is not time but outside time', Arendt writes (ibid.).

Love is crucial in the experience of the timeless *Now*: while for Augustine it is the love for God that can make humans forget their temporal existence over eternity, forgetfulness Arendt notes 'is by no means only characteristic of the love of God' (ibid., 28). In loving '[man] not only forgets himself, but in a way [he] ceases to be [himself], that is this particular place in time and space. [He] loses the human mode of existence, which is mortality, without exchanging for the divine mode of existence, which is eternity' (ibid.). But there is a problem in this self-forgetfulness and transcendence of human existence for Augustine: the Christian imperative to love thy neighbour. This is how the Augustinian journey of memory 'as a two-step process of isolation from and return to this world' (Hammer 2000, 87) becomes so important for Arendt: 'The fact that the past is not forever lost and that remembrance can bring it back into the present is what gives memory its great power'.[13] This Augustinian statement is what underpins and sustains Arendt's departure from Heidegger's orientation towards death, to the concept of natality that marks her own philosophy:

> Since our expectations and desires are prompted by what we remember and guided by a previous knowledge, it is memory and not expectation (for instance the expectation of death as in Heidegger's approach) that gives unity and wholeness to human existence. (Arendt 1996, 56)

Augustine's existential question par excellence, 'I have become a question to myself',[14] initiates a memory journey in which 'the beginning and end of [his] life become exchangeable' (ibid., 57). In remembering the past and its joys, we also transform them into future possibilities, while human existence appears as what it is: an 'everlasting Becoming' (ibid., 63), in a world that is both physical and human. It is in the realization of existence in the human world that the neighbourly love emerges, since the human world 'constitutes itself by habitation and love (diligere) [...] love for the world [...] rests on being of the world' (ibid., 66). Indeed, amidst the three configurations of love in Augustine's philosophy, 'love as craving (*appetitus*), love as a relation between man and God the Creator, and neighbourly love' (Young-Bruehl 1982, 74), it is the latter that fascinates Arendt. Neighbourly love as an existential concept is also crucial in her philosophical thought as influenced by Jaspers. As Young-Bruehl has pithily remarked, 'Augustine's three types of love are also examined with existential concepts crucial to the three dimensions of philosophizing Jaspers had formulated . . . a world-oriented love (*appetitus*), an existential love (neighbourly love) and a transcendent love (love of the Creator)' (ibid., 75). The significance of the neighbourly love in Arendt's political thought is linked to the way she reconfigured the temporal structure of human existence in her dissertation: worldly love is future orientated, transcendent love is directed towards the ultimate past, while it is only neighbourly love that exists in the present absorbing as it were 'the other modes of temporal existence and the capacities they presuppose . . . hope and memory' (ibid., 76).

By illuminating the present, the timeless space between the 'no longer' and the 'not yet', Arendt highlights *natality* as the defining aspect of human temporality and is concerned with politics as an arena where new beginnings are always possible, as history has so forcefully shown: 'The essence of all, and in particular of political action is to make a new beginning' (1994a, 321). The importance that Arendt attributes to the notion of natality has been forcefully expressed in her often-cited essay 'What is Freedom':

> Man does not possess freedom so much as he, or better his coming into the world, is equated with the appearance of freedom in the universe; man is free because he is a beginning and was so created after the universe had already come into existence *Initium* ergo *ut esset, creatus est homo, ante quem nemo fuit.*[15] In the birth of each man this initial beginning is reaffirmed, because in each instance something new comes into an already existing world, which will continue to exist after each individual's death. Because he *is* a beginning, man can begin; to be human and to be free are one and the same. (Arendt 2006b, 165–66)

Thus, while the final destination of Augustine's memory journey is God, Arendt's chosen destination is humanity, the remembrance of what binds us together, namely our birth in the world, 'for the sake of *novitas*' (1996, 55) and therefore freedom. Having retreated from the world in the quest for meaning, we thus follow an Augustinian journey of memory from the future into the past and by reaching our birth as a common experience that binds us as humans we reconcile ourselves with the world and through the experience of neighbourly love, 'as an expression of interdependence' (ibid., 104), we reposition ourselves in-the-world-with-others.[16] Love is then an existential concept in Arendt's political thought that binds together the two crucial components of her philosophy, uniqueness and plurality. In the conclusion of her important essay, 'What is Existential Philosophy', she famously noted:

> Existence itself is by nature never isolated. It exists only in communication and in awareness of others' existence. Our fellow-men are not (as in Heidegger) an element of existence that is structurally necessary but at the same time an impediment to the Being of Self. Just the contrary: Existence can develop only in the shared life of human beings inhabiting a given world common to them all. (1994b, 186)

Jeanne-Désirée was still very young when she wrote the August 1832 letter to Enfantin: although she had already raised Augustinian questions to herself, she was situated and indeed only interested in the timeless 'Now'; time seemed infinite and endless in the mind of a twenty-two-year-old proletarian girl. Jeanne-Désirée did not have memories; she was in the process of creating them though. Much later in life, while living in Brussels on her own and almost blind, she had all the time in the world to reside in the Augustinian palace of memories, remember the loves and passions of her youth and reconnect with the world through writing letters. Her first letter to Considerant on May 5, 1890, was all about memories. Since Jeanne-Désirée was not sure that the lover of her youth remembered her, she used the third-person perspective to raise the memory question and give her own part of the answer. This third-person mode of address created a space of both intimacy and distance in her amorous epistolary discourse; she would never use it again in the rest of their correspondence that marks the last year of her life.

> Does Victor Considerant remember Jeanne-Désirée? If yes, he should write her a word. She has forgotten nothing, neither Fourier, nor the feelings of the 1832 youth, and in her voluntary solitude, she lives calm and her heart is filled with memories of all her passionate life.[17]

In remembering the feelings of her 1832 youth, it was the image of a shared world that Jeanne-Désirée was reflecting upon. Her epistolary discourse is thus a beautiful exemplar of the Arendtian love for the world, an expression of her need to remember her immanence in the web of human relations and reconnect with it through the bond of social love, a concept that was at the heart of the Saint-Simonian movement: 'There is a whole world inside me; this world makes me if not happy, less and less unhappy',[18] she had written to Enfantin in the August 1832 letter. Social love seemed to surpass bourgeois moral constraints, opening up paths to existential freedom, also powerfully expressed in the love letters of her old age:

> I dreamed of free love and I knew that your feelings were engaged and that the line of your destiny had been traced. But I loved your apostolic soul and I united my soul with yours in the social love that has been the dominant passion of my life, just as it is still the dominant passion of my impotent but fervent old age.[19]

By the time she wrote the letter above to Considerant, Désirée was old enough to have realized that free love was and had remained a dream only. Social love, however, was still a possibility, 'the dominant passion' of her life, but also a central concept of the romantic socialist movements she had emerged from. It was love and not reason that underpinned the foundation of a peaceful society in the Saint-Simonian doctrine, Moses has noted (1984, 46). It is not difficult to discern Augustine's influence here, given the intense religious character of the Saint-Simonian movement. But while for Augustine, as for Arendt, love is a force of the mind, the Saint-Simonian reconfiguration of love had brought flesh back into the assemblage, making, as Moses (ibid., 47) has noted, connections with Fourierism, albeit without acknowledging it. The sex of the rehabilitated flesh, however, was unsurprisingly female: it was essentialized and proclaimed in need of regulation, through the establishment of a system of moral codes, wherein the constant and mobile human affections would be harmonized under the heteronormative love of the couple-pope.[20] Love in Enfantin's lectures was thus perceived and configured as a social force through which association would work, not only between different sexes, but also among social classes: it was on this basis that women's and workers' emancipation depended on each other, as we have already seen in Chapter 3.

Despite its heteronormative, essentialized and disciplinary nature, the Saint-Simonian take on love irrevocably troubled and shattered the waters of their community, particularly since it was linked to sexual equality, the harmonization of sexual differences, as well as women's emancipation. Love erupted as a force that took their lives by storm and was differently and unpredictably unfolded in their ideas and actions: 'You have upset and destroyed my dreams, you have not given me enough to satisfy me but you have given me enough to make me desire more',[21] Jeanne-Désirée wrote to Enfantin in her August 1832 letter. Such a powerful articulation of love as a mobile desire, an erotic force, rather than a passion is both rare and gendered, bringing forward the need for feminist genealogies of Eros to be written as I have elsewhere argued (Tamboukou 2010b, 146).

EROS OR LOVE AS FORCE

Love as a sweetbitter experience, 'impossible to fight off'[22] erupts from Sappho's verses, initiating a genealogy of Eros as force that storms Plato's *Symposium,* jumps over the gendered hurdles of romanticism and joins modernity through feminist thought that brings it to current debates and concerns.[23] To make a long story short, writing feminist genealogies of love as Eros requires that we reconsider desire and force in the way we make sense of affects, emotions and feelings. Such an approach to love does not annihilate but rather completes and complicates the Arendtian take on love, as unfolded in the previous section. Read in this light, Jeanne-Désirée's love letters make connections between love as memory of the world and love as Eros and force. What I suggest is that it is in Whitehead's process philosophy that a synthesis of these two approaches is lucidly articulated: 'The past is the reality at the base of each new actuality. The process is its absorption into a new unity with ideals and with anticipation, by the operation of the creative Eros', writes Whitehead (1967b, 276). The past is a reality and memory is a mode of perception of this reality: it is when we grasp this absorbed past that we begin to love a world, which we can no more feel on the level of presentational immediacy only. Augustine's love as a memory journey runs parallel with Whitehead's trail of causal efficacy; but not everything ends there. As we feel the past and love the world, we have already been thrown in the process of becoming other, entangled as we are with a world that is constantly changing: it is here that Eros takes over, carrying us away in the whirl of its creative force. Sappho's verses have expressed this perpetual becoming beautifully and simply: 'Eros once again limb-loosener whirls me. Sweetbitter, impossible to fight off'.[24]

While the Eros of the *Symposium* has been equated with philosophic love and the pursuit of beauty and knowledge in feminist readings of Diotima's discourse (Brown 1994, 19), Sappho's lyrics have the body as their centre piece: 'Oh it puts the heart in my chest on wings. [...] Fire is racing under skin [...] and cold sweat holds me and shaking grips me all'.[25] Eros in Sappho's lyrics is configured as a simultaneous experience of pleasure and pain; it also erupts as a vibratory force encompassed in the *Now,* which is always, already outside Time, as Arendt has argued above. Sappho's poetry then is not about 'the history of a love affair, but the instant of desire' Anne Carson has aptly commented in her poetic translations of Sappho's fragments (1998, 4). But how is desire to be understood? 'Desire moves; Eros is a verb' (ibid.,17), Carson has noted about Sappho's fragment 31. 'One of the best-known love poems in our tradition' (ibid., 12).

Drawing on Luce Irigaray's reading of Diotima's speech in the *Symposium* as a discourse opening up a third space for becomings to unfold, Linnell Secomb (2007, 23) has suggested that it is on the plane of mapping love as force, movement and becoming that the *Symposium* echoes Sappho's lyrics. In initiating the rich philosophical tradition on love, Plato has shown how much he had been influenced by Sappho's lyric poetry; it is not difficult to see why. But despite the Sapphic influence, the body and the feminine were eventually excluded from the philosophies of love, Cavarero has cogently argued: 'In Diotima's speech maternal power is annihilated by offering its language and vocabulary to the power that will triumph over it, and will build its foundations on annihilation itself' (1995, 94). In Cavarero's argument then, Plato's device to have Socrates speak through the mouth of a woman creates a mimetic effect through which a hierarchical dualism is inserted between natality as the physical birth of children and as an intellectual creativity, the birth of ideas (ibid.). In the end, natality disappears altogether from the philosophical tradition and it only returns via Arendt, as already discussed in the previous section.

It is thus the embodied link between Eros, desire and movement that I want to consider by returning to Jeanne-Désirée's letters to Enfantin and Considerant, covering as they are a lifespan of erotic lines of flight in a revolutionary woman's ultimate impossibility to love. 'Your caresses, your kisses revived me, you brought me to life, but you have caused in me a true anarchy, the living image of society',[26] Jeanne-Désirée wrote to Enfantin in August 1832. Her letter brings the body at the heart of the Arendtian immaterial bond of love and flags up the force of Sapphic Eros in bringing life back, moving things forward and making them change: 'Prosper you started it.... Finish your work, the world is against us but it will change',[27] she wrote. Jeanne-Désirée's letter poetically expresses the meaning of desire as movement; almost sixty years later—the time she started writing her last love letters to Considerant—the world had indeed seen radical changes, but how much had women felt of these changes? Not much in terms of experiencing love outside the patriarchal blinkers, Jeanne-Désirée would reveal to Considerant:

> Thank you dear friend for your affectionate response. I am very touched by the good memory that you have of my character.
> I wanted this affirmation from your part and it is perhaps what has made me search for your traces. I often had a hidden doubt in thinking that you had not considered me as a good girl; easy to give herself and easy to leave.
> Now, I will die happy having known your thoughts, I have the absolution of my main fault, the pride that has been the effect of bad training but which has broken my life and has made me suffer till now.
> I loved you passionately, Victor, but I never found a word of love to say to you, nor a caress to give you, even when you were holding me in your arms, in this little moment when you loved me a little, pride made me petrified and I will never forgive myself for this.[28]

As we know from her youth letters, pride was the seamstress' shield against patriarchal morality: 'There is a side in my life, which was compressed by my will and my pride and I came very close to be almost completely destroyed',[29] she had written to Enfantin in August 1832. In looking back at the pattern of her life, we know that she was not destroyed, but her life 'was broken' and she did suffer a lot. Having internalized the bourgeois patriarchal morality, she was uncertain about the passionate way she had embraced the idea of free love; she was fully aware of how many men of the romantic socialist movements had simply taken advantage of young women's sexual liberation. Free love was not floating in the air: it was a component of an assemblage wherein forces of desire and gendered power relations were at play.

Jeanne-Désirée, as many of her contemporaries, deployed 'technologies of resistance' (Tamboukou 2003a) within the patriarchal disciplinary regime of love, but they did not succeed in crashing it; women's struggle to love is a long durée and we are still entangled in its fierce battlefield. In this genealogical line, Claire Démar's[30] double suicide alongside her lover Perret Déssesarts in early August 1833, was one of the most dramatic moments in the way love failed women in their struggle against patriarchal segmentarities during the July Monarchy. Unfortunately, it was not the only one: Marie-Reine threw herself in the Seine only four years later, leaving a suicide note about women's impossibility to have desires and satisfy their passions (see Adler 1979, 72).

Unlike Marie-Reine and Jeanne-Désirée, Démar was not a seamstress, but she was a close friend with many of the editors and contributors of the first feminist newspaper. *Ma Loi d'Avenir*, which was published a year after her suicide by Suzanne [Voilquin], was Démar's response to the seamstresses' call to women, and particularly to Suzanne's article, 'Thoughts on the Religious Ideas of the Century',[31] published in the *Tribune des Femmes* in April 1833. As Démar explained in the foreword, she 'wanted to respond in a few lines, but [she was] carried away by the immensity of the questions she had raised' (1834, 22). She thus wrote a pamphlet instead of an epistolary article, which could not possibly fit within the page limitations of the *Tribune des Femmes*. Through Suzanne's preface to the publication, we know that there was a suicide note on Démar's desk asking for the text to be read in the Saint-Simonian community and then to be given to Enfantin. His response was that this text belonged to women and that it should be published through the *Tribune des Femmes* circles (ibid., 12–13). He must have felt very uncomfortable while reading the *Loi d'Avenir*. Despite her close relationship and admiration for Enfantin, which was generously expressed in her pamphlet (ibid., 39), Démar vehemently attacked and criticized his three principles of constancy, mobility and synthesis that he had introduced as a system of moral regulation of the rehabilitated flesh, as we have seen above:

> There are you say, constant, immobile human beings, and others who are on the contrary mobile and inconstant?—Then can you mark for me the point of *separation* between *constancy* and *inconstancy,* between *mobility* and *immobility;* where does *one end* and where does the *other begin?* Frankly, my weak and myopic eyes could not distinguish it. (ibid., 42, emphasis in the text)

Far from being rigidly structured and bounded, freedom for Démar should have no limits; it was actually through 'proclaiming the law of inconstancy that women would be liberated' (ibid., 49). Her discourse about the impossibility of separating 'spirit and matter' drew analogies with universal laws of progress: 'What then is progress, if not an eternal movement of spirit and matter, a continual passage from one idea to another, from one feeling to another, from one mode of existence to a different one'? (ibid., 43). We can see Démar's idea that life forms itself endlessly throughout matter and spirit and that everything changes, running in parallel with lines of Whitehead's process philosophy and further making connections with his thesis against the bifurcation of nature; only hers was an idea configured by a woman a hundred years before Whitehead and it came through intuition rather than the scientific knowledge of a Cambridge philosopher and mathematician.

Love in Démar's understanding was a notion entangled in multiple voices, emerging from different spaces and diffused in a variety of interpretations and understandings: 'If I were to ask the world: what is love, I would be instantly buzzed by millions of confused voices from which I would have to choose at will', she wrote (ibid., 44). Although love was a slippery notion and perhaps 'nothing but a twofold selfishness' (ibid., 45), her ideas about marriage were much better fixed: not only was marriage a form of legal prostitution, but it was also a degradation of the human species through the publicity of intimacy and the disciplinary panopticon gaze it imposed upon the couple:

> So much for the so-called legitimate union, which permits a woman to say without blushing. [...] I will receive a *man in my BED!!!*...The union contracted in the presence of a crowd is dragged *slowly* through an orgy of wines and dance right up to the nuptial bed, which is turned into a bed of debauchery and prostitution permitting the delirious imagination of the guests to follow, to penetrate all the details, *all the accidents* of the lecherous drama, played out under the name of the wedding day! (ibid., 30, emphasis in the text)

In reading Démar's radical critique of an institution still so powerful in the twenty-first century, we cannot help reconsidering Arendt's idea about the wordless nature of love, the inappropriateness of its publicity, the danger of being destroyed by the gaze. We should not confuse 'trust with publicity', Démar noted (ibid., 29). Echoing Jeanne-Désirée's wish to have some mystery in her August 1832 letter to Enfantin, Démar would ask for women to have the right 'to keep the secrets of the heart to themselves' (ibid., 49). After all, they had God, they did not need humans for confession (ibid.). Not only was mystery necessary for Démar, it was also a precondition, as well as a safeguard of women's freedom: her maxim was 'freedom without limits surrounded by mystery' (ibid., 50). Indeed, Démar articulated a very powerful critique of what was in the process of emerging: the disciplinary society that came hand in hand with humanism and the emancipatory messages of modernity: 'The "Enlightenment", which discovered the liberties, also invented the disciplines' that Foucault has famously argued (1979, 222) about, particularly highlighting confession as a disciplinary technology of power in the constitution of the *dispositif* of sexuality (Foucault 1980).

As we have already seen in Chapter 3, the seamstresses had staged a heads-on attack against bourgeois values and morals, but they remained till the end divided on the question of free love. Démar died disillusioned by the realization that *les femmes nouvelles* had ignored her radical ideas expressed in her *Call of a Woman to the People on the Emancipation of Woman*, published in 1833: 'Alone, without support, without encouragement and without the acclaim of any woman, I have already called upon the people; It does not matter what has become of my call', she wrote in the beginning of her *Loi d' Avenir* (1834, 24).

Although Démar felt she was isolated and marginalized among *les femmes nouvelles,* their newspaper had published radical and controversial ideas on matters of love. There was actually a lively 'colour duel' between the purple and the red in an article published in November 1832: 'Leave a different colour ribbon indicate how each one of us understand her freedom',[32] Suzanne had written, choosing the deep violet colour of the Dahlia as a symbol of Christian faith and endurance. 'I won't have the respect of people, I won't have the glory of the title of the spouse, but on the other hand I will have love, I will have happiness',[33] Joséphine-Félicité [Milizet] had responded. Her choice was the flaming red ribbon and her appeal was to those women 'who feel inside them the love for great things, who want love and pleasures, but also want duties and respect'.[34] It was against 'the iron yoke of Christian morality'[35] that Joséphine-Félicité was calling women wearing the red ribbon to act. Love and not Christianity was the object of her faith. But what did she mean by calling women to have faith in love?

Like Démar, Joséphine-Félicité did not believe in the constancy of love: 'Fidelity has almost always been based on nothing but fear or the powerlessness to do better or otherwise', Démar had provocatively written (1834, 49). For rebellious women like Joséphine-Félicité and Démar, love was a force, always, already in movement; what could be a constant though, was the firm belief in the power of love, the feeling that love's force must be valued above all else. Although love as a patriarchal disciplinary technology of power was fiercely criticized, it was the force of love that opened up radical futures in women's lives. On such a plane of consistency, love was crossing the boundaries of *dispositifs* of power to make connections with assemblages of desire: it was at the point of meeting desire that the seamstresses' critique of love can no more be grasped within the Foucauldian analytics of power and pleasure; instead it meets Sappho's idea of the bittersweet via Deleuze and Guattari's notion of desire, an approach to love that I will discuss next.

Interrogating the Pleasure Hypothesis

The last time we saw each other, Michel told me, with much kindness and affection, something like, I cannot bear the word *desire*; even if you use it in another way, I can't stop thinking or living that desire = lack, or that desire is repressed. Michel added, whereas myself, what I call pleasure is perhaps what you call desire; but in any case I need another word than *desire*. (Deleuze 1997, 189, emphasis in the original)

This moving exchange between Foucault and Deleuze that took place during Deleuze's visit to see Foucault in the hospital shortly before he died, has many times been cited and analysed in what has by now become a heated field of debates around desire and pleasure.[36] Deleuze himself has written that the difference between pleasure and desire was much more than a different choice of words. 'For my part', he wrote, 'I can scarcely tolerate the word *pleasure*' (ibid., emphasis in the original), and he went on to give a long list of what desire meant for him: an assemblage of heterogeneous elements, a process, an event, a haecceity, that is 'individuality of a day, a season, a life, as opposed to subjectivity' (ibid.). As I have elsewhere discussed at length, desire is diffused in the whole corpus of Deleuze's philosophical work, in the same way that power is diffused in Foucault's (Tamboukou 2003b). Perhaps after all, Foucault was right and yet when I was to choose between desire and pleasure in making sense of women's experience of love I could not see pure pleasure erupting from their narratives. My readings of the French seamstresses' political and personal writings have indeed reinforced what I have come to configure as 'the gendered ineptitude of the pleasure hypothesis'; to put it more dramatically, the illusion of pleasure has opened up the dark holes of patriarchal assemblages wherein women as 'haecceities' and events have been recurrently absorbed and erased.[37]

But here again a total rejection of pleasure would shadow and marginalize the forceful way that women have written about the intense pains and pleasures of feeling love in a long genealogical line of feminist erotics that start with Sappho's lyrics, traverse the passionate *Portuguese Letters*[38] and reach our own days with bel hooks' *Wounds of Passion* (1999). Women writing passion is a rich assemblage whose cartography has yet to be drawn. It is with the question of passion that I thus want to intervene in the pleasure/desire debate.

'What is passion?' Foucault (1996, 313) asked in a conversation with the German film director Werner Schroeter in relation to the way he had portrayed women in passion in his films *The Death of Maria Malibran* and *Willow Springs*.[39] Foucault's way of seeing was that the films were not about love, but about passion, 'a state, something that falls on you out of the blue, that takes hold of you, that grips you for no reason, that has no origin' (ibid.). More importantly for the discussion above, passion is 'an indissociable state of pleasure-pain' (ibid.), an entanglement of impersonal and unmanageable affects where 'one is simply not oneself' (ibid.). It is this deterritorialization from the self that creates conditions of possibility for radical leaps, for lines of flight to be followed. Passion is a force: it constitutes a plane of intensities that can either lead to renewed modes of existence or to death in the process of the life cycle.

Foucault's discussion with Shroeter on the passion assemblage wherein love, pain, pleasure and desire were mapped in their entanglement revolved around the affects and actions of Shroeter's cinematic personae: 'These women have been entwined in a state of suffering that links them. [...] All that is different from love. In love there is in some way or another a beloved, whereas passion circulates between the partners' Foucault had suggested (ibid., 314), while Shroeter has responded that 'love is less active than passion' (ibid.). Following the discussion of the two interlocutors, who speak of women's passion in the cinematic imagination of their director, brings to mind the mimetic effect that Cavarero (1995) has discerned in Diotima's speech in the *Symposium*, as already noted above. Although the feminine experience of love runs the risk of being occluded in the male dialogue, what is important is that by assembling pain and pleasure on the plane of passion, Foucault brings us full circle to the Sapphic *sweetbitter* erotic experience.

In this configuration, passion may be different from love, but not so much different from Eros; indeed love as Eros in women's lives has always been experienced as the *sweetbitter* feeling Sappho's amorous poetry has been about. It is in this light that I have interrogated the pleasure hypothesis, putting forward the proposition that pure pleasure has never been a component of any social and/or affective assemblage that women have been entangled in. It is always between pleasure and pain, that is, in a state of passion that women have followed lines of flight. In this sense, Deleuze and Guattari's notion of desire has always been an immanent force producing the real while incessantly transforming women's lives. Nominal histories matter in the archaeology of knowledge; this is why Foucault turned his attention to the importance of writing genealogies of how certain names, concepts and problems came to be configured in our vocabularies. Such genealogical explorations need to be grounded in the archive: it is thus to the French seamstresses' archive that I now turn again.

The way the seamstresses were divided on the question of free love but also the recurrence of this dilemma in women's lives, which reaches our own days, is I think an assemblage of riddles and contradictions that have yet to be mapped, unravelled and understood. The genealogical question is simple but simultaneously almost aporetic: Why is it that women have so spectacularly messed up their lives in matters of love, no matter how revolutionary, intellectual, philosophical or affluent the contexts of their lives have been? What makes this question more difficult is that I have never approached it through any 'macro' mode or philosophically abstract mode of understanding or analysis. I have always rejected overcoded entities or empty generalities. And yet my adventures in micro-sociology (see Tamboukou 2015b) have identified a multiplicity of recurrences of the gendered ineptitude of the pleasure hypothesis, while sometimes they have led to local and situated understandings within the limitations of what I have called 'the narrative phenomenon' of the research (see Tamboukou 2014b). I have actually come to the conclusion that this might be perhaps the way forward: collect and map as many micro and context-specific modes of understanding as possible, in the tradition of the feminist epistemological position of situated knowledges.

In this context, my reading of the feminist press of the July Monarchy has led me to an understanding, which is quite the reverse of the bulk of historical interpretations, feminist included: I have been surprised by the length and duration of what has been commonly referred to as their short-lived newspapers or short-lived movement (see Moses 1984, 230; Pilbeam 2014, 64). Were they really short? I have felt quite the opposite. For me the fact that Jeanne-Désirée and Jeanne-Victoire [Deroin] found themselves sewing, fighting and writing together in 1848—fifteen years after they had founded the first feminist newspaper—is an amazing long durée, particularly in the light of how they lived, practised and wrote difference. Desire was the force that kept them on the barricades despite their failures in matters of love, the many children they bore and brought up—often alone—the garments they had to sew to survive, the political groups they served—in short the physical, emotional, political and industrial labour they were immersed in for lengthy periods of time throughout their lives. How could I have argued that it was forces of pleasure that kept the seamstresses going after reading Jeanne-Désirée's letter to Charles Fourier, about the drudgeries of her life while living and working in London?

> The work is so unappealing that I would prefer to be in the galleys. We must work from seven in the morning until midnight at the earliest; you see there are only very short breaks during the day, so we don't really have time to eat and we are subjected to the varying caprices of the stock market; oh what a stupid business is this, this civilised industry![40]

Not only was the young seamstress disillusioned and frustrated by capitalist exploitation, she had also come to interrogate some of Fourier's ideas about the power of love that she had only recently embraced:

> You expect, my dear M. Fourier, that love will come along to distract me, the love of an Englishman, isn't this what you are thinking? In this they are the same as they are in mechanics. They can only handle the material side or a fanciful love that exists only in the imagination. I have had lovers here, I can confide this to you, but they have only given me sensual pleasures. The English are cold, egotistical, even in their pleasures, in making love, in dining. Everyone thinks only of himself. Never shall I have the sort of love I properly need. I have made my decision about it and have settled for pleasure.[41]

Jeanne-Désirée's sincere and lively letter to Fourier forcefully throws us into a material and grounded understanding of the pleasure–desire abstract philosophical debate. It was love as Eros, passion and desire, a force for life, a mutual recognition, a movement towards the other that Jeanne-Désirée was missing. Pleasure was simply a compromise for her. But as already discussed above, in interrogating 'the pleasure hypothesis' I do not want to imply, let alone suggest, that the seamstresses did not experience pleasures in their lives: Jeanne-Désirée's letter above is a testament to the opposite. But what also emerges from her discourse around desire, love and pleasure is that in the same way that desire was for Foucault a psychoanalytically invested notion that he could not bear, pleasure was for the seamstress a notion heavily invested and indeed constrained by the segmentarities of capitalism and patriarchy. It was only by following lines of flight, deterritorializing herself through the force of passion and desire that she could envision a radical future. Her letters to Fourier thus opened up heterotopic sites in the misery of her life in England and powerfully show that it was despite and not because of pleasure that the seamstresses went on working, writing, fighting and dreaming:

> My dear Mr. Fourier, if you were not a great genius, I would never dare write such silly things to you. I leave my pen roam free, certain that nothing can be lost with you and that, amid the complaints of this poor civilised creature, you will find a few seeds that will create a happy harmony between the pivot of my thoughts and your theory. This will be the only thing that will draw me out of my apathy and I always think about it in happiness; but a dry theory is only good for the spirit, I am therefore impatient to grow old, so that I can see the dawn of its materialisation.[42]

Jeanne-Désirée did indeed grow old to see the dawn of a different world for workers, but not so much for women. Writing to Considerant from Brussels, she remembered Fourier's love as reciprocal recognition, as well as the soothing impact that their correspondence had upon her life as a struggling young seamstress who was still dreaming of happiness:

> It is today the anniversary of the death of Charles Fourier in 1837. I have no doubt that you are also thinking of him, like me. What a genius man, both simple and great, full of ideas and of intelligence.
>
> On the occasion of every anniversary of those who have gone, I need to remember them, be reflective. Fourier was the console of pains; for me as for the others he loved. My youth, my social enthusiasm, my inexperience of life, inspired him to put reasoning into theory and track the reason of my sadness. 'You have so many dominant passions', he wrote to me and would urge me to believe in civilisations.[43]

Jeanne-Désirée's tender memory of Fourier brings us full circle to Arendt's reconfiguration of love as the Augustinian journey of memory that unites us with the world and the web of human relations we are part of. But our return to memory has not gone through the life of the mind only, as in Augustine and indeed in Arendt; it has also passed through the Sapphic body that vibrates by its force, forgetting and losing itself in it, following its lines of flight. It is in this light that I will now conclude this chapter by re-imagining love as a memory journey, but also as an act of affirmation and multiplication of singularities and differences, an openness to the outside, a leap into radical futures, in short love as a force within the political, which is always, already personal.

LOVE AND THE POLITICAL

'Love is nothing but joy [laetitia][44] with the accompanying idea of an external cause', Spinoza wrote in his *Ethics* (1996, 78). At the end of a very long chapter on love, it might seem somehow ironic to arrive at such a short and perfect definition. And yet it was only in the end of exploring love's multiple modes of appearance in a long philosophical tradition as well as in a multiplicity of stories and narrative forms emerging from the first feminist autonomous movement in nineteenth-century France that the salience of love in the realm of politics could ultimately emerge. Love is configured as joy, one of the three primary affects alongside desire (cupiditas) and pain (tristitia) out of which all the others are constructed in Spinoza's *Ethics*. On this plane of consistency, joy increases our power to think and act, it is 'the transition to greater activity and perfection', Genevieve Lloyd has pithily noted (1996, 90). It is indeed the Spinozist affect of joy that can best encompass the nuances between passion, desire and pleasure in the assemblage of love that I charted in the previous section. If we are to make a synthesis of Spinoza's definition then, love becomes an assemblage of affects and reasoning given that it is accompanied by the recognition of an external cause. It is actually in the art of balancing passion and reason that the force of love lies in the thought of a rational philosopher. It is here interesting to note than when literary scholars were disputing the fact that the *Portuguese Letters* that I mentioned above were written by a woman, Jean-Jacques Rousseau had argued that given the fine balance of the letters between passion and eloquence, their author had to be a man (see Kauffman 1986, 94–95).

It is on this plane of coexistence of joy as a force underpinning and sustaining thought and action with the recognition of an external cause that I want to map the seamstresses' lines of flight that erupted from their loyalty to love. 'This world makes me if not happy, less and less unhappy than the one around me',[45] Jeanne-Désirée wrote to Enfantin in the August 1832 letter that initiated the discussion of this chapter, beautifully expressing the joy emerging from the Saint-Simonian world of social love that she had immersed herself in. It was not the first time that she had felt and written about joy and happiness: 'Since I have been transformed, I feel a happiness that I had ignored till now', she wrote to her 'fathers and mothers' of the Saint-Simonian community in her *Profession of Faith*.[46] We have a perfect Spinozist image of love here: joy with the recognition of an external cause—the bond of social love that the Saint-Simonian community had inspired in the young seamstress. Feeling love was not just the context of her joy and happiness, but also the political force that would sustain and enlarge the vision of their community. Her *Profession of Faith* actually concludes with an affirmation of love as a force for personal, social [and therefore] political change.

> I offer you my industry and my work, I will use all my love to attract to the doctrine my parents and my friends and to make them participate in my happiness; I put myself entirely at your disposition, please rank me as you understand, I trust your friendly capacity to put me in a place, where I will be most useful in society and where I will be able to find my personal satisfaction.[47]

Writing to Considerant at the twilight of a long life full of action, it would be the same feeling of happiness that would erupt from remembering and dreaming of love. Having followed the Augustinian journey of memory, the seamstress would wake up to the awareness of her entanglement in the web of human relations, the Arendtian political sphere par excellence:

> Allow me my sceptical friend of rigid reasoning to affirm to you what I retain from my yesterday's dream. I opened my eyes in the midst of a gentle light and a sensation of tender calmness, as if I were hovering, moving without any awareness of movement. For some time I remained in this heavenly and earthy beatitude. The feeling remained with me as a persistent perfume. I recalled having heard Fourier describe a similar effect, which he thought was the state of the souls who love us and thus hover around us in our atmosphere.[48]

There is a perfect coexistence of matter and spirit in the way Jeanne-Désirée wrote to the lover of her youth about her dream, which fuses together the trance state of awakening, the light of the day, the beauty of the earth and heavens combined and the perfume of feeling the world in love. More importantly, she was keen to show that this was not the delirious writing of an old woman; she was fully aware that her trance writing was addressed to a sceptic, the rationalist leader par excellence, who had many times criticized—albeit not openly—the utopian and non-scientifically proven elements of Fourier's ideas (see Beecher 2001, 59). Jeanne-Désirée was conscious of the fact that she was using her feelings to address 'rigid' male rationalities. The way she counterpoises gendered differences in the formation of their thought, derives of course from the essentialized trends of her feminism, but more importantly fuses feelings with understanding and knowledge in a profound and lucid way, very much in line with the Whiteheadian prehensions that were discussed in Chapter 2: Jeanne-Désirée feels the world or rather she becomes who she is—a superject—in her entanglement with the world. What is also striking in her correspondence is the way letter writing becomes a mode of conversation, bridging the gap between presence and absence, but also between different temporalities: the time of writing and the revolutionary time of her youth.

> You are so much embroiled in my intimate thoughts, dear [...] friend, that it seems to me that you live inside me and that I speak with you at this moment. I know very well that there can be no intimacy born from habit between us, neither the expression between friends of the same sex. From my part there is the sensation of my first love and from you, the memory of my character, worthy of your loyalty. Moreover I am certain that we have the same general principles: you through knowledge, me through feelings and the simple adoration that I have had for my Fathers since my youth and which has drawn me to the apostles of social ideas and has made me responsive to sensual emotions.[49]

Happiness and joy was at the heart of Jeanne-Désirée's constitution as a political subject, Riot-Sarcey (1995, 4) has argued in her insightful studies of women's struggles for democracy in nineteenth-century France. Perhaps it is the Spinozist love as joy that offers a third space beyond pleasure and desire within which love within the political can be conceptualized. Michael Hardt and Antonio Negri have actually drawn on Spinoza to reconfigure love as a political act, 'an event [that] will thrust us like an arrow into the living future' (2005, 358). But although they link love with time, recognizing that we live in the abyss 'between a present that is already dead and a future that is already living' (ibid.), Arendt's 'no more and not yet' (1996, 15) is not included in their consideration of the troubled histories of love within the political. This is a strange omission, given that Hardt and Negri have read and criticized Arendt's approach to the revolution (2005, 78) and that in his lecture 'About Love', Hardt (2007) has referred to Augustine's notion of 'agape' as *caritas* and as a sign of freedom,[50] in the way we have also seen it in Arendt's configuration of love.

More seriously than ignoring Arendt in his lecture on love, Hardt (2007) has profoundly confused the notion of Eros confining it in the intimate sphere and even worse, within naïve romanticism: 'When you think about love in Hollywood', he has said, 'it is about love as Eros'.[51] In this light, Hardt has argued that we need to destroy the segregation between the notion of Eros as love on the plane of the personal and *agape* as the Christian theological approach of love within the community: 'It seems to me that in order to think of love as a political concept, we have to think it simultaneously as both' (in Schwartz 2009, 816). But by creating a continuum of love, linking Eros to the personal and *agape* to the political, Hardt has stripped Eros of its creative and transformative power within and beyond the personal. Here again it is Platonic and not Sapphic erotics he has considered in his analysis: 'Eros, the more common Greek word that Plato uses of course',[52] he has noted in his lecture above. But as we have already seen in the previous section, even as a purely Platonic notion, Eros cannot be configured as 'Hollywood love'. It is Eros as the pursuit of beauty and knowledge that dominates the discourses on love in the *Symposium*.

Eleanor Wilkinson has further challenged the fact that Hardt and Negri seem to recognize love as a political concept only if it is extended beyond the intimate sphere of domesticity, and they have largely ignored the dangerous liaisons between love, intimate relations, patriarchy and neo-liberal capitalism (2013, 239). But what is equally problematic in Wilkinson's critique is that she only sees love as a disciplinary technology and cannot recognize its possibility for radical transformations. Leaving aside the question of whether Hardt's and Negri's omissions and confusions are gender related, more important is the recognition that it is in the entanglement of joy, Eros and passion that love can be charted within the plane of the political. But there is an important difference here that Arendt's approach to love has highlighted: love as Eros is a force inspiring revolutions as new beginnings, but it cannot ground or sustain political projects in its name: 'What does it mean to stand for love by standing alongside some others and against other others?' Sara Ahmed has provocatively asked (2003, 1). As I will further discuss in the next chapter, we need much more than love to map the feminist interventions in the revolutions of modernity, but I will leave Jeanne-Désirée's epistolary adieu to her lover to sign off this chapter, by flagging up love's unique force in momentarily freezing the infinite *Now*:

> Adieu dear friend, true love of my youth:
>   still alive, since all contemporary feelings are affected by you.
>   I embrace you affectionately,
>   Your old friend.[53]

NOTES

1. Jeanne-Désirée to Enfantin, letter dated August, 31, 1932. BnF/BdA/FE/ Ms7608/CdG(D)/DJ/42, 1–3. Also, in Riot-Sarcey 1992, 74–77.

2. Long extracts from this letter have been translated in English and have been used on a number of studies, including Rancière 2012, 105; Beecher 2000, 76; Pilbeam 2014, 65.

3. Jeanne-Désirée to Enfantin, letter dated August, 31, 1932. BnF/BdA/FE/ Ms7608/CdG(D)/DJ/42, 1. Also, Riot-Sarcey 1992, 75.

4. I refer here to Arendt's much discussed relationship with Heidegger, which goes well beyond the limits of this chapter. For interesting insights into Arendt's worldly love relationships, see Kristeva 2001b; Young-Bruehl 1982.

5. Jeanne-Désirée to Enfantin, letter dated August, 31, 1932. BnF/BdA/FE/ Ms7608/CdG(D)/DJ/42, 3. Also, in Riot-Sarcey 1992, 77.

6. See Honig 1995.

7. See Scott and Stark 1996; Hammer 2000; Kristeva 2001b.

8. The year 1960 was the year when the thesis was first translated in English by E. B. Ashton, but Arendt was not satisfied with the translation and wanted to work on it.

9. See Arendt-Jaspers correspondence, 16 January 1966 (1993, 622).

10. The notion of the beautiful is conceived in Arendt's thought within the Kantian notion of the 'enlarged mentality' in her overall reading of Kant's *Third Critique* as his political philosophy. See Arendt's *Lectures on Kant*, particularly the seventh session (1982, 40–46).

11. Jeanne-Désirée to Enfantin, letter dated August, 31, 1932. BnF/BdA/FE/ Ms7608/CdG(D)/DJ/42, 1. Also, in Riot-Sarcey 1992, 74.

12. In explicating Augustine's notions of love as craving, Arendt (1996, 11–12) writes: 'This fearlessness is what love seeks. Love as craving (*appetitus*) is determined by its goal, and this goal is freedom from fear (*metu carere*)'.

13. Augustine's *Confessions* X, 17, 26; X, 8, 14 (in Arendt 1996, 56).

14. Ibid., X, 33, 50 (in ibid., 57).

15. This phrase comes from Augustine's *City of God* : 'That there might be a beginning, man was created before whom nobody was' (XII, 20) and is cited by Arendt throughout her work in positing man as a beginning.

16. See Hammer (2000) for a discussion of the Augustinian journey of memory in Arendt.

17. Véret-Gay to Considerant, letter dated, May 5, 1890, (AnF/10AS42/8/ DVG/57/1).

18. Jeanne-Désirée to Enfantin, letter dated August, 31, 1932. BnF/BdA/FE/ Ms7608/CdG(D)/DJ/42, 2. Also, in Riot-Sarcey 1992, 75.

19. Véret-Gay to Considerant, letter dated, June 21, 1890, (AnF/10AS42/8/ DVG/59/1).

20. These three moral principles were outlined in Enfantin's lecture on November 19, 1831. See Moses 1984, 48.

21. Jeanne-Désirée to Enfantin, letter dated August, 31, 1932. BnF/BdA/FE/ Ms7608/CdG(D)/DJ/42, 2. Also, in Riot-Sarcey 1992, 75.

22. Sappho, fragment 130, in Carson 1998, 3.

23. For an interesting discussion and overview of Sapphic and Platonic erotics from a feminist perspective, see Secomb 2007, particularly Chapter 1, 10–23.

24. Sappho, fragment 130, in Carson 1998, 3.

25. Sappho, fragment 31, in ibid., 13.

26. Jeanne-Désirée to Enfantin, letter dated August, 31, 1932. BnF/BdA/FE/ Ms7608/CdG(D)/DJ/42, 2. Also in Riot-Sarcey 1992, 75.

27. Ibid.

28. Véret-Gay to Considerant, letter dated, June 21, 1890, (AnF/10AS42/8/ DVG/59/1).

29. Jeanne-Désirée to Enfantin, letter dated August, 31, 1932. BnF/BdA/FE/ Ms7608/CdG(D)/DJ/42, 1. Also in Riot-Sarcey 1992, 75.

30. Claire Démar died in 1833 when she was between thirty-two and thirty-four years old *according* to Suzanne's preliminary note in the publication of *Ma Loi d' Avenir* (1834, 13). Very little is known about her life, apart from the fact that she had joined the Saint-Simonian circles, was involved in journalism, but was really struggling to make ends meet. See Planté 1997.

31. *Tribune des Femmes-La Femme Nouvelle* 1(15), 185–95, April 1833.

32. 'Extract of regulations which unite the New Women', *Apostolat des Femmes* 1(4), 62–64, November 4, 1832.

33. Ibid., 65.

34. Ibid., 66.

35. Ibid., 65.

36. See among others: MacCormack 2000; Robinson 2003; Kringelbach 2009; Hughes 2011; Beckman 2013.

37. Women's failure in matters of love has been a recurrent theme in my ongoing project of writing feminist genealogies. See Tamboukou 2003a, 2010a, 2013a.

38. First published in French in 1669, the book was launched as translated real-life letters that a passionate Portuguese nun wrote to her French lover who had deserted her. For a discussion of these letters, see Kauffman 1986; Tamboukou 2010b.

39. Werner Shroeter (1945–2010) is considered to be among the best of post-1968 European cinema.

40. Jeanne-Désirée to Charles Fourier, undated letter, written from 37 Duke Street, Manchester Square in London. (in Riot-Sarcey 1995, 6).

41. Ibid., 7.

42. Ibid., 8.

43. Véret-Gay to Considerant, letter dated, October 9, 1890, (AnF/10AS42/8/ DVG/66/1).

44. *Laetitia* is translated as 'joy' by Edwin Curley, but has also been translated as 'pleasure' by Andrew Boyle in the Everyman Edition of Spinoza's *Ethics*. I will be following Curley's translation in agreement with Genevieve Lloyd that although pleasure [titillatio] is included in the cluster of affects comprising joy, it is not equivalent to it, (see Lloyd 1996, 90–91).

45. Jeanne-Désirée to Enfantin, letter dated August, 31, 1932. BnF/BdA/FE/ Ms7608/CdG(D)/DJ/42, 2. Also in Riot-Sarcey 1992, 75.

46. Véret, letter to the Globe, dated September 11, 1831. BnF/BdA/FE/Ms7608/ CdG(D)/DJ/40, 1. Also in Riot-Sarcey 1992, 69.

47. Ibid., 3.

48. Véret-Gay to Considerant, letter dated, October 9, 1890, (AnF/10AS42/8/ DVG/65/2–3).

49. Véret-Gay to Considerant, letter dated September 7, 1890, (AnF/10AS42/8/ DVG/62/1).

50. Hardt 2007, 'About Love'. Presentation for the European Graduate School. Available at: http://www.egs.edu/faculty/michael-hardt/videos/about-love, part 3: 4.01/ 9.52 [Accessed, 12-2-2015].

51. Ibid., part 3: 3.01/ 9.52.

52. Ibid., part 3: 3.20.

53. Véret-Gay to Considerant, letter dated June 21, 1890, (AnF/10AS42/8/ DVG/59/2).

Chapter 5

Living, Writing and Imagining the Revolution

'We cannot die without finishing the work that has been at the heart of our whole existence',[1] Désirée Gay[2] wrote to Enfantin on February 8, 1848, shortly before she joined the demonstrations and street fighting that lasted for three days and violently ended the July Monarchy. Under the pressure of the Parisian barricades, Louis-Philippe abdicated in favour of his grandson, but the 'citizen King' had already had his chance and had failed, the French people thought, storming the Chamber of Deputies and the Hôtel de Ville. A provisional government was formed on February 24, 1848, and the Second Republic was proclaimed the following day. The February revolution[3] initiated processes for the creation of a new body politic and it was in the revolutionary spirit of the days that the seamstresses reunited demanding that women workers should be part of the struggle for democracy:

> The women who understand the grandeur of their social mission have come together to appeal to your wisdom and justice.
>
> In the name of fraternity they demand that freedom and equality should become a truth for them as it is for their brothers.
>
> It is in the name of this great law of universal solidarity, which can no more be ignored that they demand the right to accomplish all their tasks. Because it is a task for them to participate in the great work of social regeneration.[4]

Jeanne Deroin and Désirée Gay were among the six women who signed the above petition for the Comité des droits de la femme [Committee on the Rights of Woman], chaired by Bourgeois Allix in the springtime of the provisional government. Launching and signing petitions was only part of their revolutionary activities, but the above address is significant in consolidating an important aspect of the revolution that often remains shadowed:

revolutions are events that erupt marking discontinuities and ruptures, but they are also *politicogenetic phenomena* (Tamboukou 2014c), open processes for the foundation and development of a new body politic. It is thus to the discussion of the revolution as both an event and a process that I will now turn, drawing on Arendt's (1990) controversial theorization of the revolutions in modernity as well as on the Kantian image of the revolution, as discussed by both Foucault (1986b, 2010) and Arendt (1982, 2006b).

'Revolutions are the only political events that confront us with the problem of beginning', Arendt has argued (1990, 21). Imagining new beginnings and perhaps more importantly enacting them are thus at the heart of Arendt's theorization. What is important to note here is Arendt's twofold conceptualization of the revolution: (a) as a radical beginning erupting from the web of human relations and (b) as initiation of a political process that will eventually create a foundation for freedom. As I have already discussed in Chapter 4, beginning is a crucial concept in Arendt's theoretical configuration of the human condition, further shaping her understanding of the revolution within the political: 'Men are equipped for the logically paradoxical task of making a new beginning because they themselves are new beginnings and hence beginners, the very capacity for beginning is rooted in natality, in the fact that human beings appear in the world by virtue of birth' (ibid., 211).

Existentially and ontologically inherent in the human condition, the notion of beginning is also connected to freedom: 'The idea of freedom and the experience of a new beginning should coincide [and this is] crucial to any understanding of revolution' (ibid., 29). Arendt, however, makes an important distinction between liberation and freedom, two notions that are usually confused and conflated in our conceptual and political vocabularies: 'Liberation may be the condition of freedom but by no means leads automatically to it', she has noted (ibid.). Despite their incommensurability, the boundaries between the desire for liberation and the desire for freedom are porous and blurring: 'It is frequently very difficult to say where the mere desire for liberation, to be free from oppression, ends, and the desire for freedom as the political way of life begins', Arendt has aptly observed (ibid., 33). Freedom for Arendt is thus conceptualized as both negative and positive and it is in this context that she situates the revolutions in modernity, arguing that 'the revolutionary spirit of the last centuries, that is the eagerness to liberate and to build a new house where freedom can dwell, is unprecedented and unequalled in all prior history' (ibid., 35). What we are presented with in this succinct statement is a spatial configuration of the weak link of all modern revolutions: the difficulty and historical failure not to liberate from oppression, but 'to build a house for freedom', without which oppression has ultimately re-emerged in different political and social regimes of power.

It is precisely in the gap between liberation and freedom that the seam-stresses found themselves in the wake of the February revolution: 'We French women have understood that the magnificent February movement is not a political revolution, but the beginning of a social revolution',[5] they wrote on March 16, 1833, in the first of a series of manifestos and petitions that they signed and circulated during a period of intense political activism.[6] What is highlighted in the petition above is Arendt's idea of the revolution as a process, as well as its importance as a new beginning; but what is starkly different from Arendt is the importance of the social question in the revolutions of modernity that Arendt has famously castigated: 'The role of the revolution was no longer to liberate men, let alone to found freedom, but to liberate the life process of society from the fetters of scarcity so that it could swell into a stream of abundance' (ibid., 64), she critically wrote about the French revolution.

In Arendt's view, 'the social question', which for her was quite simply the problem of poverty, has been used and misused by all modern revolutions, but it has never been solved by any of them. This is because poverty cannot be addressed by political means; the rights of life for Arendt are prepolitical, in the sense that 'no government and no political power has the right to touch and to violate' (ibid., 109). In this light, the struggles of the revolution should have been about the political rights of freedom and citizenship and not about the rights of life and nature, which should have already always remained untouched and protected. But in making this distinction between natural and political rights, Arendt excluded from politics its material, legal and social conditions of possibility. It was exactly the social and constitutional guarantees of Arendt's 'given of human plurality' that the seamstresses agonistic politics brought forcefully to the fore.

Already in Chapter 3 I have discussed the thorny relation between the social and the political, particularly highlighting the seamstresses' critique of the abstract and irrelevant messages of the bourgeois politics of the July Monarchy. On the third anniversary of the July revolution, Marie-Reine had written in memory and celebration of the people's struggle and against the politics that had used and abused it: 'For the third time since 1830 the sun of July has risen; it has risen beautiful and pure as in those great days; it has risen in the middle of the sound of the cannons and in the middle of the fanfares ordered by those who have profited from the victory'.[7] Looking back at the three glorious days, Marie-Reine had tried to understand and enlighten her present keeping the revolution as its historical condition of possibility: 'Today that all the tumult has finished and the city has returned to calmness. [...] Let us have a quick look in the past',[8] she had written. In problematizing her present and her own position within it, Marie-Reine was at the heart of the two questions that according to Foucault have shaped the history of philosophy from Kant to our own days:

It seems to me that these two questions—'What is Aufklärung' and 'What is the Revolution'—which are the two forms in which Kant poses the question of his own present reality, have continued to haunt, if not all of modern philosophy since the nineteenth century, then at least a large part of this philosophy. (Foucault 2010, 20)

Marie-Reine's reflection on the July revolution forcefully shows that it is not just the history of philosophy that has been shaped by these two questions, but also the history of political action and social movements more widely. In reflecting on the past of the July revolution, the seamstress was also already looking into its future: 'People [...] could not hold any longer the heavy weight of humiliation and in the first occasion they tried to shake it off. But once they had satisfied this need, they asked: What shall we do'?[9] It is at the intersection of looking back at the same time of looking forward that the social is irrevocably entangled with the political. The burning question of 'what shall we do'? that has famously inspired Lenin's idea of the revolution[10] asks and indeed demands for social and political questions to be addressed in their interrelation in the process of founding a new freedom.

Fifteen years after Marie-Reine's interrogation of the July revolution, her friends and comrades would once again highlight the urgency of inserting the social in the foundation of a new body politic through words and deeds in the early days of the February revolution. Like Marie-Reine—and unlike Arendt—they did not separate the social from the political. As a matter of fact, they worked simultaneously in their entanglements and intra-actions through signing petitions, forming new political groups, writing articles in the revolutionary press of the days, but also founding their own feminist newspapers again as I will discuss later on in the chapter. It was in the spirit of immediate democracy emerging from the outburst of the freedom of the press, as well as from the lifting of all restrictions on the right to assemble and associate, that the seamstresses linked the right to work with the right to vote and worked simultaneously for both.

Gay was at the forefront of these struggles. On March 2 she addressed a petition for women's right to work to the Labour Commission, which met at the Luxemburg Palace under the presidency of the socialist theoretician Louis Blanc; his overall project for the reorganization of labour was the establishment of social workshops run by workers themselves. Gay's petition was addressed only a week after the provisional government had pledged 'to guarantee the livelihood of the worker with work [and] to guarantee work to all citizens'.[11] In fulfilling these promises, the Labour Commission had immediately banned subcontracting to eliminate exploitation and had reduced the working day to ten hours in Paris and eleven in the provinces. In further addressing the problem of [male] unemployment, the provisional government had decided to establish a programme of national workshops wherein men workers would receive some seed money in the form of a minimum state wage that would enable them to further develop and organize their labour.[12] But apart from the fact that this form of 'state charity' was far from Blanc's socialist ideas, women workers were not even mentioned in all these promises and projects. Their voice would be heard though, loudly so:

Citizens,
    Many isolated women are in a desperate situation, you will not want them to continue to be exposed to poverty or disorder. Good morals are the strength of the republics, and it is women who make the morals; the nation should honour women's work through your voice! With your will they should take part in the reorganisation that occurs; and you should encourage the principle of association for the work they do within their control.[13]

In gendering the February revolution's right to work, Gay highlighted the necessity for women's work to be recognized and honoured. Recognition was important since when the Luxembourg Commission devised its first list of formal occupational categories, the linen and needle trades were not included, although women's work was flagged up 'as one of our most difficult and serious problems'[14]; as such, it needed special attention but did not deserve representation in the commission. In fighting against this unbelievable exclusion, Gay particularly emphasized the fact that many women workers were isolated and indeed marginalized and erased within the deplorable conditions of home-based work, the *dispositif* of *le travail à domicile* that I have already discussed in the Introduction.

As a counteraction to isolation, Gay would flag up the principle of association retrieving it from the theoretical baggage of the romantic socialist movements of her youth. Her correspondence with Enfantin between January and April 1848 shows that it was not just memories that moved her actions: her present was fused with the ideas of her political actions in the past, enriched by the experiences of a fully active life.[15] In underlining the link between poverty and moral disorder, Gay was of course referring to the multiple entanglements between women's work, poverty and prostitution. As we have already seen in Chapter 3, the rise of sweated homework in the garment industry had led seamstresses to acquire a disreputable status: they were linked to clandestine and unregulated prostitution and they were deemed to be sexually corrupted. This vicious circle between unemployment, poverty and prostitution had become part of the social crises that had led to the February revolution, which had erupted 'in the context of a violent economic crisis that showed no signs of subsiding' (Bouyssy and Fauré 2003, 294).

Unemployment was indeed high at the time of the February revolution and that is why 'the right to work' had emerged as its rallying cry. It was thus in the spirit of eliminating unemployment that Gay wrote in her petition that 'women deserve to have a share of the honour and the well-being that our institutions will bring to the people'.[16] In doing so she was writing against two real and discursive separations: the social and the political, as well as the private and the public. She was determined that a reorganization of the public sphere of work was dependent upon a reorganization of the private sphere of the family and that the two could not be separated: 'We urgently need to create national restaurants, as well as laundries and lingeries, where people can find cheap healthy food and orderly and clean care, which cannot be created in isolation and which women reunited in association can easily organise',[17] she wrote in the postscript of her petition to the Luxembourg Commission. She also demanded that women have their own elected delegates in the commission, so that they could oversee the reorganization of their work and that unemployed women have the right to enlist in the national workshops.

In looking closely at the micro-politics of the Luxemburg Commission, Scott (1988) has pointed not only to the fierce power antagonisms between employers and workers but also to the gendered power relations between tailors and seamstresses. As already noted in the Introduction, the location of work was at the heart of these disagreements: tailors, who wanted to protect their professional status within the boundaries of the workshop, rejected home-based work. In their view, the *atelier* was well organized, had the power to divide work in a fair and equitable way and by encouraging emulation it perfected skill (ibid., 100). For different reasons both employers and seamstresses were not against '*le travail à domicile*'. Industrial homework was for employers and particularly for the new entrepreneurs among them, a stepping stone in the garment trade, while it was a factual necessity for many seamstresses who were trying to juggle work with domestic responsibilities. Even when national workshops for women were finally established in March, some women asked to take their sewing tasks at home, provided that they were paid adequately and that the whole process would be state regulated: 'If you want piece work, put it on a suitable price, and give it to women at home so that their household does not suffer', they wrote in a petition presented to Louis Blanc.[18]

In the light of these difficulties what the seamstresses needed, Gay vehemently argued, were higher wages, which they could only claim if they were appropriately trained and this was the reason why apart from the national workshops, they also needed training centres. By addressing her appeal to Louis Blanc's Labour Commission, Gay had hit the nail on its head. Her motion was further supported by women workers marching and demonstrating at the Hôtel de Ville, demanding among others, reduction of their hours of work, as well as an end to the slave work in prisons, convents and certain religious communities, as a way of eliminating unemployment. Women garment workers were at the forefront of such demonstrations since they were not new in labour activism: 'One of the earliest strikes in the July Monarchy begun as a walkout of twenty women in the hat trade', Judith DeGroat has noted, further listing a long series of women workers' street and industrial action that had often led to persecution and imprisonment (1997, 35).

Under such pressures, the provisional government announced the formation of women's workshops, *ateliers des femmes,* in late March, one month after those of men. As Gay meticulously described them in her article 'The delegates of the Workers in Paris', published in *La Voix des Femmes* on April 18, 1848, these workshops had a military structure: women workers were classified into divisions comprising one hundred women overseen by a chef and were further divided into ten brigades, led by a brigadier, while all women's workshops were under the direction of Charles Duclerc.[19] Moreover, there was a strict payment hierarchy throughout these classifications and divisions: the chef received the top wage of three francs a day, the brigadier was given half of it, while the unemployed women received only sixty centimes for each shirt that they would sew.[20] The disciplinarian regime of the national workshops thus offers a Foucauldian diagram of power par excellence and forcefully illustrates DeGroat's suggestion that 'revolutionary Paris in 1848 provided a battleground for competing sources and representations of sources of power' (ibid., 32), wherein gender relations were prominent.

But apart from the pay and surveillance hierarchy, there were other pressing problems: the newly founded ateliers needed support for buildings, work materials, furniture and equipment as well as the establishment of centres for food relief. As DeGroat has noted, out of a total expenditure of 14,174,987 francs for the national workshop programme as a whole, only 1,720,000 francs were allocated for the ateliers des femmes; it was from this meagre sum that 'rooms and equipment had to be rented, materials for the shirts purchased and the markers for bread and meals given to the poor paid' (DeGroat 2005, 1). It was mainly through charity channels that a viable milieu was eventually created but women workers soon protested against the whole system: when they were asked to elect their representatives they chose the most revolutionary ones and of course Gay was among them. She was already women's delegate to the Workers' Commission for the second arrondissement and was also appointed as *chef de division* for the atelier of the Cour des Fontaines.[21] Her appointment, however, only lasted for ten days: she was unfairly dismissed from her position and 'the door of the atelier was closed upon her by superior orders'.[22] In addition, the administration threatened to close down the atelier in case the workers chose not to follow the orders. The reason for this violent removal as well as for the disciplinary measures against all the women workers of the atelier was that Gay protested vocally against the male domination of the national workshops' hierarchical organization, as well as for the ridiculous wages that workers received for their work. In a series of articles published in *La Voix des Femmes*, Gay argued, among other issues,[23] that the ateliers did not need highly paid supervisors and asked instead for a minimum of one franc per day for all women, instead of the piece rate of sixty centimes. A minimum wage made more sense since not all women had the same skills, but they still needed to survive:

> It is impossible to talk about the obstacles that the delegates encountered in attempting to do their jobs. To enumerate the pains and the miseries that they have seen among their sisters is also impossible. They die of hunger, this is certain. The work that they give them in the workshops is a trap; the organisation of women's work is despotism under a new name and the nomination of women delegates is a mystification that men have perpetrated on women in order to get rid of them.[24]

In attacking the programme of women's ateliers, Gay also wrote against the gendered assumption that all women knew how to sew, because of which they were offered the task of sewing shirts for the National Guard as a solution to the problem of poverty and unemployment. The following dialogue presented in the first issue of *La Politique des Femmes,* the newspaper she co-edited with Deroin after their withdrawal from *La Voix des Femme,* vividly presents the inadequacies and problems of the national workshops:

> *A Woman:* When is it all going to finish? I have nothing more to hope for; my husband is unemployed, my children go barefoot and I am penniless.
>
> *A Lady:* Come to the national workshops.
>
> *An Old Woman:* You need to have good eyes to sew; I cannot do more than a shirt in two days; could you live with 6 sous per day?
>
> *A Woman:* I am a retailer; I don't know how to sew.
>
> *Many Together:* I am a laundress.
>
> And I am a cook.
>
> And I am a colourist.[25]

In staging an imaginary dialogue that drew, however, on her own involvement with the women's ateliers programme, Gay pointed to the fact that sewing was not a sort of body habit that all women grew with. Such an assumption was both degrading needle workers' skills, as well as excluding other trades from the provision of the national workshops. The journal dialogue above also brought in class antagonisms in outlining what the seamstresses perceived as failed state charity:

The Lady: If the workers were quiet, the trade would rise and everything would be better.

A woman worker: Yes, for the bosses, they will have the workers for half price and they will make them pay all the costs of the revolution.

The Lady: You are unfair; the workers on the contrary have all the benefits. They have raised the salaries and have decreased the hours of work.

The woman worker: In the law, but not in the workshops; women's salaries have been decreased everywhere; they are profiting from our misery.

The Lady: My dear friend, women's earnings are of little importance. The man is the head of the family and when he earns enough women are happy.

A Woman: And what if the man is ill or a bad person?

Another Woman: And when women are widows?

A young woman: And when they cannot get married?[26]

Interestingly enough, when the discussion about capitalist exploitation reached a difficult point in the dialogue above, patriarchy would come up in 'the lady's' discourse. Here, not even the women workers would dispute the rights of man per se: instead of a head attack to patriarchy, gender relations were nuanced and real-life difficulties were exposed in their complexity. The seamstresses' critique was therefore both against capitalist and patriarchal exploitation: 'Their socialism [...] was mingled with a certain feminism', Scott has pithily noted (1988, 104). More importantly, the hypothetical dialogue of 'a group of women in Luxemburg's court' echoes real debates within the women's political clubs as traced in some of the published minutes of their meetings:

Mme Gay talks about her petition to establish laundry and lingerie national workshops [...] she wants to establish national restaurants and also public libraries and a meeting hall [...]

Mme Duparc expresses the fear that women's and men's union in the same place would be a danger for morality.

Mme Gay disagrees and thinks quite the opposite.

Mme Eug. Foa proposes the constitution of an Institute by 20 ladies, who will assemble under the patronage of Mme de Lamartin so that they can convene conferences on the reorganisation of work and protect young women from financial and moral dangers.

The president [Eugénie Niboyet] does not want any signs of charity in whatever concerns the work of young women; she wants them to be considered in terms of their right to work, which will give them independence.[27]

Gay's dramatic outcry about how the national workshops had once more failed women is a painful reminder of Arendt's bitter remark above: the problem of poverty has been repeatedly used and abused by the revolutions of modernity, but it has never been solved. And yet the dream of the revolution has never failed women, who like Gay went on fighting. In this struggle, *La Voix des Femmes* became women's public platform from which they propagated their ideas for liberation and freedom throughout the revolutionary spring. The seamstresses who had founded the first feminist newspaper in 1832 met again on the editorial team of a daily newspaper that Eugénie Niboyet, a former Saint-Simonian and feminist journalist, initiated in March 1848.

LA VOIX DES FEMMES: STRENGTH IN UNITY

A great revolution has just taken place. A moral cataclysm faster than the waves, within hours has overflowed Paris, in a few days it has overflowed France, in a few months maybe, it will overrun Europe. [...] Liberty, Equality, Fraternity call mankind to the same prerogatives; honour this holy trinity that would give women the rights of citizenship, allowing them to rise intellectually and morally equal to men.[28]

By gloriously saluting the victory of the revolution and by underlying its national and international importance and influence, Niboyet used her first editorial to raise women's political consciousness and boldly demand their rights as citizens. Calling women into unity—'strength in unity' being its recurrent slogan—*La Voix des Femmes* became the forum for all opinions to be expressed and in the spirit of pluralism, the newspaper included articles written both by men and women. Among the men who wrote in support of the women's cause were not only academics, politicians, publishers, editors, but also unionized workers.[29] Articles in the newspaper made references to Hippolyte Carnot, minister of public instruction; Alexandre Ledru-Rollin, minister of the interior; Ernest Legouvé, who introduced and taught a course on women's History at the Collège de France; Pierre Leroux, former editor of the *Globe* as well as of the *Encyclopédie Nouvelle*; and Etienne Cabet, who was among the first to allow women to attend a man's political club—although they should remain silent in the gallery.[30] Finally, famous literary figures, both men and women, such as Hermance-Lesguillon, Pierre-Jean de Béranger and Victor Hugo also wrote articles in the newspaper.[31]

The role of the newspaper as expressed in the summary of its vision, which was included in its first twenty-five issues under the subheading, was to open up a space for women to affirm themselves on a daily basis, to identify their problems and advance 'their moral, intellectual and material interests'[32]—an assemblage derived unchanged from the editorial team's Saint-Simonian past. Apart from being a political platform, *La Voix des Femmes* was also going to be 'a library of practical instructions for women',[33] and in this light, the newspaper included a range of industrial, commercial and cultural activities as a way of encouraging women to immerse themselves in all aspects of active life. From its third issue onwards, the newspaper introduced a column entitled as 'Programme of Spectacles': it listed all theatrical and musical performances in Paris and featured in most of its last pages till the end. Apart from a mere listing of the Parisian cultural events, the newspaper introduced 'a feuilleton', that is a literary column, mostly run by the editor's only son Paulin Niboyet[34]; it also included extended drama and book reviews, as well as poetry. Finally, news from the stock market became a standard column of the newspaper in most of the issues between March and April 1848.

There were thus continuities and discontinuities from the newspaper of the seamstresses' youth: accepting men's contributions were among the most striking differences from the 1830s' feminist press. The question of signatures was raised again as an issue but it was differently handled: some articles were signed, others were not; sometimes the contributors would sign with their full names or they would just use their initials. Breaking with their previous signatory politics, the editorial team of *La Femme Libre / Tribune des Femmes*—Jeanne Deroin, Désirée Gay and Suzanne Voilquin—chose to sign all their articles.

> We recognise and value the principle of individuality, but for us this individuality must be erased before a collective being: humanity. It is because we are doing collective and social work that we have scorned the idea of signing our articles. This example does not impose anything on anybody. Everybody has the right to a point of view and is free. The responsibility of the journal does not frighten us; thus our sisters will be able to safeguard their writings by a signature, the editorial committee will only judge the merit of the work.[35]

The editors felt the need to clarify their position above in the article 'Definitive Constitution of our fraternal association'[36] where they announced the formation of their sister political club, *La Société de La Voix des Femmes*, one of many that sprang into action between February and June 1848 when

a new repressive regime was finally imposed.[37] Deroin was elected secretary
with Gay as its vice president, while Voilquin, another leading member of
the 1830s feminist press, also joined the central bureau of the club.[38] It was
from this position as well as from her involvement in the editorial team of the
newspaper that Deroin's struggles for women's suffrage were entangled with
the cataclysmic events of the February revolution. When the provisional government announced universal male suffrage on March 4, in preparation for
the April elections, Deroin took the lead in organizing a meeting on March 22
between Armand Marast, the mayor of Paris and a delegation of four women
from the Committee on the Rights of Woman:

> You proclaim: 'Election for all without exception.' We come here to ask you
> if women are included in this great generality, as indeed they are in the rights
> concerning Workers; we are even more justified in making this request since
> you have not designated them in the categories to be excluded.
>   You also say: 'There are no more proletarians' and yet if women are not
> included in your decrees, France still has more than fifteen millions.[39]

In pointing to the contradictions of the provisional government in the way
they had excluded women both from the category of 'the universal' as well as
from the multitude of 'the proletarians',[40] women asserted their right to vote,
closely intertwining it with the already recognized right to work. And yet
the only thing they got from this meeting was the promise that their demand
would have to be recognized in the new constitution that the future assembly would write after the April elections. But as it is well-known, this never
happened. The February revolution ended up in the terrible June massacres
that were detrimental for all workers, but particularly so for women, who
would have to wait another century to finally win the right to vote.[41] Deroin
could not have possibly foreseen this tragic end, as she was still living in the
revolutionary days of hope; her swift response was addressed to all French
citizens and was widely reprinted and circulated through *La Voix des Femmes*
on March 27, 1848, five days after their meeting with the mayor:

> To the French citizens,
>   The reign of brutal force has passed, that of morality and intelligence begins.
> The motives, which made our parents to exclude women from all participation
> in the government and the State, do not have any value today.
>   You have proclaimed freedom, equality and fraternity for all. Why are you
> leaving women only with tasks to fulfil without giving them the rights of the
> citizen [citoyenne]? Will women also be dispensed of their obligation to pay
> taxes and obey the Laws of the State?
>   Do you want them to become the helots of your new Republic? No citizens,
> you do not want this, the mothers of your sons cannot be slaves.

When you have abolished all privileges, you will not want to keep the most iniquitous of all and leave one half of the nation under the domination of the other.[42]

In defending women's civil rights, Deroin created a continuum between the duties and rights of the citizen and in taking up the thread of the feminist discourse of the 1830s, she promoted motherhood as women's subject position par excellence. As Scott has succinctly pointed out, the figure of the mother was an exemplary discursive site wherein rights and duties were entangled: 'An identity achieved through the performance of socially attributed duties, the very model for the meaning of reciprocity and obligation' (1996, 70). But there were other emancipatory discourses included in Deroin's political rhetoric, particularly coming from the abolitionist movement: 'The mothers of your sons cannot be slaves [and] do you want women to be the helots of your new Republic', she wrote in her address above. Anne Knight (1786–1862), the founder of the Women's Anti-Slavery Society was after all one of the six women who had signed one of the first petitions for the Committee of Women's Rights, as already mentioned above; she was also a contributor to *La Voix des Femmes,* as well as a member of its sister club, highlighting women's social and political rights and writing about the importance of emancipation.[43]

Deroin's argument about women's suffrage went hand in hand with women's right to work that Gay was propagating through the newspaper: 'We need to expose the ideas we have about reforms that we would like to see introduced in the legislation and we will have to take care of the organisation of work',[44] Gay wrote in *La Voix des Femmes* on March 30, further raising two important points for the exercise of women's rights: 'the future of our children and the peace for society'.[45] Sexual differences were nowhere challenged in the discourse of the two seamstresses and indeed in the discourse of any of the contributors in *La Voix des Femmes*: 'We do not aspire to become good citizens [citoyens], we only aspire to become good female citizens [citoyennes]', they wrote in an open letter to Ledru-Rollin, minister of the interior of the provisional government, who had signed the decree for universal [male] suffrage.[46]

In discussing Deroin's difficult task of turning sexual difference into a discourse of equality, Scott (1996) has influentially used the lens of the paradox—the struggle of French feminists both to accept and to refuse sexual difference in politics. The notion of the abstract individual bearing rights had already been shattered by the link between the right to work and the right to vote, Scott has rightly argued (ibid., 60). In this context, sexual difference was just another variable in the already socially differentiated individual and it was on this basis that Deroin built her argument for equality on the basis of difference. There were of course contradictions in this difficult task, which Scott has meticulously analysed, but my question is: Why should these contradictions be theorized as a paradox? The very notion of the paradox already presupposes a structuralist understanding of pre-existent discourses, ideas and practices: it is because such differences have already been constituted that paradoxes emerge. This is where I part company with Scott, arguing instead that her rich and nuanced analysis of Deroin's suffrage politics is much better understood within the notion of the assemblage wherein politics, ideas and practices *become* in the process of their entanglements and intra-actions with other ideas, conditions and practices. In forming relations of interiority among themselves, but also in connecting through relations of exteriority with components of other assemblages—republican and male discourses and practices in this case—the seamstresses' emancipatory politics can only be configured as complex, fluent and in the process of becoming other; in short they have a dynamic that is lost within the structural limitations of the paradox.

In putting forward the notion of the assemblage, I draw again on Arendt's lucid observation that revolutions erupt as events and then unfold as political processes; they are as I have already noted above *politicogenetic phenomena*, open processes rather than closed historical facts. As Maïté Bouyssy and Christine Fauré have pithily noted, the 1848 Parisian uprising was 'a surprise revolution' (2003, 294) in the sense that the fall of the Orleanist regime could not have been foreseen when the Parisian workers, women among them, took to the barricades. 'Revolutions are made in spite of revolutionaries', Ernest Labrousse has provocatively argued (cited in ibid.), echoing Arendt who has also suggested that that 'the revolutionary pathos of an entirely new beginning was born only in the course of the event itself' (1990, 37).

The feminist press in the February revolution opened up paths for women to emerge from the margins and shadows of the private sphere wherein even their socialist comrades as well as the radical members of the provisional government would rather have them remain. Raising women's political consciousness was at the centre of the editor's vision, who throughout her editorials, kept urging women to action: 'We have to work, not only around us but upon ourselves, to conquer through esteem the place that belongs to us'.[47] The idea of the *œuvre à faire* that I have already discussed in Chapters 1 and 3 was thus a recurrent theme in the political campaign of the first daily feminist newspaper, often expressed both in prose and in verse:

TO THE WORK [A L'ŒUVRE]
   No more uncertainties!
   No more hesitations!
   Let's pose clearly this question!

What do we want?
We want our emancipation, total and complete
That is: to be recognised equal to men in matters of intelligence.
So, let us boldly do the work.
Many of our sisters are afraid of this word:
Emancipation!
They should not tremble.
They should recede
Our work is pure.[48]

Throughout the forty-six issues of *La Voix des Femmes,* poetry became a constant form of expression in many different genres, while education was recognized as the means that would help women become independent, develop their intellectual abilities and think for themselves. In this light, the sister club of the newspaper had been explicitly organized with the aim to educate women: 'From tomorrow we are constituting two committees; one for the publication of the journal, the other to discuss the plan of public education for women'.[49] In the same line of Marie-Reine's intervention in the organization of public education for women, the contributors of *La Voix des Femmes* launched a severe critique against the nature, structure and curriculum of the education of girls, 'which submits the most natural momentum of their nature under a severe and constant discipline',[50] thus impeding rather than developing their intellectual abilities.

Following Mary Wollstonecraft's legacy, Amélie Praï, a member of the editorial team and the political bureau of the club, attacked Jean-Jacques Rousseau's functionalist take on women's education and pointed to its detrimental effects on educating women to become independent citizens and autonomous subjects of rights.[51] What the feminists of *La Voix des Femmes* proposed instead was same education for both sexes, equal provision in terms of schools and classes, as well as the organization of free classes for adults in all administrative districts. They also stressed the importance of training qualified teachers and urged young women to take the exams that were organized at the Hôtel-de-Ville.[52] As already noted in the Introduction, Deroin herself had bitter experiences of the struggle of proletarian young women to gain teaching qualifications. It was in the area of women's education that the feminist activists actually saw one of their rare victories: a bill that made education compulsory for both sexes was tabled at the Legislative Assembly of 1848 and was eventually passed in 1850 (see Dixon-Fyle 2006, 30).

In her successful campaign for the education of girls, Niboyet had often invited articles that were criticizing foreign systems of education, while pointing to their commonalities with the French.[53] Internationalizing women's cause thus became a constant editorial practice and reference of the articles in *La Voix des Femmes*: 'In order to offer more interest to its readers *La Voix des Femmes* will deal with interior and exterior politics', the first issue of the newspaper had announced in its front page.[54] The newspaper introduced a column on 'News from Abroad' and there were articles about other countries, such as Germany, England, Ireland, Belgium, Austria, Russia and Italy in all issues.[55] The European revolutionary events of 1848 were particularly highlighted and followed with reprints and citations from the European press.[56] There were also articles from international contributors, such as Robert Owen, who not only wrote to 'The Men and Women in France' to salute their struggle in the very first days of the revolution,[57] but he also visited Paris in early April, despite his old age. While in Paris, he met with the socialist members of the provisional government and also talked at Cabet's club.[58] His visit was saluted and celebrated by the editorial team of *La Voix des Femmes*; as Adrien Ranvier has noted in one of his biographical sketches of Deroin, 'Owen's trip to France in 1848, where he developed his ideas about co-operation had a great influence upon the ways that the associations expanded' (1897, 176).

It was in the milieu of its international significance that the problem of reinstating divorce was also raised through the pen of Gabrielle Soumet, a woman writer active in the politics of reforming the family law in France, who became vice president of the newspaper's sister club after Gay's withdrawal. The problem of re-establishing the 1792 divorce law, which had been revoked by the Bourbon monarchy in 1803, was presented as a moral, political and international issue, closely connected to and dependent on freedom:

> After the glorious Revolution in February [...] we have seen a poster covering the walls of the victorious Paris and this poster carried these words: *The public moral claims the reestablishment of divorce.* These words were laconic but profound. [...] Yes, it is in the name of morality that we reclaim in France the reestablishment of divorce as it exists in England, Switzerland and the United States, as it should exist in all countries where freedom is not a vain word, or a bloody derision.[59]

But it was not just middle-class women like Soumet, who wrote about the need for divorce to become legal again, extracting it from the private sphere and presenting it as a political issue of freedom par excellence. Following the 1830s' heated debates on sexuality, marriage and the right to divorce that had been staged in the pages of *La Femme Nouvelle,* a contributor signed as P. G. Ouvrière, wrote about the link between abject poverty and women's situation in abusive marriages and had urged for divorce to become the abolition of women's slavery: 'Condemned to suffer throughout their lives, is there not here a first form of slavery to be abolished'?[60] The problem with divorce in the worker's discourse was not just a political issue, but also a social one and the two were inextricably interwoven.

Its international character notwithstanding, *La Voix des Femmes* remained open to the problems and hardships of working-class women, while its sister club encouraged all women to attend its meetings in tow with their children if necessary, in spite of the dominant ideologies that considered activities outside the home detrimental for children. Women fought against such prejudices through *La Voix des Femmes*: in her article, *The sanctimonious Woman*, Praï wrote against the tendency to sacralize women's role within the family at the same time as restricting her within it and excluding her from all other civil rights and public appearances.[61]

Participation and action were indeed important for the editors of *La Voix de Femmes;* although revolutions erupt as events beyond and even despite the intentions of the revolutionaries, they demand and depend on their constant presence and involvement. It is in the political spaces of togetherness that political actors appear to each other and act in concert, Arendt has argued, within the milieu of the 'interspace' (1968, 31). Since speaking and acting in concert are so important, revolutions have historically failed whenever their political actors were excluded, or even worse persecuted. But here it is important to note that the Arendtian political actors are reborn in action: 'They do not act because of what they already are' (Honig 1992, 219); they rather become who they are in the process of appearing to each other. Moreover, they never really inhabit a unitary and stable identity, except in the stories that are told and written about them. Revolutionary praxis is thus an ongoing process for Arendt, a living organism through which freedom would be founded in the establishment of a new body politic. As already noted in Chapter 1, Arendt was deeply influenced by Whitehead's process philosophy and had particularly referred to it in *the Human Condition,* but also elsewhere in her work, where she has highlighted the importance of action in initiating political and historical processes:

> Wherever man acts, he starts processes. The notion of process does not denote an objective quality of either history or nature; it is the inevitable result of human action. The first result of men's acting into history is that *history becomes a process*, and the most cogent argument for men's acting into nature in the guise of scientific inquiry is that today, in Whitehead's formulation, 'nature is a process'. (Arendt 2006a, 62)

It is on the Whiteheadian plane of process then that Arendt was fully convinced that public life and direct democracy were *sine qua non* conditions for freedom and the role of the revolutionary councils was crucial in realizing direct democratic practices: 'The claim for participatory democracy

[...] derives from the best in the revolutionary tradition—the council system, the always defeated but only authentic outgrowth of every revolution since the eighteenth century' (1972, 98–99). In Whitehead's vocabulary then the clubs that sprang into action during the February revolution were moments of concrescence in the flow of political processes. Seen from a Foucauldian perspective, they also became heterotopic spaces of freedom and although they were ultimately dissolved they did create a historical precedent, a model of revolutionary praxis to be emulated in the future. The revolution should not be evaluated in terms of its immediate effects, or its possible success or failure, but rather in terms of its aura in enacting memories of revolt and hopes for a different future, Kant has insightfully argued:

> The revolution, which we have seen taking place in our own times [...] may succeed or may fail [...] a phenomenon of this kind which has taken place in human history *can never be forgotten.* [...] For the occurrence in question is too momentous, too intimately interwoven with the interests of humans and too widespread in its influence upon all parts of the world for nations not to be reminded of it when favourable circumstances present themselves, and to rise up and make renewed attempts of the same kind as before. (Kant 2011 [1798], 182, 184, 185)

The February revolution came to a tragic end during 'the bloody June days'[62] when the proletarians took to the barricades again to protest against the government's decision to close down the national workshops and therefore to disentangle its political projects from guaranteeing work for all. But this time the people were defeated: they were either killed, imprisoned or exiled, like Victor Hugo and Louis Blanc, whose idea about the reorganization of labour had been used and abused by the provisional government. But while 'the bloody June' marked the end of the February revolution, its fall had begun much earlier with the gradual exclusion of its political actors—many militant seamstresses among them. The latter soon joined forces around a new newspaper that was less ambitious than *La Voix des Femmes,* but much more focused on women workers' interests and on socialism as a political project more widely.

LA POLITIQUE DES FEMMES: 'THE ECHO OF THE DISINHERITED'

La Voix des Femmes shut down on June 20, only two days before the uprising began; it had already intermitted its publication for a month, between April 29 and May 29, just after the disastrous results of the national elections, where the moderate republicans and the party of order took the majority, leaving the socialists with only 80 seats out of its 880, despite the massive turnout of the first democratic elections in France held under [male] universal suffrage.[63] When the newspaper resumed its publication, on May 29, 1848, it introduced a column with news about the National Assembly sessions, highlighting the fact that the socialist representatives were already in the process of being persecuted: in the issue of June 1–4, there was a report from the May 31 session, when Blanc had been accused for having encroached and oppressed the National Assembly and a committee had been formed to investigate these allegations.[64] It was not the first time that the newspaper had defended Blanc: already before the elections Blanc had received threats to the point that women workers had decided to march in protest to defend his work: 'Long live Louis Blanc! Long Live the organisation of work!' was the rallying cry of that demonstration, reported in *La Voix des Femmes*.[65]

The hopes and socialist ideas of the February revolution and the first daily feminist newspaper fell together but the seamstresses' revolutionary spirit did not: *La Politique des Femmes* had already emerged on June 18, 1848, run by Gay, Deroin and Voilquin. The 1830s' seamstresses' gang was again together, although only Gay was still a dressmaker; Deroin had become a teacher and a journalist, while Voilquin had trained as a midwife. But given the seamstresses' commitment to the social question why did they name their newly founded newspaper *La Politique des Femmes?* Maybe it was because they had already realized what much later in life the exiled Deroin would succinctly articulate in an open letter to Leon Richer's newspaper *Le Droit des Femmes*: 'Duty and right are correlative. But to exercise one's right and to fulfil one's duty it is necessary to have power'.[66] It was indeed the question of power not only between women and men, but also among women themselves that the first issue of *La Politique des femmes* highlighted in the already mentioned dialogue between an enlightened bourgeois woman and a group of working-class women gathering in the Cour du Louvre.[67] Apart from vividly dramatizing the inadequacy of the national workshops for women, the imaginary dialogues were a narrative mode that the seamstresses used to insert class antagonisms in their political rhetoric without openly attacking bourgeois women with whom they were fighting together for suffrage rights. Later on, 'hypothetical narratives' (Riessman-Kohler 1990) would also become a way of avoiding censorship as the freedom of the press gradually came under attack after the June 1848 insurgency.

A seamstress: They have to increase our wages; we don't want to pay for the beautiful apartments and toilettes of our bosses any more.

Another seamstress: It is our work and our money that make their fortunes.

A socialist worker: If you shout like this you will do nothing to change things. Our force is in calmness and perseverance. [...] We will not achieve anything if we do not learn how to reason.

A voice: How can we learn that?

A socialist: By observing, reflecting and searching for education and most importantly by loving each other and by uniting towards useful work.

The Lady: My dear friends, here is one of you, who speaks wisely. I like such workers and I am ready to join them in order to explain morality to those who are less enlightened.

A Voice: We do not need any lessons in morality.

The socialist: You have to give us the opportunity to be moral before you preach us.

The Lady: This is how I understand it. Also several of my friends and I would like to devote ourselves to the workers and organize them.

A Voice: We do not want ladies as our patrons.

The Lady: I am only your friend and nothing else.

The Socialist: Well then, help us to organize according to our tastes and our ideas, instead of trying to organize us according to yours.

The women: This is it! We want to live as we feel and to be happy in our own way![68]

'Help us to organize according to our tastes', the socialist worker asked the lady. But what does taste have to do with politics? Or as Arendt has put it, 'Could it be that taste belongs amongst the political faculties'? (2006b, 211). In addressing this question, Arendt (1982) drew on Kant's *Critique of Judgement*—initially entitled as *Critique of Taste*—the work that in her view 'contains perhaps the greatest and most original aspects of [his] political philosophy' (2006b, 216). But why? As a faculty of the mind, judgement does not derive from logical operations, Arendt explains; it rather emerges from the phenomenon of taste, which Kant 'understood as an active relationship to what is beautiful' (ibid.). Although taste deals with particulars and is configured within subjective conditions, its political aspect unfolds in relation to Kant's notion of *enlarged mentality*: 'The power of judgement rests on a potential agreement with others' (ibid., 217). It is this possibility of collective agreement in matters of taste that can liberate judgement from its individual limitations and ultimately lead to an enlarged way of thinking and judging—the fact for example that many of us admire the Parthenon and/or enjoy Aretha Franklin's music—within the aesthetic milieu of agreement and active relationship with 'what is beautiful'. In this light, 'the capacity to judge is a specifically political ability [...] to see things not only from one's own point of view but in the perspective of all those who happen to be present (ibid., 218).

In drawing on taste to express their differences with the bourgeois feminists of their times, the seamstresses further added corporeal and visceral components in Arendt's conceptualization of taste as a political ability: 'We want to live as we feel it',[69] they all cried out as a response to the lady's attempt to discipline and moralize them. It is here that Whitehead's process philosophy succinctly reminds us that 'action weaves itself into a texture of persuasive beauty' (1967b, 51). Indeed, beauty need not be only an ideal schema on the level of the sublime: it is in nature, in the body and of the body, inherent in the Spinozist joy of political action that I have already discussed in Chapter 4. On the plane of the philosophy of the organism, the seamstresses were not disputing the fact that there was a platform of agreement with the feminist politics of the bourgeois women; but the reality that the latter had not tasted the lived experiences of poverty and destitution-imposed limitations upon their understanding, although it left open the possibility of seeing things from the seamstresses' perspective. 'Help us to organize according to our tastes' thus beautifully encompasses the need for unity, which was the rallying cry of *La Voix des Femmes,* with the recognition of class differences among the feminists of the Second Republic, which was the reason that the seamstresses had taken the decision to start their own newspaper, *La Politique des Femmes,* 'a newspaper appearing on Sundays, published for women's interests and for a Society of Workers'.[70]

With Gay as its director, *La Politique des Femmes* run in parallel with the *Association mutuelle des femmes,* a political and cultural group that attempted to organize and educate women workers for social change. It was high time young women workers spoke; they had come of age in the course of the revolution and 'wanted to live in their own way' Gay argued in her first editorial through the voices of the women workers, as staged above.[71] What she also highlighted in her short editorial was the fact that although women's political aim was the same with men's, their perspective was different and thus 'we must each have our originality', so that 'under the vast banner of socialism women's politics can march in front alongside men's politics'.[72] Women's active involvement in politics was also seen within an international context, wherein Italy, England and the United States were particularly mentioned:

Paris is not the only city where women take active part in politics. In Italy they fight alongside men for the freedom of their countries. In England and America that have been holding public lectures with big audiences. In Leicester a club of women chartists presided by madam Cully has organised a feminine society.[73]

In highlighting the importance of women's involvement in politics, the association and the newspaper tried to create conditions of possibility for young workers to take front stage: sessions were organized where poor women were encouraged to narrate their experiences and relate to each other through story-telling. The seamstresses' political club thus enacted the narrative scene of recognition and communication bringing together the personal, the social and the political in an assemblage that would later shape the consciousness raising movement of second-wave feminism: 'in women's struggle, the symbolic revolution—the representation of oneself and of one's fellow women in relation to the world—is fundamental and must come first' (The Milan Women's Bookstore Collective as cited in Cavarero 2000, 55).

The feminist maxim that the personal is political was thus powerfully encompassed in the title of the seamstresses' newspaper, but only for a very short period. The first issue appeared in the same week that the June uprising erupted, followed by the infamous decree that prohibited women's participation in political clubs; not only were women denied the right to vote, they were excluded from the sphere of politics by law: 'Women and minor children may not be members of a club nor may they attend the meetings', Article 3 of the 'Décret sur les clubs' brutally stipulated.[74] Moreover, the Republican government re-imposed the caution tax on all publications, which made the seamstresses' newspaper both legally and financially untenable. The second and last issue of *La Politique des Femmes* appeared in early August as a dissenting voice within a regime of oppression and persecution to thank its supporters, but also to say 'au revoir' to its readers in the spirit of hope and perseverance:

> The support that we demanded in our first issue was offered. Men gave us the protection we asked for and women came to provide help.
>
> But the intervening events not only delayed the publication of our second issue, but also will most probably force us to suspend the publication of the newspaper for lack of money to pay the caution tax. [...] Yet we hope and we know how to wait. It is by no means a definitive adieu: au revoir![75]

Despite the gloomy editorial introduction, the seamstresses went on to demand from the government to change the law of excluding them from clubs. Their claim was very much based on the necessity and complementary aspect of sexual difference. Entitling their article as 'Eve's daughters', they asked: 'What harm will we be doing by going to a club with our husbands'?[76] But their discourse was also critical, ironic and sarcastic: 'The time has long passed when women naively believed in men's superiority',[77] they wrote, symbolically presenting their public involvement as a sign of progress brought about by the working classes. 'Why are you afraid of women'? they provocatively asked, 'Let them search for happiness in freedom'.[78]

I want to stay in this request, where the search for happiness and freedom becomes a political slogan in dark times. Freedom was always associated with happiness for Gay, Riot-Sarcey has commented (1995, 3, 4); it was necessary in the minutiae of her everyday life, but it was also projected in the future either through her personal letters or the articles and petitions she wrote and circulated. Happiness is a troubling notion for feminists, as well as a politically dangerous injunction, Ahmed has influentially argued (2010). It was in the pursuit of individual happiness that revolutions were derailed from the political project of building a house for freedom and lost sight of the importance of public happiness, which is only attained in action, Arendt has famously maintained (1990). And yet happiness, both personal and public, has been traced as a refrain in the discourses and practices of revolutionary women in my project of writing feminist genealogies.[79] How is this possible?

Taking Gay's political discourse on happiness as my starting point, I want to rethink happiness within the political. Already in Chapter 4 I have looked at Gay's beautiful letters to Enfantin, Fourier and Considerant and have considered how joy as a primary affect is at the heart of Spinoza's configuration of love. What I want to do here is to consider joy as the sine qua non of political collectivities and struggles. As Susan Ruddick has pithily noted there is 'a connection between joy and empowerment—the argument that we organise encounters to maximise joy' (2010, 22) in a rich field of contemporary interpretations and indeed inflections of Spinoza's philosophy.[80] The question that such approaches respond to, namely 'how we fashion a new political imaginary from fragmentary, diffuse and often antagonistic subjects' (Ruddick ibid., 23), was at the very heart of the seamstresses' political problematic during the time of the February revolution and in its aftermath. Posing the question of political collectivities at the core of a revolution shifts the interest from the conditions of possibility that made it possible to the event itself, its multiple modes of expression, as well as its real and imaginary possibilities.

Although addressing a farewell to its readers in the mode of an 'au revoir', the second issue of *La Politique des Femmes,* as well as its sister association, also raised the problem of how it was possible to form a new body politic through creating 'a paideia, a formation a culture', which is what thought needs according to Deleuze (1983, 110). It was through a new culture that the seamstresses believed that they could mobilize new modes of thought, as well as new alliances that were previously unforeseen, unthought-of—what Gatens and Lloyd, inspired by Spinoza, have theorized as 'collective imaginings' (1999). Happiness and joy, both individual and collective were integral to the seamstresses' gesture towards a radical futurity. Interestingly enough, sorrow was also part of this affective encounter, the sadness of having to say au revoir to their readers. And yet 'it is the destabilising moment of the encounter which might be joy or sorrow' Ruddick argues that carries possibilities for forming new political subjects and new collectivities (2010, 24). Why is that?

For Spinoza, humans collaborate with one another to enhance their power for action; this is not suggested as a moral proposition—humans should collaborate—but as a matter of fact, an immanent process of how things work, changes happen and the world moves forward. Drawing on Spinoza's theory of how bodies are in a continuous process of affecting and being affected, Moira Gatens and Genevieve Lloyd have argued that 'freedom is not a possession of the autonomous individual, but rather an ethicopolitical practice [...] a collective process of *becoming*-free' (1999, 146). Spinoza's proposition on the immanence of collectivities relates to his concept of the very essence of things, which also underpins Whitehead's configuration of actual entities: 'The philosophy of organism is closely allied to Spinoza's scheme of thought', Whitehead announced in the very beginning of *Process and Reality* (1985, 7). Although Spinoza's 'morphological description is replaced by description of dynamic process' (ibid.), 'an actual entity satisfies Spinoza's notion of substance: it is *causa sui*' (ibid., 222), and the universe itself 'a creative advance into novelty' (ibid.).

It is on the plane of 'creative advances into novelty' that joy and happiness become constitutive and not derivative components of the assemblage of the seamstresses' political practices; such affects have left traces of their expression in the articles that they wrote while still in the whirl of revolutionary action. As Ruddick has aptly put it, for Spinoza, 'The expansion of our capacity to act is at once relational, produced by mutually reinforcing collaborations, and the outcome of a complex interplay of affect and reason' (2010, 26). In this context, joy and happiness became the passage alongside which the seamstresses moved from the experience of feeling joy to the phase of conceptual understanding, expression and enactment of political discourses and practices, which included the formation of associations and their multiple publishing activities.

But while the political was flagged up in the newspaper's title, it was not separated from the social and its material conditions of possibility. Both issues of *La Politique des Femmes* presented a carefully designed project for a commercial association of seamstresses, a co-operative which in contrast with the humiliating structure of the *ateliers des femmes,* offered a model for a social workshop of seamstresses, very much in the line of Blanc's socialist ideas for the reorganization of labour. Entitled as 'Studies for an association'[81] the project was first published as a draft, open to suggestions; it comprised ten articles outlining its organizational structure and economics and included a detailed costing for its initial foundation, which came up to the sum of 10,000 francs. While following the ten hour workday, as legislated by the provisional government after the February revolution, article 6 of the new co-operative stipulated that 'the workday will start at 8 o'clock in the morning and finish at 6 o'clock in the evening. There will only be half an hour for lunch. (This arrangement is taken so that women in returning home at 6 o'clock can do their housework and dine with the family)'.[82] What is interesting in this article is not only the gendered inflection of the law, but also the need to have it in brackets. Bracketing gender was the seamstresses' tactic for reinserting gender in the labour legislation without openly attacking or undermining patriarchy. Despite their cautions, however, the Republican government was adamant: politics was denied to women. Although the seamstresses did manage to secure the caution tax through the support of former Saint-Simonian friends and comrades[83], their newspaper had to drop politics from its title; it appeared on August 21, 1848, as *L' Opinion des Femmes* with Deroin as its director this time.

L' OPINION DES FEMMES: GIVING REASON TO DREAM

The truth! Sacred purpose without which nothing can be undertaken. Truth! The light, which alone can illuminate the filthy cesspool of our backward society; it can make us recognise the ugliness and depravity, as well as the excesses and miseries in opposing them with what is good, the beautiful.[84]

In writing triumphantly about the power of truth in the first issue of *L' Opinion des Femmes*, its unknown author signed as 'M' firmly situated the newspaper's vision and scope at the centre of an enlightened era to come. Interestingly enough, truth and beauty are linked in the discourse of the article, strengthening Arendt's argument about the political dimension of aesthetics in Kant's *Third Critique*, as we have already seen above. The author's engagement with the power of beauty and truth was not immaterial, however. In appropriating Enlightenment discourses, the author was rather confronting what Foucault (1976) has configured as 'regimes of truth'.[85] It was in the attempt to criticize regimes of power and truth that poverty was identified as one of the main problems that women workers had to fight against, particularly since their abject conditions were not even recognized and named, let alone addressed by the newly elected Republican government: 'Each of us should get up from the lower position that has been imposed upon us, to speak out with nobility and dignity about our overlooked needs, our crushed instincts, our violated destiny and rights'.[86] It was for women then 'to prepare the way to truth' and all women should be part of it, 'each had her own work to do';[87] the way to truth was an *œuvre à faire* for all women.

In this line, revealing lies and myths about the family was an interesting game of truth to engage with: 'The family is a fiction for the worker',[88] an unsigned article putting forward the formation of associations provocatively suggested; even when they manage to get together for a short time in the evening they are all exhausted and all they can talk about is their pains and miseries: 'For the proletarians the family is not a source of joy, but of suffering, of deprivations and of anxieties'.[89] Written on the aftermath of 'the bloody June days', the article above was using the project of associations as an antidote to the problem of social unrest; by deconstructing the myth of the family it actually became helpful for the women workers, who had once again been relegated within the constraints of the private. Its inclusion in the first issue of *L' Opinion des Femmes* shows that their feminist and working-class priorities notwithstanding, the seamstresses were trying to forge cross-class collaborations in advancing their cause. They were trying to survive politically within dark times and amidst immense difficulties, but they were determined to persevere.

Sticking to the importance of education would thus remain as one of their outmost priorities as the article about the 'Society for the Mutual Education of Women' showed; its aim was to promote women's reunion either in forming industrial associations or for the purpose of intellectual enlightenment and education. Moreover, the society would be the link between women of all conditions, as well as between existing associations; it would offer women workers free education and would also publish newspapers and brochures. Apart from the already known *Politique* and *Opinion des Femmes,* the society also announced the forthcoming publication of *Les Ouvrières Parisiennes,* a bi-monthly newspaper on the modes and the industry, run exclusively by workers.[90] Tristan's influence—albeit with inflections—can be clearly traced in the seamstresses' struggle to find ways to associate despite their exclusion from the political. But while Deroin announced that the second issue of the newspaper would appear on September 22, it never did.[91] *L'Opinion des Femmes* folded after its first issue; it would reappear again in January 1849, the year when Deroin became the first woman to stand as a candidate for national elections. In her appeal to the electors of the Seine department, published in *L'Opinion des Femmes* on April 10, 1849, she asked her fellow citizens to honour the republican dogmas of liberty, equality, fraternity for all, women and men:

A legislative assembly composed entirely of men is as incompetent to make laws that regulate a society composed entirely of men and women as would be an assembly composed entirely of the privileged to decide on matters concerning the interests of workers, or an assembly of capitalists for upholding the honour of countries.[92]

Following trails of her 1848 electoral campaign[93] publicized through pamphlets, brochures and a series of articles in *La Voix des Femmes,* Deroin proclaimed herself a citizen [citoyenne] drawing on the link between rights and duties as the legal and moral foundation of universal citizenship and by making an appeal to the necessity of speaking and acting the truth: 'By posing my candidacy for the Legislative Assembly, I fulfil my duty; it is in the name of public morality and in the name of justice that I demand that the dogma of equality no longer be a lie',[94] she wrote in response to Proudhon's vitriolic attack through the pages of his socialist newspaper that he edited, *Le Peuple.* Despite his socialist ideas and principles, Pierre Joseph Proudhon (1809–1865) had vehemently attacked women's civil rights since the early 1840s arguing that their options were constrained between being 'a housewife or a courtesan' (cited in Thomas 1948, 61). It goes without saying that feminist activists—Deroin among them—had spilt a lot of ink in responding to the discourse of 'la femme au foyer', the idea that women's position was to preserve the household as a sanctuary of humanity in the cruel bourgeois world. Against the prevailing notion of 'the social' as an object of scientific inquiry, as well as a domain for government regulation and protection, Deroin reframed it as a repository of political rights, with the figure of the mother at its heart:

> But it is mainly the sacred function of motherhood, which some oppose as being incompatible with the exercise of the rights of the female citizen [citoyenne], which imposes on the woman the duty to ensure the future of her children and gives her the right to intervene, not only in all acts of civil life, but also in all acts of political life.[95]

If the 'care of the self' was a precondition for the young Athenian men's politicization (Foucault 1988b), the motherly care for others would become for the French feminists the foundation of women's involvement in politics, a feminist mode of governmentality: 'Up until now politics has not been the art of governing people, but of oppressing them [...] this is why women must claim the right to intervene [...] to transform this politics of violence and oppression',[96] Deroin's article on women's mission went on. In posing an ethics of care at the heart of politics, Deroin transformed the notion of the social from a space of necessity and dependency to a space of action, thus annihilating its separation from the political; the latter was reconfigured as the art of governing—ironically enough, the object of Foucault's critical inquiries a century later. Her decision to stand for the legislative elections was made despite her socialist comrades' attacks and defiance, but also against her overall heavy overload, as a mother, worker and journalist. Gay's letter to Deroin carries traces of how overworked these women activists were:

'We are so much preoccupied dear friend that we have not been able to examine clearly our project for the association before the general assembly, so it won't take place tomorrow', she wrote, but she highlighted how much she always counted on Deroin's leadership.[97]

But although Deroin worked towards pushing away violence and oppression from the field of politics, violence was there to stay: in August 1849, *L'Opinion des Femmes* published a draft for a federation of workers' association, *L' Association Solidaire et Fraternelle de Toutes les Associations Réunies*.[98] The project was founded on the intersection of three fundamental rights: sovereignty, work and consumption, which were all underpinned by the socialist idea of solidarity and redistribution along the lines first expressed by Blanc: 'from each according to their ability, to each according to their need'.[99] The association would materialize the right to work by providing tools, raw materials and interest-free loans for its members. On submitting the finished products of their work, the workers would receive vouchers that they could use to obtain food and other products. Apart from workers, farmers would also be invited to participate, while the association would also see to the social organization of education on all levels, including vocational training, housing, as well as health insurance and retirement benefits. The democratic and egalitarian organization structure of the whole project was outlined in fifty-two articles, regulating the function of a central committee, which would oversee five subcommittees on production, consumption, finances, education and litigation. The plan also included structures for the organization of cultural and family life, as well as regulations for the annual general assembly; it covered 4 pages of the newspaper and was signed by Deroin. As Serrière has noted, this was not just a plan for an association, but rather a utopian plan for the reorganization of the whole society: 'The future always ends up giving reason to dream', she poetically noted (1981, 38). Given the overt socialist direction of the plan, it is not difficult to understand that the government intervened swiftly: *L' Opinion des Femmes* was fined with five thousand francs for publishing against the anti-associationist laws and was forced to close down.

SEAMSTRESSES IN DARK TIMES

It was not the first time that the seamstresses had to fold a newspaper, so they went on with their political activities. Although they no longer had their own press platform to speak from, their ideas were published elsewhere: *La Democratie Pacifique,* a Fourierist newspaper run by Considerant had always supported them. Despite the government persecution, the association was formally constituted on November 22, 1849, and by May 1950, 400 workers' associations had joined forces under the umbrella of the federation, which had also attracted 104 producer co-operatives. This time, the seamstresses had gone too far threatening capitalism and liberal economy; on May 29, 1850, the police stormed Deroin's apartment during a meeting of the Central Committee and arrested all its members, 38 men and 9 women. Apart from 27 men, Deroin, her old Saint-Simonian friend Pauline Roland and Louise Nicaud, a representative of the laundresses' association were finally charged with the crime of political conspiracy against the government.[100] They were imprisoned for five months, while waiting for their trial, which took place on November 14, 1850.

Although Deroin and Rolland were initially accused of trying to over-throw the government by a violent revolution, they were finally interrogated about their private life: the reasons Deroin kept using her maiden name, while Roland had refused to get married altogether choosing to have children out of wedlock. At the same time, their socialist comrades, as well as their defence lawyers put pressure on them to refuse their involvement in the leadership of the workers' association and leave men to be charged for this as more politically appropriate: 'I had been urgently begged, in the name of the association, not to acknowledge that I was the author of the project or of the act of Union of the associations', Deroin wrote in a statement included in the papers that she entrusted to Adrien Ranvier (1909, 823). Deroin confronted the male prejudices of her judges: 'I must protect against the law by which you want to judge me. It is a law made by me; I do not recognise it', she boldly stated (cited in ibid., 423–24). When it came to her socialist comrades' demands, however, she gave in: 'Not wanting in the presence of our adversaries, to start a debate among socialists on the socialist outlook, I contented myself to answer the question that was put to me: "No I have nothing to say for the associations". But it is evident', she bitterly added, 'that this could not have done any service to the workers' (Deroin 1909, 823).

Both Deroin and Roland were given a prison sentence of six months, which they served leading an ascetic life of studying together, 'as if they were reading Schiller', Riot-Sarcey has noted (1994, 259). They also went on writing revolutionary pamphlets, brochures, journal articles and letters 'from the depths of the jail which still imprisons our bodies, without reaching our hearts',[101] as they movingly wrote in a letter they sent from Saint-Lazare's prison to the *Convention of the Women of America* on June 15, 1851. Their letter unfolded as a short history of women's struggles, as well as of the failure of the 1848 revolution to found a new body politic, a house for freedom: 'Your courageous declaration of Woman's Rights has resounded even to our prison, and has filled our souls with inexpressible joy',[102] they wrote drawing on the political power of joy in enacting 'collective imaginings' (Gatens and Lloyd

1999). But while joining their American sisters 'in the vindication of the right of woman to civil and political equality',[103] they concluded by highlighting the need for solidarity and union with the working classes: 'Only by the power of association based on solidarity—by the union of the working-classes of both sexes to organise labour—can be acquired, completely and pacifically, the civil and political equality of woman, and the social right for all'.[104]

Deroin was released in early July 1851 and resumed teaching as a way to grapple with her own family crisis: her children had been scattered in schools away from Paris, while her husband who had lost his job on the grounds of the family's political involvement and had developed a serious mental illness (see Gordon and Cross 1996, 96). But things were going to get worse: after resisting Napoleon's coup d'etat in December 1851, Roland was arrested and incarcerated again and in June 1852 she was deported to an Algerian penal prison. Deroin was actively involved in organizing support for the victims of political persecution and she also published the first volume of her *Almanach des Femmes* (Deroin 1852). Seeing, however, her friend and comrade brutally treated and fearing her own persecution, she finally chose the road of exile: in August 1852, she fled to London and stayed there for the rest of her life in the company of her children, but not of her husband who died from exhaustion while trying to join his exiled family.

These were dark times for the seamstresses: Gay, who had retreated from public life at the end of 1849 (Riot-Sarcey 1994, 252), was also forced to take the route of voluntary exile in 1864, following her husband Jules Gay who had lost his permit to publish in France. Voilquin emigrated to Louisiana in 1848, but she returned to France in 1860. Roland was less fortunate: although she was released from prison after the intervention of public intellectuals such as George Sande and Béranger, she died in Lyon in December 1852 after falling ill in the course of her voyage back from Algeria. Still, their work went on in their newly adopted countries.

The Seamstress as a Pariah

The era of the revolutions had come to a halt and the seamstresses had become 'social pariahs' Deroin wrote (1852, 19) in the first volume of her *Almanach des Femmes,* a publication that started in Paris in 1852 but was eventually transferred to London. It was not the first time that the figure of the pariah appeared in the discourse of nineteenth-century feminists in France. Tristan had already drawn on it to configure her autobiographical experiences of walking the streets of London and of travelling as a single woman: her diaries had the figure of the pariah in their very title.[105] Reflecting on Tristan's experiences, Eleni Varikas has looked at the genealogy of the pariah, arguing that 'the metaphor of the "pariah" provides [...] an idiom of the critique of arbitrary authority and the persisting social and political exclusion' (2010, 60).

The figure of the pariah also appears throughout Arendt's work as a courageous truth-teller amidst particularly risky situations. In her book, *The Jew as Pariah*, Arendt (1978) has actually painted the portrait of four *pariah* figures: (a) the *schlemihl* or Lord of Dreams, the people's poet as exemplified in the poetry of Heinrich Heine, (b) the conscious pariah as illuminated by historical figures such as Bernard Lazare, (c) the always suspect as Charlie Chaplin's cinematic hero and (d) the Kafkian hero. All four figures are portrayed as outsiders of their geographies, times and social worlds, but with differentiated attitudes, practices and effects that I have elsewhere discussed at length (see Tamboukou 2012b).

Drawing on Arendt's figures, I thus want to sketch the Parisian seamstress as a 'conscious pariah', but also as a Kafkian hero. Through political involvement, the seamstress became a rebel and her agonistic practices brought her in confrontation not only with the forces that marginalized her but also with trends of integration, the forces that compelled her to downplay her difference in order to be recognized as a speaking subject, the author of her words and deeds. When she was not recognized as a citizen, although she had been asked to fulfil her duties as a legal subject, she had to address the Kafkian aporia par excellence: 'You are not of the Castle and you are not of the village, you are nothing at all' (Arendt 1987, 84).

This is what the Parisian seamstress as a Kafkian pariah struggled with: the right to be a subject who could choose her name, have her right to work protected and be allowed to enjoy simple things like a home, work, family and citizenship. Normal existence became impossible for her and she was pushed to the road of exile, the road of prison or the road of death. And yet the stories she wrote about her life and experiences in the newspapers, brochures, pamphlets and letters that she published and distributed enlightened some of 'the villagers' and made them see 'that the rule of the castle is not divine law and, consequently, can be attacked' (ibid., 88). If the spaces of contemplation and thinking became the shield of the Kafkian hero, it was the spaces of writing that sheltered the seamstresses in exile.

As already noted in the previous section, the first volume of the *Almanach des Femmes* was published in 1852 in Paris, while Deroin was still involved in supporting political prisoners and exiles.[106] After *La Politique* and *L'Opinion des Femmes*, choosing *Almanach* as a title of her publication might seem strange, particularly since the *Almanach* appeared as a continuation of *L'Opinion*; its subscribers were actually asked to notify any change of address to the editor, so that they could receive the *Almanach des Femmes* and other brochures (Deroin 1852, front matter). In her introduction, Deroin herself felt the need to justify the title: 'Today an Almanach should not only indicate variations in temperature and the courses of the stars, but also the variations in the diverse tendencies of the spirits and the progress of the social truths that contain the prophesy of a better future' (ibid., 9).

It is quite obvious that the choice of the title was a tactic to avoid censorship under the laws that had totally suppressed the freedom of the press and had prohibited political debates in general.[107] But in appropriating a title of women's popular magazines, Deroin also challenged common sense perceptions about what women should read. The use of plural form for truth is quite striking, particularly considered in the light of the Foucauldian idea of 'regimes and games of truth' that I have already discussed above. But it has to be noted here that Deroin only used the notion of multiple truths sarcastically: 'Is it not this, the truth, the whole truth and nothing but the truth'? she wrote in concluding a letter 'to the author of the universal dowry'[108] published in the second volume of the *Almanach* (1853, 78). Finally, the ironic reference to 'prophesies for a better future' not only shows Deroin's creative inventiveness, but also reveals the fact that political hope was a constant light in dark times: 'Resistance is the privilege of the oppressed' (ibid., 10), she wrote in introducing her second volume, 'to allow the oppressors to accomplish their iniquitous projects, would be to become their accomplish, to imitate them in their rage, would be to lower one's self to the same degree of perversity' (ibid.).

Flagging up resistance in the introduction of the second volume was indeed Deroin's narrative mode of showing that women's struggle would go on irrespective of its difficulties and bleakness and beyond national borders and language barriers. The *Almanach des Femmes/Women's Almanack* (1853) appeared as a bilingual publication in London in the very first year of the editor's new life in Shepherds Bush. It was a difficult year not only because of the harshness of relocation, despite the support and help of her socialist friends in London, but mostly because it was in London that she heard about Roland's and her husband's death: 'One year has elapsed since the publication of our Almanack and sad and fatal events have taken place during this period', she wrote in the very beginning of her introduction (ibid., 9). But these 'sad and fatal events' winged her pen: in castigating the cruelty of Roland's death she asked her readers to revisit a genealogy of brave women who had paid with their life the price of freedom:

> Pauline Roland is no more!
> She has fallen victim to the cruel horrors of African transportation. The martyrdom of this holy and noble woman adds to the shame of our adversaries. It forms the last jewel in the crown of the new emperor of France, in that crime begotten blood bought crown! (1853, 212)

Roland's death thus enacted the aura that makes all failed revolutions the Kantian events 'never to be forgotten' in Deroin's moving adieu to her friend and comrade: 'We behold thee still: we experience thy influence still, thou [inspitest] us, thou [confirmest] us, thou [encouragest] us to persevere. Adieu! Adieu!' (ibid., 224). But it was not just the sad deaths that Deroin had to deal with in her first year in London. Surviving in a foreign metropolis was also a challenge: as Vaughan Baker has noted, on arriving in London without speaking English, Deroin 'must have been frightened and depressed' (1997, 3). Although there is no information about who helped her to settle down, Knight—who she had worked with in Paris, as we have seen above— must have been involved. Baker (1997, 14) also notes that there was an assistant group for French political refugees in London, which had been set up by Blanc who had also fled to London after the June uprising.[109]

Deroin lived at various addresses in Shepherd's Bush, where she took up the needle again to earn a modest living for herself and her family, including her invalid son,[110] who she looked after till his premature death in 1887 (see Pilbeam 2003, 288). As Baker has noted, apart from the fact that other French émigrés already lived in Hammersmith, 'her location in an area of heavily concentrated laundry work' (1997, 4) was surely related to her search for work opportunities. She also gave private lessons and as already noted in her pen-portrait she tried to run a school, which turned out to be a financial failure. Although there were ups and downs in her financial situation, Deroin was mostly struggling to make ends meet.[111]

Life was thus a real struggle for Deroin and attending to the importance of women's work was not just a socialist idea but also a bare necessity, a daily fight for her own survival. Quite interestingly, the last entry of the 1853 *Almanack*, following Roland's obituary, was the announcement of the 'North London Women's Association and Home' at 31 Red Lion Square, Holborn: 'Established 3 years since with the view of supplying the public with good and substantial work [...] and providing regular employment for needle women at such prices as to deliver them from the oppression of middle men and slop sellers' (Deroin 1853, 237). The idea of workers' association and the need for improving women's position in the industry thus remained the central focus not only of her writing and publishing activities, but also a pressing reality she lived with, although her financial precarious position was somehow alleviated when in 1880 the government of the Third Republic granted her an annual pension of 600 francs as a compensation to the proscripts of the previous regime (Serrière 1981, 41).

But despite all financial difficulties exacerbated by language barriers, Deroin became organically involved in the London socialist circles. She met William Morris, who gave the oratory in her funeral (Ranvier 1908, 318) and together with her eldest daughter Cécile they became members of both the Socialist League and the Hammersmith Socialist Society (Baker 1997, 8). For Ranvier, she was 'one of the leaders of the English socialist party'

(1908, 318), an assertion that can be verified according to Baker by her socialist activities recorded in William Morris' newspaper *The Commonweal* as well as in the records of the Hammersmith Socialist League (1997, 2). Thus, although all three volumes of the *Almanach* had a rich diversity of themes, including articles on women's education, as well as their civil and property rights, celebratory announcements of women's achievements in art and science, critical views vis-à-vis the death penalty, reports against women's slavery and even ideas about animals' rights and vegetarianism, the overall focus was and remained on the importance of work: 'True liberty for women as for men is the complete development and the free exercise of all their faculties and true equality is the right to participate in the social work for the wellbeing of all, which can only be accomplished by the organisation of work' (Deroin 1852, 70). Moreover, the *Almanach* retained the dialogic form of the seamstresses' newspapers since the days of *La Femme Libre*. Heated epistolary debates developed among its contributors, both men and women, making it an open democratic platform for questions around women, work and gender relations.

WRITING TO BECOME OTHER

The seamstresses of the July Monarchy and the 1848 revolution found themselves scattered in all corners of Europe in the second half of the nineteenth century, but while in exile they still managed to open up paths in the European social movements of their times and new geographies. Jeanne-Désirée's[112] letters in the twilight of her life offer a vivid picture of their undefeated optimism and determination, which went on abidingly throughout their lives. In writing to Considerant on September 1, 1890, Jeanne-Désirée reflected upon their lives in struggle and about the value and legacy of their socialist ideas. She seemed very conscious of what they had achieved, but she was also bursting with plans about what they could still strive for, despite the fact that they were both octogenarians:

> The books of our social values will be very much researched in a future nearer than one fears, but for the moment they are smothered by a banal literature. [...] We must address ourselves to the illiterate, to the crowd anxious to know what is wanted by these human beings who do not have their banners blessed. [...] It would be good to do for the scientific utopia what Jean Macé, Verne, Flammarion, and Hetzel have done to popularise the experimental sciences. We must write [...] to produce work through the channels of numerous societies. In short, we must inject theory into action, starting with children and women within cooperative schemes.[113]

Even more strikingly, the seamstress' plans were not only about ideas and knowledge, but also about action: 'We must prepare for the magnificent phalanstery [...] the communes [...] the groups of industrial armies',[114] her fervent letter went on. Although she recognized that her discourse might be considered as a utopian vision, she was not afraid to admit that imagination was her chosen reality 'Though I could be taken for a visionary, in fancy I already live in this new world and I have the ideas that I would like to be able to write about'.[115] Her perception of her life in exile is also striking: 'I didn't use to like either Belgium, or the Belgians. I moved here against my will. [...] And, well, now that I am as free as I have never been, I live here voluntarily and I feel more and more attached to them, having learnt to know them'.[116]

Having written profoundly and tenderly about her life in exile, Jeanne-Désirée would not only give away the mystery of her passionate involvement, but also of her recurrent disappearances from the editorial and activists' groups as well as the workers' associations that she had so tirelessly worked to put together: 'After the struggle I used to fly off into the clouds of reverie, where I fashioned an ideal world for myself. Real, earthly life has always been painful for me',[117] she wrote to Considerant in July 1891, shortly before she died. Following lines of flight, the seamstress would deterritorialize herself from the striated spaces of the counter-revolution regimes, while writing letters, brochures and pamphlets was a set of practices entangled in her 'technologies of resistance' (Tamboukou 2003a). Writing has always been a technology of the self, a mode of self-transformation, Foucault has influentially argued: 'One tries to modify one's way of being through the act of writing' (1987, 182). It is the seamstresses' practices of writing so as to become other that I will further consider in the next chapter, taking up the genre of autobiography as a vibrant mode in the narrative assemblage of writing the self.

NOTES

1. Gay to Enfantin, letter dated February 8, 1848, Bibliothèque de l'Arsenal/ Fonds Enfantin/Correspondance Divers/7728/153, 1–2, (BnF/BdA/FE/CD).

2. Following Gay's and Deroin's signatures in their 1848–1851 writings, in this chapter, I will refer to them with the names they had chosen to be identified with in this period.

3. There is a rich body of historical studies around the February 1848 revolution, with de Tocquevilles' *Recollections* (2009) being the classic source. See also Jones 1991, for the wider context of the 1848 European revolutions.

4. Petition for the 'Committee for Women's Rights', Archives Nationales, series C*2430, C2231, no 1723, cited in Riot-Sarcey 1994, 182. It was signed by Jeanne Deroin, Ann Knight, Désirée Gay, de Lohgueville, A. François and J. Deland.

5. The petition above came from the 'Society for Women's Emancipation' and was addressed to the provisional government. Archives Nationales, Bb 30/307, 6802, cited in Riot-Sarcey 1994, 188.

6. According to Rémi Gossez, labour historian of the Second Republic, between February and May 1848, 640 petitions were addressed to the Labour Commission, 63 of them were from women workers, and among them, 18 from the garment trades. (See Bouyssy and Fauré 2003, 296)

7. *Tribune des Femmes [La Femme Nouvelle]*, 1(19), 260, August, 1833.

8. Ibid., 261.

9. Ibid. [emphasis in the original].

10. I refer here to Lenin's famous text, 'What is to be done', first published in 1902. According to Arendt, Lenin was the last heir of the French Revolution in the sense that he sacrificed the freedom of the soviets to solve the problem of the poor (1990, 66).

11. *Le moniteur,* February, 25–26, 1848, cited in Bouyssy and Fauré 2003, 295.

12. For a detailed discussion of the labour reforms and actions of the provisional government, see Gossez 1967.

13. Petition addressed by Désirée Gay to Louis Blanc on March 2, 1848; reprinted in *La Voix des Femmes,* (2), 2, March 22, 1848.

14. Speech by Philippe Buchez, president of the Constituent Assembly in a meeting of the mayors of the 12 Parisian arrondissements (cited in Bouyssy and Fauré 2003, 296).

15. There are 14 extant letters from Gay to Enfantin between 1846 and 1860 and 6 of them were written between January and April 1848: January 1; February 8, 25, 26; March 7 and April 4 (BnF/BdA/FE/CD/7728/151-164).

16. *La Voix des Femmes,* (2), 2, March, 22, 1848.

17. Ibid.

18. *La Voix des Femmes,* (24), 1, April 15, 1848.

19. Duclerc was also undersecretary of state for Finance and was himself assistant of Emile Thomas, who was the director of all national workshops.

20. See Gay's article 'The Delegates of the Workers in Paris', *La Voix des Femmes,* (26), 2, April, 18, 1848. For more discussion about the organization and problems of the National Workshops for Women, see Thomas 1948; Rowbotham 1993; DeGroat 1997, 2005; Bouyssy and Fauret, 2003.

21. See 'How they treat women after February 1848', in *La Voix des Femmes* (28), 1–2, April 20, 1848.

22. Ibid.

23. See *La Voix des Femmes*: 'Our Principles', (10), 1, March 30; 'To the citizen Cabet' (11), 31, March 31; 'Keep your promises', (13), 2, April 2; 'The Delegates of the women workers of Paris', (26), 2, April 18; 'How they treat women after February 1848', (28), 1–2, April 20.

24. 'The Delegates of the women workers of Paris' in *La Voix des Femmes,* (26), 2, April 18, 1848.

25. 'Un group des femmes dans la cour du Louvre' [A group of women in the court of Louvre], *La Politique des Femmes* (1), 1, June 18–24, 1848.

26. Ibid.

27. Minutes of the April 2, 1848 public meeting of *La Société de La Voix-des Femmes,* published in *La Voix des Femmes,* (14), 2–3, April 3, 1848. See also ibid., (17), 2, April 7, 1848.

28. Ibid., (1), 1, March 20, 1848.

29. See 'Elections' letter sent to the Parisian electors by Eugène Stourm, who signs as a typographer-worker, on April 1, 1848, reprinted in *La Voix des Femmes,* (16), 2, April 6, 1848. Stourm had collaborated with the revolutionary seamstress Julie Fanfernot in editing the brochure *L'Etincelle* in 1833.

30. See among others: announcements about Leroux's candidacy, *La Voix des Femmes* (1), 4, March 20, 1848; the success of Legouvé's course, ibid., (5), 2, March 25, 1848; 'To the citizen Cabet' by Niboyet, Gay and Deroin, ibid., (11), 1, March 31, 1848.

31. See Hermance-Lesguillon, 'L'Arbre de la Liberté', ibid., (13), 3, April 2 and (33), 1–2, April 26; Béranger, 'A Wilhem', ibid., (11), 1; Victor Hugo, 'Opinion de Victoire Hugo sur la condition des femmes' ibid., (17), 1–2, April 7.

32. Summary of the newspaper's vision under the subheading, 'Daily socialist and political newspaper, organ of everybody's interests'. It appeared in all issues between 1 and 25, but was dropped for the rest of the issues between 26 and 46.

33. Ibid.

34. See 'Feuilleton du Journal la Voix des Femmes' in *La Voix des Femmes,* issues 7, 8, 12, 13. Jean-Alexandre Paulin Niboyet (1826–1906) was himself an author writing comedies and travel novels under the pseudonym of Fortunio Niboyet.

35. *La Voix des Femmes,* (5), 1, March 25, 1848.

36. Ibid.

37. As Moses (1984, 128) has noted, 171 newspapers emerged in Paris during this period alongside the massive multiplication of political clubs that we have already mentioned in Chapter 3.

38. See letter 'to Citoyen Cabet' signed by Niboyet as president, Gay as vice president and Deroin as general secretary in *La Voix des Femmes* (11), 1, March 31, 1848. See also Voilquin's first article on an assembly of midwives in ibid., 2. Gay withdrew as vice president in early April, as the minutes of the April 6 session record Gabrielle d' Altenheym Soumet and Jeanne-Marie as vice presidents of the club, with Voilquin as a member. (ibid., (17), 2, April 7, 1848).

39. *Liberté,* égalité, *fraternité. Les femmes* électeurs *et* éligibles [Texte imprimé], BnF.8- LB54- 423.

40. In proclaiming universal suffrage for all men, the provisional government had also dramatically announced, 'From the day of this law there will no longer be proletarians in France' (cited in Scott 1996, 60).

41. French women first voted in the 1945 municipal elections.

42. *La Voix des Femmes,* (7), 3, March 27, 1848. A different translation of the whole article can be found in Bell and Offen 1983, 247–48.

43. See 'Minutes of La Société de *La Voix-des Femmes*', public session of April 6, 1848, published in *La Voix des Femmes,* (17), 2, April 7, 1848. See also Knight's letter to M.A. Coquerel, reprinted in ibid., (24), 3, April 15, 1848.

44. Ibid., (10), 1, March 30, 1848.

45. Ibid.

46. 'A M. Ledru-Rollin' in ibid., (20), 2, April 11, 1848.

47. Ibid., (3), 1, March 23, 1848.

48. Ibid., (9), 1, March 29, 1848, emphasis in the original.

49. Ibid., (5), 1, March 25, 1848.

50. Ibid., (21), 2–3, April 12, 1848.

51. Ibid., 3.

52. Ibid., (32), 2, April 24 and 25, 1848.

53. See article signed by L. Du Park, editor of another newspaper, *L'Athénée des femmes,* comparing the deficiencies of the French and Algerian educational system in ibid., (6), 3–4, March 26, 1848.

54. Ibid., (1), 1, March 20, 1848.

55. See among others: Bettina von Arnim's 'The Misery in Germany', ibid., (2), 1–2, March 22, 1848.

56. Among the significant revolutionary events that the news of *La Voix des Femmes* followed were: the January revolution in Palermo, Sicily; the meeting of the Heidelberg Liberals that called for a *Vorparlament,* the resignation of Metternich in Vienna, the violent uprisings in Berlin, Frederick William's IV promises of reform and the declaration of war against the Habsburgs by Piedmont in March; the Great Chartist meeting on Kennington common in London and the entry of Prussian troops in Schleswig in April; the meeting of the Pan-Slav Congress in Prague in early June. See Jones 1991 for an overview and discussion of these events. The Irish issue was also a constant feature of the newspaper's interest.

57. The address was sent from London on February 27, 1848, and was reprinted in *La Voix des Femmes*, (5), 2, March 25, 1848.

58. See Desiree Gay 'Robert Owen in Paris' in ibid. (15), 3, April 4 1848 and Gabriel Soumet's 'The club of Citizen Cabet' in ibid., (16), 3, April 6, 1848.

59. 'Extracts from the *Courrier de Paris'* reprinted in *La Voix des Femmes,* (37), 1, May 29, 1848. The article is signed as G. S. [initials for Gabrielle Soumet].

60. Ibid., (11), 2, March 31, 1848.

61. *La Femme moralisatrice,* ibid., (31), 4, April 23, 1848.

62. For a more detailed discussion of the events between June 22 and 26, 1848, see among others: Amann 1975; De Tocqueville 2009 [1969].

63. For a critical discussion of the April elections, see among others, Fasel 1968.

64. *La Voix des Femmes,* (39), 2, June, 1–4, 1848.

65. Ibid., (25), 2, April 16 and (26), 2, April 18, 1848.

66. 'Les tours', letter in the series 'La récherche de la paternité', in *Le Droit des Femmes,* October 7, 1883, cited in Scott 1996, 70.

67. *La Politique des Femmes,* (1), 1, June 18–24, 1848.

68. Ibid.

69. Ibid.

70. Ibid.

71. Ibid.

72. Ibid.

73. Ibid., 2.
74. *Décret sur les clubs,* July 28, 1848, in Bell and Offen 1983, 249.
75. *La Politique des Femmes,* (2), 1, August 5, 1848.
76. 'Eve's Daughters' in ibid.
77. Ibid.
78. Ibid.
79. As I have argued elsewhere in my work, joy has been a saturating affect of women's collective lives in education, as well as of the feminist movement more widely (Tamboukou 2003, 84–85, 161). It has also been a recurring theme in Emma Goldman's and Rosa Luxemburg's letters (Tamboukou 2013b, 2014c).
80. See among others: Deleuze 1988; Gatens and Lloyd 1999; Hardt and Negri 2005.
81. *La Politique des Femmes* (2), 2, August 5, 1848.
82. Ibid.
83. It was Olindes Rodriques and Hortense Wilde, writing under the pen name of Henriette who saved the seamstresses' newspaper. See Dixon-Fyle 2006, 42.
84. 'De la Vérité', *L'Opinion des Femmes,* (1), 2, August 21, 1848.
85. Apart from his 1976 interview, 'The Political function of the intellectual', the notion of 'the regimes of truth' is recurrent in Foucault's work and expresses his overall argument that truth and power cannot be separated.
86. 'De la Vérité', *L'Opinion des Femmes,* (1), 2, August 21, 1848.
87. Ibid.
88. 'Project for an association of all proprietors and of all those who are interested in maintaining order', in ibid., 1.
89. Ibid.
90. 'Société d'éducation mutuelle des femmes' in ibid., 2
91. 'Faits Divers' in ibid.
92. *L'Opinion des Femmes* 2(3), 2, April 10, 1849.
93. Campagne électorale de la citoyenne Jeanne Deroin, et pétition des femmes au people, March 16, 1848. BNF, Fol-Lb55-505.
94. Ibid., 2 (4), 5, May 1849.
95. 'Woman's mission in the present and in the future' in ibid., 2(2), 2, March 10, 1849.
96. Ibid.
97. Désirée Gay to Jeanne Deroin, letter dated February 10, 1849. Bibliothèque Historique De la Ville de Paris, Archives Marie-Louise Bouglé/Autographs/Désirée Gay/10-2-1849/CP4247.
98. *L'Opinion des Femmes* 2 (6), 3–6, August, 1849.
99. *'De chacun selon ses facultés, à chacun selon ses besoins'* was used by Louis Blanc, who Gay had collaborated with in the Luxemburg Commission, in his 1851 work, *Plus des Girondins.* The slogan was of course popularized through Marx's 1875 *Critique of the Gotha Programme.*
100. Ranvier's account (1897, 1908, 1909) is the classic source for this period of persecution, imprisonment and the trial. See also Thomas 1948; Serrière 1981; Moses 1984, Riot-Sarcey 1994 and Pilbeam 2003 for further discussions and analysis.

101. 'Letter to the Convention of the Women of America', June 15, 1851. It was first published in *History of Woman Suffrage*, I, 234–37 and was reprinted in Bell and Offen 1983, 287–90.

102. Ibid., 287.

103. Ibid., 289

104. Ibid.

105. *Pérégrinations d'une paria*, first published in 1838.

106. See Ranvier 1909, Serrière 1981 and Baker 1997.

107. These oppressive press laws were imposed by Napoleon III, after his coup d'état in 1851 and remained in power for almost 20 years (see Moses 1983, 151).

108. Through the pages of the *Almanach* the author had argued that the government should institute a 'universal dowry' for mothers in recognition of their role. This suggestion created a lot of angry responses and debates about the danger of infantilizing women and reducing them to their maternal role instead of recognizing their full rights as citizens.

109. For a discussion of the conditions of French political exiles in London, see also Zévaès 1924, 345–75.

110. Deroin's son was suffering from hydrocephaly, according to Serrière 1981, 41.

111. Baker has meticulously looked at the Hammersmith Poor Rate Book, the Hammersmith Lighting Rate Book and the Hammersmith and Kensington directory to trace Deroin's financial situation (1997, 14–15).

112. I return here to the name of her epistolary signatures.

113. Véret-Gay to Considerant, letter dated, September 1, 1890, (AnF/10AS42/8/DVG/61/1–3).

114. Ibid.

115. Ibid.

116. Ibid.

117. Véret-Gay to Considerant, letter dated, July 6, 1891. (AnF/10AS42/8/DVG/68/3).

Chapter 6

Creativity as Process

Writing the Self, Rewriting History

'I am free!! I have deposed my rights on the altars of humanity! I have liberated a man from a love that was not shared. [...] Yes, I say it with pride: I have put a man into the world, I have given him to *everyone*',[1] Suzanne Voilquin wrote to the imprisoned Enfantin in early 1833 in a letter announcing her decision to divorce her husband Eugène. Not only did Voilquin pronounce herself divorced in full defiance of the laws that prohibited it, she also reversed the discourse of the powerless deserted woman by presenting the divorce as her decision to liberate her husband from the shackles of a loveless marriage. But she was swift to note that by liberating her husband she had also freed herself: 'Since this separation I have remained *alone* before the world—My reconquered freedom has allowed me to work more effectively for the freedom of my sex',[2] she wrote in concluding the article. What is particularly striking is that she decided to reproduce this personal letter in the very last issue of *La Tribune des Femmes,* where she defended women's demand for the right to divorce by revealing the troubled story of her own. A slightly different version of this divorce story reappeared three decades later when Voilquin published her *Souvenirs* (1866), the only autobiography from the women of the first autonomous feminist movement in France.

Despite its rarity, this autobiography has never been translated into English in its entirety, although lengthy extracts from its first chapters are included in two edited volumes, both published in 1993. What is further intriguing is that the translated extracts in these two volumes appear with two slightly different titles: 'Suzanne Voilquin: Recollections of a Daughter of the People' in (Traugott 1993) and 'Suzanne Voilquin: Memories of a Daughter of the People' in (Moses and Rabine 1993). Apart from the different connotations between 'recollections' and 'memories' in philosophical approaches to the study of memory,[3] none of these titles conveys in full the original title of the autobiography: *Souvenirs d'une fille du peuple ou La Saint-Simonienne en* Égypt, *1834–1836* [Memories of a Daughter of the People or The Saint-Simonian in Egypt, 1834–1836]. As Voilquin explained in the preface to her autobiography, this double title was not accidental: not only did she want to narrate 'the poignant sorrows' (1866, vi) of her life, but she also felt that the harsh experiences she went through as a member of the Saint-Simonian circles in Egypt had to be told.[4] But although the autobiography comprises forty chapters organized in six parts, only sixteen of them in parts 4 and 5 (19–35) are about her experiences in Egypt. And yet 'A Saint-Simonian in Egypt' appears as the main title in the original publication, with 'Memories of a Daughter of the People' as a subheading. It is also important to note that Voilquin's name does not feature in the title, as in the two translated extracts above.

I have already discussed the problems and troubles of translation in Chapter 2, but what I want to highlight here is the bibliographical and historical confusions that such differences in titles have created in the archive of nineteenth-century French feminist writings. I further want to draw attention to the conceptual problems that appear when handling the discursive formations of women workers' autobiographical writings, particularly considering issues around 'the author's function' (Foucault 1989), already discussed in Chapter 2. As Patti Lather has pithily commented, 'Translation is always producing rather than merely reflecting or imitating some "original"' (2000, 15), further suggesting that all we can hope for when in translation is 'echoes that reverberate the original' (ibid.) and mobilize it in new contexts.

The aporias of translation notwithstanding, feminist theorists have long argued that autobiographical writing offers a deeper understanding of women's consciousness, but they have also pointed to the fact that gender, class and race intersect in decisively bending the autobiographical canon.[5] 'The self is something to write about, a theme or object (subject) of writing activity', Foucault has famously suggested (1988b, 27) in the context of his genealogical inquiries around truth, power and the subject. Such writing activities create an assemblage of narrative modalities of power and forces of desire wherein discourses around the self are generated, inscribed and enacted, but also disputed, negotiated and reversed.[6] Seen from this perspective, women's autobiographical writings have operated as a critical Foucauldian technology of the self, but they have also created what Maggie Humm has succinctly configured as 'a rhythm in a system of moments' (1989, 45).

It is with the seamstresses' autobiographical rhythms that I want to drift along in this chapter. In doing this I follow Voilquin's narrative, but at the same time I make 'rhizomatic connections' (Deleuze and Guattari 1988) with two autobiographical documents written and published in the first half of the twentieth century: Jeanne Bouvier's *Memoirs* (1983/1936) and Marguerite Audoux's autobiographical novel, *L'Atelier de Marie-Claire* (1920).[7]

Jeanne Bouvier (1865–1964) was a French seamstress, born in the south of France to a peasant family. She became a silk worker at the age of eleven after a financial disaster that left her family penniless. In 1879 she moved to Paris, where she worked as a domestic and she finally trained as a dressmaker. She got involved in labour politics and became an ardent trade unionist in the French garment industry, as well as a leader in the international women's labour movement.[8] After her retirement, she threw herself in the pleasures of research and wrote four historical studies, as well as her *Memoirs*.[9] Marguerite Audoux (1863–1937) was born in the centre of France; after her mother's death and her father's abandonment, she grew up as an orphan. She first worked in the country as a shepherdess and farm worker, but in 1881 she moved to Paris where she eventually became a seamstress. Through her involvement in the Parisian bohemian literary circles, she was encouraged to write and publish her own novels.[10]

Although both Bouvier and Audoux were born in the second half of the nineteenth century—around the time that Voilquin's *Souvenirs* appeared—their work was published in the early twentieth century, a sociopolitical and historical context, which is different from the July Monarchy—the period this book has focused on. As we have already seen in the Introduction, women's workforce in the garment industry rose significantly throughout the nineteenth century, an increase that came hand in hand with a dramatic proletarianization of their condition. What is particularly significant for the period that both Bouvier and Audoux moved to Paris to become seamstresses is the technological revolution that the advent of the sewing machine had brought to the garment industry, becoming 'the gentle and docile companion of any working-woman—whether her skin be white, red, black or yellow' as one of the many brochures circulated by the Singer sewing machine company widely advertised (cited in Coffin 1996, 74). It seems that the spirit and mentality of 'the united colours of Benetton' campaign had its predecessors back in the nineteenth-century garment trade, where signs of diverse cultures became the spin of economic, political and social transformations.[11] Apart from the economic and technological changes in the garment industry, the political climate in France was also different at the turn of the nineteenth century, particularly after the 1871 Commune wherein women workers had once again been heavily involved. Despite the defeat of the Commune, feminist activism had re-emerged in the French political scene and had significantly influenced the sociopolitical and cultural formations of the Third Republic.[12]

I am aware of these differences in shaping the conditions of possibility that these autobiographical documents have emerged from. This is why I have used Deleuze and Guattari's (1988) notion of *rhizomatic connections* as a conceptual tool that allows for multiplicities to connect horizontally—like rhizomes—on a plane of consistency: women workers' condition in the garment industry, where abrupt changes and ruptures coexist with surprising and unexpected continuities.[13] It is actually on the latter that my interest lies in making *rhizomatic connections* between and among these three autobiographical documents. As I will argue, it was the autonomous feminist movement of the July Monarchy that created conditions of possibility for the figure of the woman worker/writer to emerge, very conscious of her uniqueness in the cultural histories of her time: 'I believe I am the only worker who has become a writer. Marguerite Audoux, who is also a seamstress is a novelist, but I feel attracted by historical research',[14] Bouvier wrote in an article in *La Française* in 1928. Within the genealogical framework of the book, the seamstresses' writings of the early twentieth century are tangible and rare effects of the nineteenth-century political and cultural activities of their predecessors; together they create an assemblage of women workers' radical cultural practices in the formations of modernity that has yet to be fully explored and appreciated.

AUTOBIOGRAPHICAL RHYTHMS:
BETWEEN PAST AND FUTURE

'So that you can understand my life, dear child, I have to unfold my first years in a few pages; the past gives birth to the future', Voilquin wrote in the opening lines of the first chapter of her autobiography, which was addressed and indeed dedicated 'to Suzanne, my adopted daughter and my beloved niece' (ibid., v), the child she loved and cared for, after her brother's premature death. As we have already seen in the previous chapter, Voilquin fled to the United States at the end of 1848, disillusioned by the crush of the February revolution, but unlike Deroin and Gay who lived and died in exile, she returned to France in 1860. It was after her return that she wrote her autobiography, which was published six years later. Giving an account of herself when she was already sixty-seven years old, Voilquin looked back at a life full of actions and passions, but being 'a daughter of the people' she did not want to stand up as an exceptional or charismatic individual. Thus, her autobiography does not follow the canon of the autobiographical self-raising from the multitude and becoming the mirror of his era—a strong male tradition of *Confessions* that starts from Augustine and culminates in Rousseau.[15] It rather follows trails of working-class autobiographies where the self is embedded in its social and political context, in an attempt to create a collective voice of the multitude, its experiences and its struggles.[16] In this light, the fact that her name does not appear in the title of her autobiography is important, while its insertion by later translations creates conceptual misunderstandings, as I have already noted above. It is here that White's (1987) argument that narrative form imposes restrictions and limitations upon the content becomes important in shaping the discursive framework within which life stories take up meaning in the archives of history (see Tamboukou 2013b). But apart from 'the content of the form', what are the themes that emerge in Voilquin's *Souvenirs* and how do they make connections with the early twentieth-century autobiographical documents? This is what I want to discuss in the next sections.

Writing the Good and the Bad Mother

In telling her life story to her niece, Suzanne drew a genealogical line where her mother was a crucial figure: 'Although dead for more than forty years, she is still as alive in me now, as at the moment of our separation', she wrote in the very first pages of her *Souvenirs* (1866, 3). Apart from the fact that the figure of the mother was central in Saint-Simonian discourses, her tragic absence has also become a recurrent theme of literary engagements with the autobiographical self: 'My mother, the most noble and proud of creatures, succumbing to exhaustion and wretched poverty, while my father was dreaming about saving the human race', the famous artist Rosa Bonheur had said about her father Oscar-Raymond Bonheur—one of the leading figures of the Saint-Simonian movement—in recounting her life story to her portraitist and lover Anna Klumpke (2001, 154).

Although absent from her novels, as she died when Audoux was only three-years-old, her mother features prominently in her name: Audoux was actually the author's maternal name, which she consciously took up rejecting her father's name Donquichote. This was a symbolic gesture against the cruelty of a father who abandoned the author and her sister after their mother's death. It was in the name of the mother that Audoux wrote her novels, following trails of the Saint-Simonian battle against the patriarchal name in the nineteenth century. Perhaps as a sign of mourning for her mother, all mother figures in Audoux's novels are either abandoned, unhappy or dying. Sandrine is the most tragic figure of the seamstresses' group in *L'Atelier de Marie-Claire:* she was born in the country, fell in love with the son of a Parisian family, got pregnant, gave birth, left her child behind with her mother and went to Paris to work as a seamstress. Still in love and in a relationship with Jacques, the father of her child, they never married, although they had a second child together. Unsurprisingly, her beloved abandoned her to marry the bride of his parents' choice, while Sandrine died from sadness and exhaustion: 'Like the others I looked at the empty place but at the same time I saw once more the sad eyes and the tired smile of Sandrine on the Saturday before, and I understood that, on that evening, she was at the end of her life' (Audoux 1920, 56).

Sandrine's sad story, which takes up seven chapters out of the eighteen of the novel, encapsulates real-life experiences of many young seamstresses in Paris in the nineteenth and early twentieth centuries. It exposes the hypocrisies of the bourgeois society and reveals young women's fate within it. 'The crisis of nineteenth-century working class poverty was particularly acute for young and single women. Many left their families in the countryside and migrated alone to the cities', Moses has noted (1984, 27). The figure of young women workers who had to work hard in the city, while supporting their illegitimate children in the country has become well-known through the figure of Fantine in Hugo's *Les Misérables.* Unlike Hugo, however, Audoux did not leave Sandrine to fall into prostitution, she let her die instead—a fate that was more worthy of the best seamstress in the atelier. As Moses has commented, 'Working-class women were victimised by capitalism and by sexism' (ibid., 31); it would thus fall upon women workers/authors to restore their fellow workers' dignity, even if this had to be done through the romantic literary trope of the dead woman/lover/mother.

Against the genealogical line of mothers' hagiographies, Bouvier's mother emerges as an exception. Throughout her memoirs, Bouvier recounts her mother's cruelty in making her work hard for the subsistence of her whole family, without showing any signs of tenderness or gratitude:

> My mother spent the night with me, shaking me whenever, in spite of myself, I began to fall asleep. She was telling me, 'Don't fall asleep. You know very well that you mustn't sleep. Tomorrow we won't have any bread. I was making superhuman efforts to stay awake.' (1983, 59)

The striking image of a destitute mother shaking her daughter's body to keep her awake so that she could go on working for the sake of the family's bread, forcefully brings in gendered experiences in the memory of work: a young working girl feeling exhausted, hungry, cold and unprotected in her own home, which is also her workplace. Despite her agonies, Bouvier could see the desperate situation her mother was in and worked hard to alleviate it; years later, however, when she had already moved to Paris, she was devastated to find out how little her sacrifices had been appreciated. In opening up an unlocked trunk, she read some old letters accusing her of selfishness and cruelty: 'Your sister earns sixteen francs every two weeks, gives me ten, and when I have no bread to eat, she hangs on to her money. She is a heartless daughter' (ibid., 90), her mother had written to her younger daughter. Bouvier was traumatized and her love for her mother was irrevocably wounded: 'She doesn't love me', she wrote, 'That's why she always punished me so harshly' (ibid., 91). Apart from some visits to her homeland, her mother would never enter the discourse of her memoirs again—she had become Bouvier's bad object. But either cherished or vilified, the figure of the mother is inextricably interwoven with poverty, a recurrent theme in women workers' autobiographies.

The Gender of Poverty

'The years that followed the Restoration[17] were excruciating for workers to live through. So misery, our long time acquaintance came once again to knock at our door', Voilquin poignantly wrote (1866, 22–23). Poverty is inscribed in her *Souvenirs* as an abject condition annihilating any hope for progress and change. Moreover, living in poverty was not only a condition imprisoning the workers within the daily struggle for the bare necessities of life. As already shown above, poverty was also very much a gendered experience par excellence and has remained so to our own days: 'This sad visitor weighed principally upon my mother, who out of devotion for her loved ones took upon herself the greatest part of the burden', Voilquin noted with sadness (ibid., 23). Her mother died from illness within conditions of abject poverty, in the same way Bonheur's mother had, as already noted above.

The ghost and fear of poverty marked the lives of working women; it is no wonder that it would fall upon them to take it up as a social problem and transform it into a political one when the time of the revolutions came, as we have already seen in Chapters 3 and 5. But apart from political actions, poverty also influenced individual lifestyles and directions. Bouvier has written extensively in her memoirs about her frugal lifestyle, saving for a little cottage in the country where she could retire in comfort: 'When my young fellow workers in the shop would say, "I want a beautiful dress, a handsome hat," I would tell them, "Me I want a little house in the country"' (1983, 98). Her dream of returning to the country went hand in hand with her fear of poverty knocking again at her door: 'I was recalling the sad days of my childhood, the days when I was hungry. I did not want to have an old age without bread. I wanted my old age to be better than my childhood. This perspective gave me the courage to work' (ibid.). Thus, when the girls in the atelier were joking about the boredom of country life she would respond: 'I'll never get bored as long as I am sure that I will never go hungry' (ibid.).

What is also striking is that poverty was not just a fear of the future but also a component of the garment industry during the slack season, when seamstresses would experience the miseries of forced unemployment, bluntly expressed in their writings: 'The end of December brought with it the dead season and we had to separate once more', Audoux plainly wrote in her novel (1920, 38), recounting the dark days of having to leave the atelier she worked for and miss not only her wages but also the friendship and company of the girls she was working with. The ebbs and flows of the garment industry interfered with the body rhythms of going hungry and cold, ultimately becoming the rhythms of her narrative: 'I suffered with the cold too and I wanted to light a fire, but there was neither stove, nor fireplace in the room' (ibid., 46).

But as already noted in the Introduction, despite its harshness the dead seasons of the garment industry also offered some time off work for the seamstresses to engage with cultural and political activities. Of course, such cultural escapes were only a possibility for those seamstresses who had managed to save something during the high season or had created alternative networks of employment through personal clients: 'For some time I had had clients who would have me work at their homes during the dead season. I would thus escape the period of unemployment, which gave me a certain comfort', Bouvier wrote about her tactics of survival (1983, 97). Here again, such 'technologies of resistance' (Tamboukou 2003a) were only available to workers like Bouvier and Désirée Gay before her, who had become skilful dressmakers; it was not something seamstresses of a lower status, like Audoux, could ever achieve. It is thus no surprise that it was only seamstresses among the labour aristocracy that became active in politics and engaged in the intellectual life and movements of their times. The role of education was crucial here.

The Adventure of Education

Education or rather the lack of it comes up early in Voilquin's reminiscences. She wrote powerfully about the sorrow, anxiety and anguish of searching for knowledge: 'Many times in public concerts and in museums, I would feel my tears flow. In those tears there was a mingling of the happiness of aspiring to the unknown with the despair of never being able to attain it' (1866, 20). Tears flowing down the young girl's face create a visceral image of women's desire for education and would become a constant theme of their future campaigns. As a Saint-Simonian writer, Voilquin felt no restriction whatsoever in exposing the force of her emotions, powerfully interrelating the intellectual and the material in the assemblage of the social and cultural conditions she had emerged from. Happiness [bonheur] and despair [désespoir] were entangled in her experiences of seeking for knowledge, and reading opened up heterotopic spaces in the constraints of her environment: 'I passionately loved reading; I could indulge in this penchant in the evening next to my mother on condition that I read to her, while she worked' (ibid.). Passion, joy, happiness, indulgence fill up and indeed overflow from the writer's discourse alongside her tears. Moreover, reading to her mother in the evening while she was engaged with most probably needlework created a different pedagogical context for working-class girls than those of their brothers.

Work was never separated from learning for working-class women who became of age as writers and political activists in the assemblage of work, labour and action, thus defying through their practices the boundaries that

Arendt (1998) configured in her analysis of the human condition. 'Sometimes I brought with me a book wrapped up in the same paper as the bread for my lunch', Audoux wrote in her autobiographical novel (1920, 41), recounting at the same time how uncomfortable she felt when her patron and co-workers kept asking her about her passion for reading:

> The *patron* turned over the leaves and gave it back to me quickly, and in a scolding tone he said, 'You have a passion for reading, eh?' This reproof had been flung at me so often that I had acquired the habit of excusing myself by replying that I only read in odd moments, or during the night when I could not sleep. (ibid.)

While recognizing the importance of reading in making up for the formal education they lacked, the seamstresses would also point to its discursive limitations: 'Instead of that solid instruction that young girls are now beginning to receive, I extracted from these novels false notions about real life', Voilquin wrote (1866, 20). Education was an adventure for young working-class women, a process with unforeseen outcomes. Although lamenting her lack of formal instruction, what Voilquin had not fully realized even at the moment of writing her autobiography was that education in her times was often full of dead ideas she had been spared. Seeing the world without the blinkers of scholastic education, she was therefore in no need of 'unlearning' useless notions and prejudices. There is always a need of 'unlearning' in the process of education, Deleuze (2004) has influentially suggested in his major philosophical work, *Difference and Repetition*: getting away from what has been segmented as knowledge so that one can follow lines of flight in new terrains of questions and problematizations.[18] As Whitehead has further noted, 'Education in the past has been radically infected with inert ideas.... This is why uneducated clever women, who have seen much of the world, are in middle life so much the most cultured part of the community' (1967c, 2). Voilquin would be a perfect exemplar for Whitehead's critique of the deadlocks of education.

In this context, Voilquin's *Souvenirs* is a paradigmatic text of the possibilities and limitations of the seamstresses' cultural movement, vividly portraying how she immersed herself in philosophical literature: 'Reading became the only distraction I wanted to taste' (1866, 35), she wrote, reflecting upon the dark period she entered after her mother's death. Following Voltaire's urge to 'crush the infamous',[19] she threw herself in the negative philosophies of her time. Her autobiography thus lucidly reveals the philosophical and literary archive that would later underpin and inform her reviews and cultural interventions in the feminist newspapers she edited and contributed: 'From Voltaire I only read his theatre with interest; I preferred Rousseau; from him

I read with joy *Emile* and mostly the *Nouvelle Héloïse*. [...] I no longer felt the same after this reading'. Like writing, reading also has a transformative effect upon the self, it is a *technology of the self* in its own right, Foucault has succinctly suggested (1997, 211).

Voilquin was not unique in managing to educate herself in spite of constraints and limitations and against the odds of her social class restrictions. Already in Chapter 3 we have seen how Marie-Reine Guindorf threw herself in the project of educating working-class women, while in Chapter 5 we discussed the workers' educational associations that Jeanne Deroin founded with Désirée Gay and Pauline Roland. Although the newspapers and associations that the self-educated seamstresses founded were short-lived and crudely persecuted, their legacy was long-standing. It inspired and shaped a cultural movement among women workers that went well into the twentieth century, particularly flourishing after the World War I, when the eight-hour working day was established—a change that opened up time and space for workers' intellectual lives. This is how Bouvier wrote about her experiences of knowledge and education:

> During many years, I carried out regular research. [...] I was interested in this intellectual work that brought me satisfaction every day. I was also learning so many interesting things, that I had never thought about; I found such a big number of documents, either in the National Library, or in the National Archives. [...] The study of questions around work and particularly women's work is exciting; and it has its rewards as long as the researcher manages to reconstitute a past of struggles, of injustices and miseries that workers or a category of employers had to endure. (1983, 216, 227)

Although she never had the chance to follow a proper education, Bouvier found her way to knowledge through the paths of the National Library in Paris, in the evenings of her workdays, 'the proletarian nights' that Rancière (2012) has so influentially written about. The price she paid for choosing to be a seamstress, an activist and an intellectual was that she never married or had a family; as she movingly wrote in her memoirs: 'One cannot have everything: material goods and intellectual satisfaction; I much prefer the latter' (ibid., 183). But in acknowledging the personal sacrifices she had to make, she also wrote passionately about the joys of knowledge, research and intellectual creativity: 'In the midst of material difficulties there remained a big, a very big satisfaction: to be able to indulge in intellectual work and more particularly in research that has allowed me to write my four volumes' (ibid). The passions and joys of intellectual life were indeed important for the young seamstresses, who chose to live as single women in a heterosexual patriarchal society. But how did it feel to live without love as a single working woman?

The theme of love and its failures has been forcefully inscribed in their auto-biographical writings.

Erasing Love

I was still looking at the work of my good old authors, but I was forced to admit my preference for works of romance, since they spoke more to the imagination. Mesdames Cottin and de Genlis, the charming storytellers of that period, were my preferred ones. From the savant Madame de Staël I read with pleasure her *Delphine* and *Corinne,* the new Sappho in whom, it is said, she wanted to paint her own triumphs and real sorrows. (Voilquin 1866, 36)

As already discussed above, philosophical readings changed the way Voilquin saw and understood the world; and yet, she was not afraid to declare her love for romantic fiction. But it was not just romantic literature: it was more specifically women writers that charmed the young working-class woman creating a world wherein she could re-imagine herself and her relations with others. However, there was such a huge gap between the imaginary worlds of her readings—the fictional figures she lived with in one of the many modes of existence that Souriau's (2009) philosophy has revealed as possible—and the reality of cruel love, dramatically narrated in the fourth chapter of her autobiography: 'Let me briefly paint for you this first love; through it I was elevated onto a luminous world for a few moments, but the man who had made me live in such ethereal heights threw me brutally into an abyss', she wrote (Voilquin 1866, 38). Voilquin's experience of love was much more bitter than it was sweet: it is a shocking story of sexual abuse under the eyes of her family, who did very little to protect her. Following the dialogic mode of her autobiography she told her niece how she met a young medical student in her brother's house, how the whole family orchestrated a match making, how she was initially seduced by the romantic idea of love and how she was eventually abandoned and rejected:

Toward dusk, when we were alone in my room, he became violent, out of control, and committed such a brutal assault against me that I was horrified. I screamed out; my sister and brother came in; I ignore what Stanislas told them to explain the state I was in. (ibid., 43)

Like many young girls of her times—and ours—Voilquin was repeatedly accused of 'indifference [...] having a cold heart [...] incapable of loving' (ibid, 41). Her narrative account of sexual violence as a symptom of her unjust heteronormative society was a bold act, particularly considered in the context of her times and geographies. But in her view this was not 'a case to remain silent about' (ibid., 38). She felt that telling her story of sexual abuse was her 'duty to re-establish the facts' (ibid.) and get the records straight. Her story was addressed to women in general and her niece in particular: 'You and all women will judge me' (ibid., 39), she wrote, defying the stigma that the revelation of her story carried with it.

While Voilquin boldly wrote about her own experiences of violence and sexual abuse, Audoux wrote about abandonment and desertion in recounting Sandrine's story as already discussed above. Having herself been betrayed by the lover of her youth, what Audoux repeatedly wrote about in her novels is women's impossibility to love as an effect of their powerless position in the heterosexual matrix. The way she portrays her fiancé Clement towards the end of the novel is striking:

> Then Clement joined us. I saw him coming from afar. The upper part of his body retained much of its freedom, but there was something, I could not tell what, that made him heavy below. And he always made me think of a tree that had moved without taking from the earth any one of its roots. (1920, 229)

We will never know, whether she married him or not, as the novel ends with the death of the matron of the atelier and its final dissolution, while a young seamstress was singing 'in her merry falsetto voice: *Paris, Paris, paradis de la femme'* (ibid, 239). Audoux wrote pessimistically about the failures and aporias of romance, but love is completely absent not only from Bouvier's memoir but from the whole body of her archived papers. We know that it was Bouvier herself who bequeathed her papers to the archives of Marie-Louise Bouglé library at the time of her retirement. The absence of love from her papers is thus a carefully crafted 'archival technology of the self' (Tamboukou 2014d). In looking after her legacy, Bouvier must have carefully edited all traces of her private self, apart from the stories she chose to include in her memoirs and love was not one of them. Being a single work-ing woman herself, Bouvier preferred to write about the strange experience of not having a family:

> One also finds people in our times, who criticise women's work, since they consider that their right place is at home. In this case every woman must have a home; but myself and so many other women have never found somebody who could offer us a home or the possibility to rest.[20]

We know that 'these people' who criticized women's work emerged in the Parisian socialist circles well before Bouvier's times, as already examined in Chapter 5 through the heated debates of the women of 1848 with Proudhon and his followers. But what is also interesting in Bouvier's article above is that the end or absence of love marks the beginning of work and the consolation it can give to women's life troubles.

Writing the Memory of Work

The sad story of Voilquin's cruel love concludes the first part of her *Souvenirs*, opening up the importance of work in reclaiming the joys of life: 'I had to find again the force to live' (1866, 50), she wrote before turning to the fifth chapter of her autobiography, which recounts her experience as a young working woman in the Parisian needleworld: 'The first house of embroidery, where we were accepted as workers was in Rue Saint-Martin' (ibid., 56), she wrote. Drawing maps of workplaces was important as the route to work was one of its many challenges:

> Our task however, was rough; we had to be at work at seven o'clock sharp, and, before undertaking such a long race to arrive on time, we had to carry out hastily all our household chores. If some details put us behind, Mrs Martin did not admit any excuses, neither did she offer any pardon, we had to pay in kind, that is, make up for those few minutes at the end of the workday. When our days were prolonged in this way, I had a ghastly fear of meeting on our return one of those despicable men who make a game of accosting young working women and frightening them with shameful proposals. (ibid., 57)

Voilquin's brief and vivid account of the daily space/time race between work and home paints a colourful picture not only of the home/work continuum in the gendered experience of work, but also of the complex capitalism/patriarchy assemblage the Parisian needle workers were entangled in. Bouvier has also written about the dangers that young seamstresses faced while walking back home after working late at night in their Parisian ateliers: 'In this atelier they used to make us work very late, without having dinner [...] these late nights would go on till two o'clock in the morning' (1983, 88). Working till the early hours of the day without dinner was only part of the problem, however. The bigger challenge was how to return home at the end of the night shift, fighting against the dark and the cold: 'The Seine carried along huge icicles and large piles of snow were hitting the riverbanks. I had to walk for three quarters of an hour to reach home' (ibid.). In going through such difficulties, Bouvier was hopeful that things would soon change after the 1892 law that imposed regulations upon the working hours, disallowing night work for women among other adjustments. But this law was never equally followed in practice as Audoux's stories of her own experiences of working late in her Parisian atelier vividly depict:

Our long evenings continued. We spent one night in every two finishing the
most urgent work. There were nights so hard to endure that sleep in the end van-
quished us, and the *patron* found us asleep with our heads on the table. We were
all stiff with the cold and the cheek, which we had rested on our arm remained
marked for a long time. (1920, 79)

And yet work was not only about exploitation, power and domination.
Lines of flight and forces of desire simultaneously and incessantly erupt from
the segmented spaces of the Parisian garment industry. Disciplinary as it was,
the embroidery workshop opened up smooth spaces for Voilquin's young
sister, Adrienne:

Because of Adrienne, I was happy we had fallen into the milieu of this swarm
of mad young women. My sister was livened up again in their company. Until
then she had suffered more than I from the changes in our lives and from our
lowly position. [...] Thus when the gaiety of this young atelier won her little by
little, I was so happy to see her vital force achieve a better equilibrium and her
youth blossom out at last. (1866, 57)

Despite the harshness of the working conditions, the Parisian ateliers were
also places of homosociality for young working women. Friendship was
important in their lives as it created a smooth space within the segmentarities
of capitalism and patriarchy. Women workers have repeatedly written about
how much they cherished and valued their relations with the other girls:
'I found many young women of my age at the atelier. I became friends with
one of them very soon and we were not preoccupied at all with what the other
workers did or said', Bouvier wrote in her own memoirs (1983, 81). Audoux
has also joyously portrayed the relations of the group of young seamstresses
in the opening pages of *L'Atelier de Marie-Claire*:

In spite of the crowd I saw Sandrine immediately. [...] It was Monday. Our
summer slackness was coming to an end and we were returning to the workshop
to begin the winter season. Bouledogue and little Duretour were waiting for us
on the pavement, and big Bergounette, whom we could see coming along on
the opposite side, crossed the avenue, without heeding the traffic, in order to be
with us sooner. For several minutes there was gay gossip in our group. Then the
four stories were climbed quickly. (1920, 5)

It was thus the youth and boldness of the young seamstresses that would
challenge the regime of fear in the route of returning home late at night after
a long day of hard work:

It was quite different with my proud and pretty Adrienne. She would say to me
laughing at my cowardice, 'Dear sister, aren't I here? (She was barely fifteen)

'Should the occasion comes, then you will see that *valour does not follow the number of years!*' As a matter of fact, one evening, she proved it to me; around nine o'clock, we were in the Rue du Temple near Saint Elisabeth's Church; we were stopped by the gross words and filthy gestures of a miserable man. As always I stood there trembling and unable to speak before this abuser. Adrienne, on the contrary, had a moment of sublime energy. She managed to find such a resolute tone, while brandishing an enormous key before his eyes, that he withdrew.' (1866, 57–58)

Gender and generation are skilfully interwoven in Voilquin's account of women workers' 'technologies of resistance' (Tamboukou 2003a) while walking the city. In an Arendtian way, her story seizes the moment of her younger sister's sublime energy—narrative becomes the vector of the young woman's force. But this is also a story that as Arlette Farge has argued brings women at the heart of the city, challenging classed perceptions and schemas of women's urban mobility in modernity: 'The archive speaks of the Parisian woman and makes her speak . . . through glimpses, it reveals a lively sketch of her as she lived, juggling the many uncertainties of social and political life' (1989, 33). Voilquin's *Souvenirs,* Bouvier's *Memoirs,* as well as Audoux's autobiographical novel have thus become part of the archive of women's work in modernity, but they also carry traces of the seamstresses' agonistic politics as I will further discuss.

Narrating Political Action

The years between 1830 and 1838 were for Voilquin a period of 'exceptional existence' (1866, 77), during which her life was transformed by her Saint-Simonian faith and apostolic life, the details of which are narrated in the seventh chapter of her *Souvenirs:* 'From this moment, we said goodbye to friends who did not want to follow us, adieu to the societies of pleasure that did not speak to their souls any more' (ibid., 78). It was in this context that her involvement in the first feminist newspaper was also portrayed: 'In the beginning of August 1832 [...] two proletarian girls [...] published a small weekly journal under the title of *La Femme Libre.* At their request, I wrote in the second issue a very timid article calling women to a pacifist crusade' (ibid., 95). It was the beginning of a new activity for Voilquin, but surprisingly enough the story of her involvement and collaboration in the first feminist newspaper is differently presented in *Souvenirs* than in her last article in the *Tribune des Femmes:* 'Soon after, these young persons, fascinated by Fourier's theories [...] withdrew, leaving the direction of our little newspaper to me. Désirée Véret, the founder was the first to withdraw and then Reine Guindorf followed swift', she wrote (ibid., 96). Not only was Guindorf's involvement in the newspaper diminished, but the newspaper's role was overall demoted and downplayed: 'Our poor little newspaper, created and continued by proletarian women without fortune, position or formal education that could enlighten our way, remained without prestige and never had a real influence upon people' (ibid.). It seems that in writing her *Souvenirs* as a testament of the Saint-Simonian legacy, Voilquin wanted to erase the traces of the feminists' political breach with the movement. In writing her memoirs she was rewriting herself and the social histories of her time. After all these were only the first chapters of a memoir that was to be about the Saint-Simonian activities in Egypt, a theme that was already flagged up in the title of her book. What we therefore have here is 'political autobiographics' at work, the creation of a discursive regime, wherein narratives of truth, experience and political action are knitted together.[21] What I want to highlight here is that rather than reading Voilquin's *Souvenirs* at face value, her autobiographical document is situated within a complex network of discursive limitations, power relations and forces of desire that have created its conditions of possibility. It is thus the author's function as a Saint-Simonian and not as a feminist that configures the discursive regime of this document.

Interestingly enough, it is the author's function as a 'syndicaliste feministe', highlighted in the subtitle of her memoirs that marks Jeanne Bouvier's political autobiographics. As a matter of fact, Bouvier seems to be much more conscious and aware of such discursive limitations: her memoirs are structured along the lines of 'How I became a syndicalist' (Chapter 2) and 'How I became a writer' (Chapter 3), with a final supplement of 'How I became a feminist'. Although Bouvier tried to separate her political orientations in her memoir, becoming a feminist as well as a trade unionist seems to have emerged together, triggered by the publication of a feminist newspaper that was to have a long-lasting impact among bourgeois and working-class women, actually revealing interesting cross-class collaborations:

> In 1897, a feminist journal was launched by Mme Marguerite Durand: *La Fronde,* a daily edition on feminist rights. [...] One of my clients Mme Norat was an ardent feminist. She became an assiduous reader of this journal and while I was trying her dresses, she was talking to me about women's rights and the injustices of the law with regard to women. In this way, every fitting session was a lesson in feminism. [...] One day she told me: 'I am surprised that an intelligent woman like you has not subscribed to the union of your trade.' [...] This invitation to unionise seemed to me extraordinary. Unionise, me? Why? I confess that I did not understand anything. (Bouvier 1983, 101)

Despite her fears and hesitations, Bouvier joined the union. Chapter 2 of her memoirs recounts her initial ignorance about what was talked about in the various meetings that she was attending and finally her joy of being part of demonstrations, singing 'The International' with other workers. It was indeed this feeling of togetherness that animated Bouvier's life in ways that she had not thought about before, although she had always enjoyed the company of fellow workers, as we have already seen above. Throwing herself in the passion of politics, Bouvier soon climbed the union's hierarchy and became one of its few women leading figures, not only in France but also in the international labour movement. Her papers include innumerable letters from women trade unionists all over the world, many of whom she would meet in person, whenever they visited Paris.[22]

For Bouvier, working and developing personal friendships with a network of international women was among the pleasures of being a feminist and a trade unionist. After all, it was these friendships and connections that kept her going through her harsh times with her comrades in France. Like many other women trade unionists, Bouvier fell out with the CGT leadership and stepped down as a vice president of the International Committee of Labour in 1923, but soon after this crisis, she threw herself into research and writing. Indeed, writing became for Bouvier not just a life passion, but also a way of talking back as a single woman to her social world in general and to her comrades in particular, a practice that can also be traced in American women activists in the garment industry (see Tamboukou 2013c, 2014e). But in recounting her adventures and struggles in the union, Bouvier concealed and silenced many of its internal conflicts. Her allegiances to the workers' movement were stronger than her disputes and disagreements, thus charting the order of discourse of her own 'political autobiographics'.

Following Lines of Flight

In choosing '*La Saint-Simonienne en* Égypte' as the title of her memoir, Voilquin most prominently showed that her two years as a Saint-Simonian in Egypt were the most important worth narrating. In linear terms, two years of a long life is 'a short time'. But in Voilquin's narrative, *Chronos*, the measurable, linearly sequential conception of time has been absorbed by *Aion*, time as duration where past and future coexist in the continuously contracted moments of the present.[23] In terms of mobility, Voilquin's life was indeed exceptional. Not only did she travel all over France before sailing off for Egypt; on returning to France in 1836 she found out that she could not make ends meet and once again she set off for Russia, where she worked as a midwife for seven years, between 1839 and 1846. In the last chapter of her memoirs, Voilquin recounts her sadness while her brother and a group of friends have accompanied her to St Germaine to say farewell:

I embarked there on one of those big ships that sail down the Seine till Rouen. After having embraced all my friends, as well as my brother, who I would never see again, the ship turned and set on its route; we were waving handkerchiefs until the river bank [...] disappeared from my view. From that point until my arrival in Rouen, I did not see, neither did I take interest in anybody; everything was absorbed in my dark thoughts, sad premonitions made my tears flow without realising it. (1866, 492)

On arriving in Rouen, she was met again by a last group of friends, who warmed her heart, brightened up her last day in France and created sweet memories, that stayed with her as 'the end of an era' (ibid., 493). Voilquin returned to France in 1846, but after the suppression of the 1848 revolution, she emigrated to Louisiana and it was only in 1860 that she eventually returned to France for good. Her adventures in Russia would be recounted in her unpublished manuscript *Voyage en Russie,*[24] while very little is known about her twelve years in New Orleans.

Michel de Certeau has noted that 'we travel abroad to discover in distant lands something whose presence at home has become unrecognisable' (1988b). Dislocation opened up for Voilquin's restrictive gendered spaces and radicalized the politics of self-formation, creating conditions of possibility for active experiments in life. Voilquin was an exceptional traveller, particularly given her working-class background as well as her limited financial situation: she lived a nomadic life par excellence, while travelling emerges as crucial technology of the self throughout her autobiographical writings.

But while travelling became a mode of existence for Voilquin, it only emerges as a pleasant and unforeseen break in Bouvier's memoirs: 'I had an extraordinary impression, while I was feeling the boat sweetly moving away from the shore. It seemed to me that there was nothing tying me to my country anymore, that all the bonds had been broken', Bouvier wrote on recounting her voyage to Washington to attend the first International Congress of Women Workers in 1919 as one of its two French delegates (1983, 125). This feeling of existential freedom, while sailing away from one's country is a recurrent theme in women workers' autobiographical writings, a transitional moment when memories of the past and images of the future blend and fuse in the experience of the traveller (see Tamboukou 2003a, 2009). But apart from her personal impressions, Bouvier wrote vividly about the politics of her travels both in her memoirs, as well as in numerous journal articles. She had a clear political eye to understand differences and similarities among nations and to criticize national governments, without hurting international bonds and solidarity among workers. Her article in *Madame et Citoyenne* about her experiences abroad is filled with acute observations, gratitude, admiration, but also irony and humour:

I confess that my first impression was a bit confused and I have retained much
of the inevitable trouble landing in a country whose language is unknown,
the hustle and bustle of the crowd, the crushing sensation that give the fifty
storey houses gave you. [...] But what a cordial welcome awaited us from the
American delegates on our first visit! We felt immediately at our ease: we found
a family. [...] But the Government's attitude towards the International Labour
Conference [...] was truly unique. Not only did the government systematically ignore the work of the Conference, but we felt much hostility: we were
the 'undesirables'. Some U.S. newspapers have even said that we should be
deported or imprisoned as 'Bolshevik'! Quite charming, is it not?[25]

The article goes on recounting their constant company with interpreters,
their sightseeing trips, as well as the opportunities they had to learn about the
different organizations of workers' education in the United States. Her report
of the business of the Congress highlighted its important resolutions, but
did not include the many tensions that arose among the delegates, including
disagreements around questions of race, about who could count as a worker
and whether women workers should be protected or seek equal treatment as
men.[26] Solidarity and fraternity were more important for Bouvier, particularly
as the Congress represented a feminist response to women's marginalization
from the newly founded International Labour Organization:

This was the first International Women's Congress. We already knew about its
inevitable disputes, but what prevailed during its meetings, was the great feeling
of human fraternity. Thus, a place was reserved for German delegates and an
association of black women was accepted by acclamation.[27]

Throughout her life, Bouvier worked hard to materialize many of the resolutions of the Women Workers' Congress above, from different positions in
her life not only as a worker and trade unionist, but also as a researcher and
writer. The story of her travels was more in line with her political autobiographics than with any other genre or mode of travel literature. Writing about
her travels was part of the *œuvre à faire*, a theme that I will now take up in
concluding the seamstresses' autobiographical chapter.

ŒUVRE À FAIRE

If we are to address the question about whether this being exists, the answer
should not be 'yes' or 'no', but rather 'more' or 'less', Souriau (2009, 196)
has provocatively suggested in his philosophical exploration about the mode
of existence of the work to be done. Existence for Souriau is simply work
in progress: it requires a making, but also an establishing act. In this sense,

virtual and concrete existences are always interrelated and it is the continuous passage from one to the other that we should be tracing. This search is actually a drama in three acts: (a) virtual work or *œuvre à faire,* (b) concrete work in progress and (c) the creator and her responsibility towards the promise of the *œuvre à faire* (ibid., 205). In looking at the seamstresses' autobiographical writings, Souriau's philosophical exploration of the mode of existence of the *œuvre à faire* created a plane of consistency for diverse life-history trails, as well as literary modes of autobiographical representation to be assembled.

What was particularly interesting in bringing together the three acts of the autobiographical drama as outlined above was the material basis of the seamstresses' *œuvre à faire,* put simply the way the concrete processes and objects of their work created conditions of possibility for the virtual work to be imagined and captured. Here it is important to note that Souriau rejects not only both the idea of finality and futurity for the 'work to be done', but also the idea of a project as these configurations exclude the experience felt in the process of making. 'If you consider the *œuvre à faire* as a project', he writes, 'you miss, the delights of discovery, of exploration, in short the experiential input in the historical route of the advancement of the work' (ibid, 207). In this light, a carefully predetermined trajectory of the work excludes the experience of unexpected encounters in the process of realization. Rather than designing her steps, the creator should put more effort in letting herself immerse in the experience of making: initiating a new process is the crucial movement here. 'We determine what is going to come by exploring its path', writes Souriau (ibid., 208). Instead the creator has to subsume herself to the will of the work, to enable its autonomous realization.

If the seamstresses had not thrown themselves to 'the will of the work', nothing at all would have happened. They would have remained in the initial stage of fear and intimidation enacted by their lack of education in front of 'the work to be done'. Bouvier's memoirs have left a vivid trace of these first moments of panic when Georges Renard, professor of labour history at the Collège de France, asked her to write the history of linen-good workers as part of fifty-eight volumes comprising *La Bibliothèque sociale des métiers* [The Social library of trades] that he was editing:

> When alone, I was thinking: 'M. Georges Renard has been deluded about my value and my knowledges. No, it is not possible for me to accept to write a book, I have always suffered by my ignorance. [...] How can I write the history of the lingerie and its workers?' It is true that in the course of my long career as a trade unionist, I got to know the social questions for better or for worse; but to translate them in paper and compose them in a book, it seemed insurmountable! (1983, 214)

Despite the difficulties, Bouvier threw herself in the pleasures of research and produced a rare study of the French linen-goods industry in the twentieth century that has become an invaluable source in women's labour history.[28] 'You have written a book and you will write others' (ibid., 216), Renard had told her when she delivered her manuscript and indeed research and writing became Bouvier's lifelong passion. What this chapter has shown is that Bouvier's intellectual achievement did not emerge out of the blue: it was rather a component of the assemblage of women workers' radical practices, which are inextricably entangled in the political, social and cultural formations of modernity. The seamstresses' autobiographical writings are traces that can take future researchers to a rich genealogical archive full of greyness and dust, waiting for more digging and excavation.

NOTES

1. *Tribune des Femmes-La Femme Nouvelle* 2 (11), 176, April 1834.

2. Ibid., 179.

3. Recollection is a search in something bodily for an image, according to Aristotle, Casey had pithily noted in his important phenomenological study on remembering, thus highlighting the visual component of recollections (2000, 37).

4. For a historical analysis of the Saint-Simonian life and activities in North Africa, see Pilbeam 2014.

5. See among others: Humm 1989; Steedman 1989; Stanley 1992; Smith and Watson 1998; Cosslett et al. 2000.

6. For Foucauldian approaches to autobiographical writing, see Gilmore 1994; Tamboukou 2003a. For an extensive discussion of narrative modalities of power and desire, see Livholts and Tamboukou 2015, particularly Chapters 6 and 8.

7. None of Bouvier's books has been translated into English, although lengthy extracts from her *Memoirs* are included in Traugott's (1993) collection of French workers' autobiographies, alongside Voilquin's. Due to the popularity of Audoux's first novel, *Marie Claire* (1910), its sequel, *L'Atelier de Marie-Claire* was translated into English in 1920, the same year of its French publication.

8. For more biographical details, see Bouvier's *memoirs* 1983 [1936]. See also Traugott 1993 and Tamboukou 2015c, 2016. Her papers are housed in the Bibliothèque Historique de la Ville de Paris, under the *Archives Marie-Louise Bouglé*, (BHVP/AMB/FJB).

9. *Deux époques, deux hommes* (1927); *La lingerie et les lingères* (1928); *Histoire des dames employées dans les postes, télégraphes et téléphones, de 1714 a 1929* (1930); *Les femmes pendant la révolution* (1931), *Mes Mémoires* (1936).

10. For more biographical details about Marguerite Audoux and her work, see her own autobiographical novels (2008 [1910, 1920]). Audoux also wrote a collection of short stories, *Valserine et autres nouvelles* [Valserine and other stories] (1912) and three more romances that are all autobiographically inspired: *De la ville au* Moulin

[From the Mill to the Town] (1926), *The Fiancée* (1932) and *Douce Lumière* [Soft Light] (1937). For literary studies on her work, see Garreau 1991, 2004. All her books can be accessed at the Internet Archive: https://archive.org/

11. For a rich discussion of the effects of the sewing machine in the French garment industry, see Coffin 1996, particularly Chapter 3.

12. See Moses 1984; Scott 1996 for French feminist politics at the turn of the nineteenth century and Thomas 2007 [1967] for women's involvement in the Paris Commune.

13. As Deleuze and Guattari have pointed out, instead of 'plotting a point' and 'fixing an order', rhizomes make connections with a multiplicity of heterogeneous elements (1988, 7).

14. *La Française,* 17-11-1928, BHVP/AMB/FJB/B20/Divers.

15. See Anderson 2001, for a rich discussion of the autobiographical canon, particularly Chapter 1.

16. For a range of approaches to women workers' autobiographies, see among others: Stanley 1984; Zandy 1990; Swindells 1995; Hollis 2004; Gagnier 1987.

17. Voilquin refers here to the Restoration of the Bourbon monarchy following Napoleon's fall, between 1815 and 1830.

18. See in particular Chapter 3 on 'The Image of Thought'.

19. Reference to Voltaire's famous epistolary urge, 'écrasez *l'infâme*'.

20. *La Française;* 17-11-1928, (BHVP/AMB/FJB/B.20/Divers).

21. In creating the notion of 'political autobiographics', here as elsewhere in my work (Tamboukou 2013a, 2014e), I have drawn on Gilmore's (1994) notion of 'autobiographics'.

22. See *Bibliothèque Historique de la Ville de Paris, Archives Marie-Louise Bouglé, Fonds Jeanne Bouvier,* Boite 17, Correspondence, (BHVP/AMB/FJB/B17/Cor).

23. See Deleuze 2001 for a discussion of *Chronos* and *Aion* in Stoic philosophy.

24. Written in 1869, the manuscript was eventually deposited in the Bibliothèque Marguerite Durand. It was annotated and published by Maïté Albistur and Daniel Armogathe in 1977.

25. Bouvier, 'Au Congrès féminin International' in *Madame et Citoyenne,* c. 1919, (BHVP/AMB/FJB/B.20/Divers).

26. For a discussion of the 1919 First International Congress of Working Women, see Vapnek 2013.

27. Ibid.

28. For commentaries about Bouvier's work, see among others: Coffin 1996; Green 1997.

Conclusion

Reassembling Radical Practices

'In rereading my letter I stay convinced of the necessity of a school of scientific utopianism, which will teach utopias of poetic grandeur [...] the ideal is possible',[1] Désirée Véret, veuve Gay, noted in a postscript to one of her last letters to Considerant, written from her apartment at St. Gudule place in Brussels on September 17, 1890. As already discussed in chapter 5, it was not the first time that she had written passionately about the political reality and importance of utopias, which she wanted to see elaborated and developed:

> Let us found together or with our friends the school of scientific and social utopianism. Let us resuscitate the modern innovators. Utopia has been the mother of exact sciences and, like many fertile mothers she has often produced embryos that were sterile or too fragile, embryos born prematurely or under bad circumstances. Utopia is as old as the organised world. She is the vanguard of the new societies. And she will fashion society, harmony, when human genius makes it a reality through learned demonstrations that dissociate her from obscurities and temporary impossibilities.[2]

The revolutionary seamstress' deep conviction about the possibility of the ideal in the twilight of her life is striking. The way she related it to science is also important, while the feminine gender of utopia in the French language [l'utopie], nicely lends its grammatical form to the metaphor of the mother of sciences.[3] In writing about the urgency of founding a school of scientific and social utopianism, the seamstress was fully aware of utopia's shortcomings: 'the fragile and/or sterile embryos'[4] that were born from it; but she still had confidence in the radical futures that utopian and socialist ideals could open up. More importantly, she perceived the real as an assemblage of actualities and potentialities, things that have been realized and others that have not

195

become concrete yet, but they inhere in the actualities of the present, opening up imaginary glimpses to the future. As I have elsewhere discussed at length (Tamboukou 2010b), such a perspective is very much in line with Deleuze's (2004) theorization of the real as a fusion of the actual and the virtual, an inflection of Bergson's philosophy of time that has also largely inspired current feminist theorizations of the imaginary (see Grosz 2004, 2005).

'What history gives us is the possibility of becoming untimely, of placing ourselves outside the constraints, the limitations and blinkers of the present', Elizabeth Grosz has pithily noted (2004, 117). In writing at the end of a fully active life, the seamstress had not only lived history, she had actually had time to reflect upon it. Moreover, by having written political narratives herself and by having read those of her contemporaries she had learnt a lot from the historical events she had been entangled with: 'I am devastated with the new Belgian socialists. I think that the general strike is a utopia, a mere illusion. We must have an international congress',[5] she wrote to Considerant. While reflecting upon the trends and programmes of the Belgian labour movement she was conscious of her position as a bystander: 'I am a simple spectator of the movement',[6] she wrote, remembering the strikes in 1866 'when we were part of the [First] International'.[7] In thus looking back at the ebbs and flows of the social movements and revolutions that she had been part of, the seamstress had some understanding about the possibilities of future formations and becomings. Hers was an eventful life, but because she had lived for so long, in so many different countries and through so many crucial eruptions and events, she could reassemble their traces left in the personal and political narratives of their protagonists:

> The other day I was re-reading *The New Industrial World*; *The Theory of the Four Movements* and your work on *Social Destiny*.[8] What serious pages to read. Although experimental, they explain the organisation of work much clearer than most brochures that are currently published.[9]

In rereading some of the important writings of both Fourier and Considerant, Véret-Gay was adamant that they should form the basis of a school of scientific and social utopianism that could help orientate the young writers and social leaders of Europe at the turn of the twentieth century: 'There is no shortage of young writers who are ready to enter a new road and search to orientate themselves. It is for us to put them in the right path',[10] she wrote in the same letter above. In highlighting the responsibility of the older generation to educate and illuminate the youth, the seamstress was once again within the philosophical milieu of the *œuvre à faire*. As already discussed in chapter 6, the creator's responsibility for Souriau is to immerse herself in 'the will of the work' (2009, 208). It is in this context that he suggested the withdrawal of the old to the young and/or of the teacher to the student in the area of education (ibid). In this light, creativity is a collective process since when we create we are never alone, Souriau argues (ibid., 215).

Through Véret-Gay's letters to Considerant we actually have a glimpse of the dialogue that goes on between the creator and the work that keeps raising questions and in doing so it guides and steers the process, opening up paths that lead to its final concrescence, a socialist world of peace and justice for the seamstress. In the same way that Souriau looks for the poet of 'the great, the immense poem that would fill human beings today' (ibid., 215), the seamstress looks for the founders of a school of scientific and socialist utopianism. Her quest throws a different light in the way the nineteenth-century French feminist movement has been read and understood: sometimes stifled under labels such as Saint-Simonianism or Fourierism, other times restricted within concepts such as 'the spiritual' or 'the paradox', as already discussed and criticized throughout the book.

What comes to light instead from the seamstresses' words and deeds is 'how matter matters' (Barad 2007) in the way the first autonomous feminist movement in Europe emerged and unfolded. It is here that their 'ephemeral' associations, short-lived publications and failed revolts have been perceived differently in the light of process philosophy and the importance of the event: conceptual tools and theoretical perspectives that have informed the analysis throughout the book. As Whitehead has argued, 'events are the ultimate realities' (1967b, 236), occasions where something emerges into actuality. But the event is also configured as 'a spatio-temporal unity with contemporaries (present), memories (past) and anticipation (future)' (Whitehead 1967a, 72). It is within this philosophical framework that the seamstresses' personal and political narratives are themselves conceptualized as events: they carry memory traces of revolutionary processes, illuminate the writers' lived experiences and finally foreshadow future potentialities, then and now. As the seamstress Julie Fanfernot[11] poetically put it in the single brochure of *L'Etincelle* that she co-edited with Eugène Stourm in 1833:

> Why is it that the brilliant image of those brief instants appears to be merely a fleeting vision in the dark labyrinth where we have come to stray? [...] The reason is that we, like those condemned to the mines, accustomed to the darkness like them, could not sustain the glare of such a bright light.[12]

In seizing the fleeting moments of revolutionary events that would have otherwise been forgotten and erased, such narratives become actual occasions wherein novel perspectives emerge: the seamstresses' mode of rewriting history. The Foucauldian genealogical approach was catalytic in this archaeological process of excavating the seamstresses' narratives. What surfaced as a niggling surprise is the messiness of the archive of nineteenth-century French seamstresses: its dispersion in many different archival places, its subordination and indeed suppression under different and confusing cataloguing practices. Documents were lost and found in famous libraries such as *la Bibliothèque Historique de la Ville de Paris*, and there does not seem to be a logic or some kind of system as to why some documents have been grouped or placed in the way they are, while there is no coordination between actual and digitized documents.[13] Even more painfully, there are errors, discrepancies and inconsistencies in the feminist bibliography, while there are omissions of page references, issue numbers and even authors' names in many bibliographical references of the existing feminist body of literature.[14] The feminist archive in itself is an *œuvre à faire* for future feminist researchers and it is to this œuvre that I hope this book and its accompanying archival blog will be contributing.[15]

Revisiting the archive of nineteenth-century feminism with a sensitivity to the life of its life documents has opened up different vistas of conceptualization and understanding. In the process of the research that underpins the writing of this book I have allowed myself to drift along the rhythms of the documents that I have been reading, analysing and writing about. Following Lefebvre's rhythmanalysis (2004), I have tried to listen to the rhythms of the documents I was reading, imagine the space/time continuum of their production, as well as the social and political conditions of their emergence.

Locating the various addresses of the first feminist newspaper was in itself a concrete experience in the spatiality and materiality of nomadism: it was from their homes that the seamstresses wrote and published, the same places where they would most probably work to make up for the meagre wages of their needlework. When an editor withdrew, the address would also change: 17 Rue du Caire was Jeanne-Désirée's home for the first four issues; the newspaper then moved to 11 Rue du Feaubourg St Denis, Marie-Reines's address after Jeanne-Désirée's withdrawal. Both addresses were at the heart of Sentier, the Parisian garment area industry, but when Voilquin became editor the social and political geography of the newspaper also changed: 26 Rue du Cadet and 37 Rue de Bussy (today Buci) were in much more elevated areas of Paris, since Voilquin's husband was an architect and she had climbed up to his social position. Finally, in its second year, the newspaper acquired a professional status with proper bureaus at 21 Rue des Juifs—Ferdinand-Duval today.[16] The geography of the newspaper thus reveals an intriguing history, or maybe the history of the journal can be starkly traced in its geography: its different addresses are thus the material traces of economic and social differences in the editorship, as well as in the theoretical and political orientation of the journal. Such differences were further inscribed in the themes, topics and debates of the journal that I have already discussed in chapter 3.

In retracing the seamstresses' steps and addresses in Paris in April 2015, I could still see and feel these differences: I could literally listen to their rhythms in the way Lefebvre (2004) has suggested that we should do. Hanna Hallgren (2015) has suggested that travelling should be taken as a method of inquiry, offering a detailed account of how travelling opens up space for experimenting with the possibilities and constraints of what we can know. Entangled in the speed of travelling, 'the "I/eye" is in the verb, in that the subject of the text is moving and is thus wrapped up in movement', Hallgren has argued (2015, 88), but she has also pointed to the fact that the situated position of the traveller researcher should be considered in terms of the perspectives that differences such as gender, race and class among others can facilitate or inhibit. Travelling to Paris during the last phase of writing the book opened up unexpected vistas in my understanding of the seamstresses' Parisian world, which went well beyond the final checking of the archival sources, which was initially my reason for going there.

By following the spatio/temporal rhythms of the first feminist newspapers, I could also see how they were deeply influenced by the turbulent politics of their times. *La Voix des Femmes* interrupted its publication a day after the disastrous results of the April 1848 elections. *La Politique des Femmes* was launched in the same week of the bloody June days: no surprise why it took a whole month for its second issue to appear and why it was forced to change its name after the July 29 decree that explicitly excluded women from the very experience of politics altogether. *L'Almanach des Femmes* was first published in Paris, but it was transferred to London after the harsh persecutions that followed Bonaparte's coup d'état in the end of 1851. If such conditions of possibility are not taken into consideration, this continuous change of names, addresses and editors seems like a pointless wandering and indeed loses the politically significant element of how much the nineteenth-century feminists were continuously ridiculed and persecuted not just by the state power, but also by their very socialist comrades. But apart from revealing the harshness of the political reality that the French feminists went through, the multiple geographies of the feminist newspapers are also traces of lines of flight, forces of deterritorialization and reterritorialization in the long revolutionary durée of the nineteenth century: they powerfully express the political force of nomadism.

Rhythms, both real and imaginary, are constitutive of our archival practices and therefore of the knowledges that can derive from them. One of the themes that has forcefully emerged from the seamstresses' genealogical archive is the importance of internationalization and the role of the labour movement in forging, supporting and sustaining universal ideas, as well as real and material links. Throughout the book I have followed the seamstresses and their sisters in struggle moving around Europe, crossing the Atlantic, supporting each other in exile, translating each other's work, writing letters, signing petitions. Not only did the nineteenth-century feminist movement transcend national boundaries, it actually developed and unfolded within an international matrix, despite language barriers, travel restrictions and the many wars, revolutions and conflicts that shook Europe during this period. As Bonnie Anderson has succinctly observed, it is precisely its international character and perspective that 'makes this movement seem so modern' (2000, 2).

What is also striking is the current urgency of its historical demands and concerns: poverty and child raising, motherhood and domestic labour, education and job opportunities, prostitution and (modern) slavery, sexual violence and rape, the need for independence and autonomy both material and intellectual. It goes without saying that if we focus on women's position in the garment industry, the material milieu of the whole book, the similarities become unbearably disturbing, even uncanny. It is in the greyness of such difficulties that the seamstresses' revolutionary voices and their lifelong confidence in the power of joy, happiness, association and friendship sound so soothing, then and now:

> I have had a life full of affections and passions but I found happiness alone and I have been able to unscrupulously evoke memories that social conventions have made me keep them hidden at the bottom of my heart for fifty years. My letters must have seemed to you unique but I needed you to know about the past and the present of my life so that we can talk and you can be a friend from whom I no longer have secret thoughts. Write to me about your ordinary days, about people and about brochures, I like chronicles![17]

In responding to Jeanne-Désirée's desire for 'chronicles' I have thus chosen to conclude the book by drawing a cartography of space/time events in the long durée of nineteenth-century feminist praxis and thought. It is in the entanglement of macroscopic processes and microscopic events that the complexity, force and also contemporaneity of their movement powerfully emerges, as a feminist assemblage par excellence that surrounds and inheres in today's problematics, ideas, politics and imaginaries.

CHRONICLES AND TIMESCAPES

1789   French Revolution
1791   Abolition of the seamstresses' guild and all guilds in France
         The *Chapelier Law* forbidding workers' associations is introduced
         Olympe de Gouges: *Déclaration des droits de la femme et de la citoyenne*

1792 Mary Wollstonecraft: *A Vindication of the Rights of Woman*
September 20: Divorce becomes legal in France
1793 *November 3:* De Gouges is executed in Paris
1801 Suzanne Monnier-Voilquin is born in Paris
1802 Napoleon is elected consul for life
1803 *April 7:* Flora Tristan is born in Paris
1804 The Napoleonic civil code is established
1805 *December 31:* Jeanne Deroin is born in Paris
1807 Abolition of the Slave Trade Act is passed
1808 Charles Fourier publishes *Theory of the Four Movements*
October 12: Victor Considerant is born
1810 *January:* New Lanark is established in Glasgow by Robert Owen
April 4: Désirée Véret is born in Paris
June 22: End of the First Empire
1812 Marie-Reine Guindorf is born in Paris
1813 Owen's first edition of *A New View of Society*
1815 *June 18:* Waterloo battle
1816 Divorce is abolished
1820 Magazines de nouveautés are established in Paris (1820–1830)
1823 Anna Wheeler moves to France, meets Fourier, translates his work
The Anti-Slavery Society is founded
1825 William Thompson: *Appeal of One Half of the Human Race, Women, Against the Pretensions of the Other*
Suzanne Monnier marries Eugène Voilquin
1827 Women's Anti-slavery Associations are formed in Britain (1827–1831)
1829 First sewing machine by the French artisan Barthélemy Thimonnier
Bazard publishes first volume of the *Exposition of the Doctrine of Saint Simon*
1830 Fourier publishes *Le Nouveau Monde Industriel*
Wheeler publishes *The Rights of Women*
Enfantin publishes the second volume of the *Exposition*
April: Saint-Simonian lecture series start
July 27–29: *Les Trois Glorieuses,* the July Monarchy begins
August–September: Workers' strikes particularly among the typographers
1831 *January:* March of hostile tailors against the sewing machine in Paris
April: The Russian army invades Polland
July: Thimonnier's sewing machine project is withdrawn
Saint-Simonian organization of working-class neighbourhoods
Deroin writes her 'Profession of Faith'
September 11: Véret writes her 'Profession of Faith'
November: Break between Enfantin and Bazard
November 19: Enfantin's lecture on the regulation of love

November 22: Julie Fanfernot is tried for attempts to provoke revolts

November 28: Women are excluded from the Saint-Simonian hierarchy

November–December: Revolt of the silk workers in Lyon

1832 *January 22:* The Saint-Simonian Halls are closed

February: Cholera epidemic in Paris (February–May)

April: The Saint-Simonian newspaper *Globe* folds

April 20: Enfantin and forty apostles retreat to Ménilmontant

May: Véret writes the appeal *To the Privileged women*

June 5–6: Republican uprisings in Paris

June 10: Véret sends her open *Letter to the King*

August 15: *La Femme Libre* is published

August 28–29: Saint-Simonian trial in Paris

August 31: Véret sends her famous love letter to Enfantin

September: Voilquin joins the Apostolat des Femmes

October 20: Véret sends her farewell letter to Enfantin

November 4: Véret withdraws from the Apostolat des Femmes

Deroin marries Antoine Desroches

1833 Julie Fanfernot and Eugène Stourm publish the only issue of *L'Etincelle*

Véret moves to London, gets involved in Owenite circles

Guindorf withdraws as editor of *La Tribune des Femmes*

June 28: The Loi Guizot passes, girls are not included

August 3: Claire Démar commits double suicide

August: Enfantin leaves for Egypt

September–November: Wave of strikes: tailors create a 'national workshop'

Wheeler publishes the *Letter from Vlasta*

The Abolition of Slavery Act is passed

1834 *April:* Insurrections in Lyon and Paris

Véret returns to Dieppe, works as a dressmaker

Voilquin publishes Claire Démar's *Ma Loi d'Avenir*

Voilquin leaves for Egypt

Considerant publishes *Destinée sociale*

1835 Guindorf-Flichi gives birth to a little boy

The Saint-Simonian project in Egypt falls apart

1836 Voilquin returns from Egypt, lives for a short time with the Flichis

1837 *June:* Guindorf commits suicide in Paris

October 10: Fourier dies

Véret marries Jules Gay

Enfantin returns to France

1838 Gay has her first son, Jean

Tristan publishes *Pérégrinations d'une paria* (1833–1834)

1839   *May 5:* Voilquin leaves for Russia

1840   *July:* International tension and a wave of nationalism in relation to Egypt

July–September: Workers' agitation and strikes

Publication of the workers' newspaper *L'Atelier* (1840–1850)

November: Leaders of a coalition of tailors are sentenced to five years

Louis Blanc publishes *Organisation du travail*

Etienne Cabet publishes *Voyage en Icarie*

The Gays try to found an Owenite school in Châtillon-sous-Bagneux

Tristan publishes *Promenades dans Londres*

Wheeler retires from active work

Attempts to exclude women from the World's Anti-Slavery Convention in London; Anne Knight campaigns for equal rights for women

1841   *July: L'Humanitaire,* a materialist communist journal is published

September: Street agitations in Paris

Olinde Rodrigues publishes *Poésies sociales des ouvriers*

1842   Gay has her second son, Owen

The Fourierist colony in Brazil falls apart

1843   Tristan publishes *The Workers' Union*

1844   *November 14:* Tristan dies in Bordeaux

1845   *September:* Thimonnier renews his patent and manufactures sewing machines

1846   Voilquin returns to France

Knight moves to France

1847   *January:* Economic crisis and food riots in Buzançais

The Ten Hour Act is passed in Britain

Knight produces the first known leaflet of women's suffrage

1848   *January*: Revolution in Palermo, Sicily

February 3: First mission leaves Le Havre to found Icaria in Texas

February 8: Gay sends a letter to Enfantin about the revolution

February 22–25: The February Revolution in Paris

February 25: The Second Republic is established; a provisional government is formed; the right to work is proclaimed

February 26: Creation of national workshops for men only

February 27: Owen's sends an address to the men and women of France

March 2: Limitation of working day to ten hour;

Gay's petition to Louis Blanc for women's right to work

March 2: Underpaid labour in prisons, convents and barracks forbidden

March 4: Universal male suffrage is granted

End of press censorship

Abolition of imprisonment for debts

March 16: Deroin's campaign for women's civil rights begins

Antoine-Andre Giles' proposition in the name of artists, workers, authors and teachers

March 20: *La Voix des Femmes* is published

March 22: The Committee on the Rights of Women meet the mayor of Paris demanding the right to vote: they are rejected

March 24–April 14: Women workers march for the right to work

March 25: *La Société des Droits des Femmes* is founded

La Société de La Voix des Femmes is founded

March 27: The Vesuvians demand shelters for homeless girls

Deroin's appeal to the French citizens for women's suffrage

March 29: Women's national workshops are established

March 1–November 1849: Austrian Empire Revolutions

April 4: Owen visits Paris to meet the provisional government

Women workers demonstrate in support of Louis Blanc

April 5: Gay is elected delegate of the women workers of the 2nd arrondissement

April 10: Great Chartist meeting on Kennington Common in London

Hubertine Auclert is born

April 15: Petition by Citoyenne Dubois for a minimum wage

April 18: Gay criticizes the hierarchy of women's workshops

April 20: Gay is dismissed from the national workshops

April 23: National Constitutional Elections

April 29: Elections results: the conservatives win

La Voix des Femmes intermits its publication

May 5: First meeting of the National Assembly

May 15: Revolt in Paris, workers invade the National Assembly

May 29: *La Voix des Femmes* resumes its publication

June 21: Dissolution of the national workshops

June 23–26: The Bloody June days: barricades in Paris

Gay and Deroin form the *Association Mutuelle des Femmes*

June 18–24: *La Politique des Femmes* is published

June: Louis Blanc flees to England

June: Meeting of the Pan-Slav Congress in Prague

July 5: The assembly funds a project for Workers' Associations

July 28: Decree excluding women from political clubs

July: Deroin launches a *cour de droit social pour des femmes*

August: Second and last issue of *La Politique des Femmes* is published

August 21: First issue of *L'Opinion des Femmes* is published

November 4: The French Constitution is voted

December 10: Louis Bonaparte is elected president of the Republic
Second attempt to run the school at ChâtillonsousBagneux by the Gays
Wheeler dies
Voilquin emigrates to New Orleans

1849 Cabet joins with the Icarians in New Orleans
January: *L'Opinion des Femmes* is relaunched
May 13: Deroin stands as a candidate for the Legislative Elections
June: Gay and Deroin are funded to create an Association for Lingères but the project doesn't take off
August 3–6: L'Opinion des Femmes is fined and forced to close down
September: Deroin and Roland form the Association for Socialist Teachers
November 22: The Workers' Association is formerly constituted
Louise Otto publishes *Women's Newspaper* in Germany (1849–1852)
Louise Dittmar publishes *Social Reform* in Germany
Amelia Bloomer publishes *Lily* in the United States
Considerant goes to exile in Belgium

1850 *April–May:* Restrictions on universal suffrage
May 29: Deroin is persecuted and imprisoned
November 14: Deroin's trial in Paris
June 15: Deroin and Roland send a letter from Saint-Lazare's prison to the *Convention of the Women of America*
July 3: Deroin is released from prison
Bill that makes education compulsory for both sexes is voted

1851 Knight works for the Sheffield Female Political Association
August and December: The Women's Newspaper in Germany publishes two articles on 'Johanna'
December 2: Napoleon Bonaparte's coup d'etat: persecutions and exiles
December 11: Victor Hugo takes the road of exile

1852 Deroin publishes the first issue of *L'Almanach des Femmes* in Paris
Second generation of department stores in Paris (1852–1869)
June: Roland is sent to a penal prison in Algeria
August: Deroin flees to London fearing persecution
July: Mathilde Franziska Anneke reprints Deroin and Roland's letter from prison in the German newspaper she published in New York
December 15: Roland dies in Lyon on her return to France

1853 Second issue of *L'Almanach des Femmes* is published in London
Deroin's children join her in London

1854 Third issue of *L'Almanach des Femmes* is published in London

1855   Gay wins a prize at the *Exposition Universelle de Paris*
Considerant establishes a Fourierist colony in Texas (1855–1857)

1858   *November 17:* Owen dies

1860   Voilquin returns to France

1861   American Civil War

1862   Deroin founds a school for French exiles in London
November 4: Knight dies near Strasbourg
World exposition in London

1863   Marguerite Audoux is born.

1864   The Gays take the road of exile
September 1: Enfantin dies
September 28: International Workingmen's Association in London
Dissolution of the Icarian community in Cheltenham
Workers Manifesto in France

1865   Jeanne Bouvier is born

1866   Voilquin publishes her *Souvenirs*

1866   Gay becomes acting president of the Women's Section in the International Workingmen's Association

1867   World Exposition in Paris
Loi Durury on the education of girls passes

1868   The Gays move to Geneva (then to Turin and finally to Brussels)
Désirée Gay publishes *Éducation rationnelle de la première enfance*

1869   Léon Richer founds the newspaper *Le Droit des Femmes*
Victor Considerant returns to France after the failure of the colony in Texas

1870   Richer founds the *Association for the Rights of Women*

1871   The Parisian Commune

1876   The Gays move to Brussels

1877c   *January:* Voilquin dies in Paris

1878   Women's Rights Conference, Auclert brings up the question of women's suffrage, but it is rejected as premature

1879   Bouvier moves to Paris and becomes a seamstress

1880   Deroin joins the Socialist League in London
The Third Republic grants Deroin a pension of six hundred francs

1881   Audoux moves to Paris and becomes a seamstress

1882   *November:* Richer founds the *Ligue Française pour le Droit des Femmes*

1883   Richer publishes *Le Code des Femmes*

1884   The *Chapelier Law* is abolished
Divorce is re-established.

1887   Deroin's invalid son dies

1890   *May–July 1891:* Véret-Gay writes twelve letters to Considerant

1891c. Véret-Gay dies in Brussels (last extant letter July 7)
Le Droit des Femmes is suspended
1893 *December 27:* Considerant dies
1894 *April 2:* Deroin dies in London, William Morris gives her oratory

NOTES

1. Véret-Gay to Considerant, letter dated, September 17, 1890, (AnF/10AS42/8/ DVG/63/4).
2. Véret-Gay to Considerant, letter dated, September 9, 1890, (AnF/10AS42/8/ DVG/62/1-2).
3. Utopia's grammatical gender is also feminine in the Greek language, where its etymological root lies: [ἡ οὐτοπία].
4. Véret-Gay to Considerant, letter dated, September 9, 1890, (AnF/10AS42/8/ DVG/62/2).
5. Véret-Gay to Considerant, letter dated, September 17, 1890, (AnF/10AS42/8/ DVG/63/1).
6. Ibid.
7. Ibid., 2–3
8. Véret-Gay refers here to Fourier's works, *Le Nouveau Monde Industriel* (1829–1830) and *Théorie des quatre mouvements et des destinées générales* (1808) and to Considerant's *Destinée sociale* (1834). For an overview and critical discussion of these works, see Beecher 1986, 2001.
9. Véret-Gay to Considerant, letter dated, September 1, 1890, (AnF/10AS42/8/ DVG/61/1).
10. Ibid.
11. Very little is known about Julie Fanfernot apart from the fact that she was in the July, 1830 barricades and then joined the Saint-Simonian and Fourierist circles. A short episode from her life is recounted in the sixth chapter of the *Mémoires épisodiques d'un vieux chansonnier Saint-Simonien* by Vinçard Aîné.
12. *L'Etincelle*, signed prospectus: Julie Fanfernot, décorée de juillet, BnF, FOL- LC2- 1357.
13. The second issue of *La Politique des Femmes*, for example, is digitized by Gallica, but not the first one. When there are only two issues anyway, such a selection seems at least odd.
14. Moses (1984, 128), whose book has been a classic and very useful reference source, erroneously gives March 19 as the date of the first issue of *La Voix des Femmes*, the first daily feminist newspaper of the French revolution.
15. See: https://sites.google.com/site/mariatamboukou/the-book-archive.
16. See the book archive for a cartography of these addresses: https://sites.google.com/site/mariatamboukou/the-book-archive/mapping-the-seamstress
17. Véret-Gay to Considerant, letter dated, August 15, 1890, (AnF/10AS42/8/ DVG/60/1).

Archival Sources and Bibliography

Archives Nationales de France (AnF)

- Fonds Fourier et Considérant 10AS/1-10AS/42
  - Considerant (1798–1893)/10AS/26-29/Correspondance des membres, classée par ordre alphabétique des expéditeurs, 1832-1890/10AS/42/ Dossier 8, Lettres de Désirée Véret, veuve Gay (1830–1891). Also in microform: 681Mi/57-75.

Bibliothèque Nationale de France (BnF)

- Bibliothèque de l'Arsenal/Fonds Enfantin ou Fonds Saint-Simonien/
  - Ms7608/Correspondance du Globe (Dames)/Deroin (Mme)/Profession de foi/39 (1-44). [in microform]
  - Ms7608/Correspondance du Globe (Dames)/Désirée (J.)/4 lettres/40-43 [in microform]
  - Ms7728/76-G1/Correspondances diverses/ Désirée Gay au Père Enfantin/14 lettres/151-164. [in microform]

Bibliothèque Historique De la Ville de Paris (BHVP)

  - Archives Marie-Louise Bouglé/Fonds Jeanne Bouvier
  - Archives Marie-Louise Bouglé/Autographs/Jeanne Deroin/9 lettres/ CP4247
  - Archives Marie-Louise Bouglé/Autographs/Désirée Gay/2 lettres/ CP4247

- La Voix des Femmes /Texte imprimé, journal quotidien/ Dir. E. Niboyet/ N° 1 (1848, 20 mars)-n° 46 (1848, 18 juin) /FM27395 volume 55
- Bulletin de la Société d'histoire de la revolution de 1848, sous la dir. de Georges Renard/Texte imprimé, périodique bimestre. Paris: F. Rieder, 1904-1916. T. 1, n° 1 (mars/avr. 1904)-t. 12, n° 46 (janv./févr. 1916), ISSN 1155-8814/8-PER-0513-(01)

Bibliothèque de l'Hôtel de Ville (BHdV)

- La Politique des Femmes-périodique, 2 vol. /18 juin -5 août 1848/MI20, Sur microformes (In : Bobine n. 13)

Bibliothèque Marguerite Durand (BMD)

- Deroin, Jeanne. Dossier documentaire/ Texte imprimé/DOS DER
- Voilquin, Suzanne-1801-1877/Voyage en Russie/ Texte manuscript /
- 091 VOI mf.
- Baker, Vaughan Burdin/Jeanne Deroin: the years in exile /Texte imprimé, 1 vol (16p) / Western Association of French History, Saskatoon, Saskatchewan, October 15–18, 1997/Broc. MF 1674

Digital Archive Sources

Bibliothèque National de France-Gallica la bibliothèque numérique de la BnF http://www.bnf.fr/fr/collections_et_services/bibliotheques_numeriques_gallica.html

- Apostolat des Femmes-La Femme Libre
- http://gallicalabs.bnf.fr/ark:/12148/bpt6k85525j/f5.image   [Accessed, 18-4-2015]
- La Tribune des Femmes
- http://gallicalabs.bnf.fr/ark:/12148/bpt6k855277/f1.image   [Accessed, 18-4-2015]
- La Politique des Femmes (2nd volume only]
- http://gallicalabs.bnf.fr/ark:/12148/btv1b53014119q/f1.image [Accessed, 18-4-2015]
- L'Opinion des Femmes
- http://gallicalabs.bnf.fr/ark:/12148/bpt6k68491/f3.image   [Accessed 18-4-2015]
- Jeanne Désirée *Lettre au roi, écrite sous l'impression des évènements 5 et 6 juin 1832*. [Letter to the King written under the impression of the évents of 5 and 6 June 1832] accompanied by *Aux Femmes Privilégiées* [To the Privileged Women]. (BnF, FRBNF37303490)

- http://gallicalabs.bnf.fr/ark:/12148/bpt6k85529x/f8.image   [Accessed, 18-4-2015]
- *L'Etincelle,* signed prospectus: Julie Fanfernot, décorée de juillet http://catalogue.bnf.fr/ark:/12148/cb30417733v/PUBLIC [Accessed, 18-4-2015]
- *Liberté,* égalité, *fraternité. Les femmes* électeurs *et* éligibles http://gallicalabs.bnf.fr/ark:/12148/bpt6k5698434k/f3.image [Accessed, 17-5-2015]
- Campagne électorale de la citoyenne Jeanne Deroin, et pétition des femmes au peuple. [Campaign of the citizen Jeanne Deroin and petition of people's women]: http://gallica.bnf.fr/ark:/12148/bpt6k109896h.r [Accessed, 15-11-2014]

REFERENCES

Primary Sources

Aîné, Vinçard. *Mémoires épisodiques d'un vieux chansonnier Saint-Simonien* Available: http://gallica.bnf.fr/ark:/12148/bpt6k114966n.r=julie+fanfernot.langEN [Accessed, 17-4-2015].

Audoux, Marguerite. 1912. Valserine and other stories. New York: Hodder and Stroughton.

Audoux, Marguerite. 1920. *Marie-Claire's Workshop,* translated by Frank. S. Flint. New York: Thomas Seltzer. Available on line at: http://books.google.fr/books?id=fzM0AAAAMAAJ&oe=UTF-8 [Accessed, 18-4-2015].

Audoux, Marguerite. 1926. De la ville au moulin. Paris: Fasquelle.

Audoux, Marguerite. 1932. La fiancee. Paris: Flammarion.

Audoux, Marguerite. 1937. Douce Lumière. Paris: Grasset [posthum].

Audoux, Marguerite. 2008. *Marie-Claire* [1910] *suivi de L'Atelier de Marie –Claire* [1920]. Paris: Grasset [in print].

Bouvier, Jeanne. 1927. Deux époques, deux hommes. Paris: Radot.

Bouvier, Jeanne. 1928. *La lingerie et les lingères*. Paris: G. Doin [BHVP].

Bouvier, Jeanne. 1930. Histoire des dammes employées dans les postes, télégraphes et telephones, de 1714 a 1929. Paris : Les Presses Universitaires de France.

Bouvier, Jeanne. 1931. Les femmes pendant la révolution. Paris : E. Figuière

Bouvier, Jeanne. 1983 [1936] *Mes Mémoires: Une syndicaliste féministe, 1876–1935.* Paris: La Découverte/Maspero [BHVP].

Daubié, Julie-Victoire. 1869. *La Femme Pauvre Au* Dix-Neuvième Siècle, 2nd edition, volume 2. Paris: Ernest Thorin. Available though Gallica: http://gallica.bnf.fr/ark:/12148/bpt6k842840 [Accessed, 2-1-2015].

Démar, Claire. 1834. *Ma Loi d' Avenir, par Claire Démar. Ouvrage posthume, publié par Suzanne.* Paris: Imprimerie de Petit. Available through Gallica: http://gallica.bnf.fr/ark:/12148/bpt6k1025035g.r [Accessed, 10-6-2014].

Deroin, Jeanne. 1852. *Almanach des Femmes pour 1852: 1re année.* Paris: Jeanne Deroin [BHVP].

Deroin, Jeanne. 1853. *Women's Almanack for 1853, in the English and French Languages /Almanach des Femmes, Seconde Année.* London: J. Watson [BHVP].

Deroin, Jeanne. 1854. *Almanach des Femmes pour 1854: Troisième Année.* Londres: J. Watson [BHVP].

Deroin, Jeanne. 1909. 'Le Testament d'une feministe de 1848'. Edited by Adrien Ranvier, in *La Révolution de 1848: Bulletin de la société d'histoire de la révolution de 1848* (5) 1908–1909, 816–25 [BHVP].

Fourier, Charles. 1808. Théorie des quatre mouvemens et des destinées générales. Lyon: A. Leipzig. Available through Gallica: http://gallicalabs.bnf.fr/ark:/12148/bpt6k106139k/f1.image [Accessed, 3-5-2014].

Gay, Désirée. 1868. *Éducation rationnelle de la première enfance: manuel à l'usage des jeunes mères.* Paris: Adrien Delahaye Libraire and Geneva: J. Gay et Fils. Available at: https://play.google.com/store/books/details?id=pblbAAAAcAAJ&rdid [Accessed, 16-5-2015].

Lucas, Alphonse. 1851. *Les Clubs et les Clubistes.* Available at: http://gallicalabs.bnf.fr/ark:/12148/bpt6k74948v/f4.image [Accessed, 17-5-2015].

Ranvier, Adrien. 1897. 'Une féministe de 1848' In *La Revue Féministe* (2), 65–89 and 166–98 [BMD].

Ranvier, Adrien. 1908. 'Une feministe de 1848: Jeanne Deroin' In *La Révolution de 1848: Bulletin de la société d'histoire de la révolution de 1848* (4) 1907–1908, 317–55 [BHVP].

Ranvier Adrien. 1909. 'Une feministe de 1848: Jeanne Deroin' In *La Révolution de 1848: Bulletin de la société d'histoire de la révolution de 1848* (5) 1908–1909, 421–30; 480–98 [BHVP].

Riot-Sarcey, Michèle. 1992. *De la liberté des femmes: 'Lettres de Dames' au Globe (1831–1832).* Paris: côté-femmes editions (in print).

Riot-Sarcey, Michèle. 1995. 'Lettres de Charles Fourier et de Désirée Véret: une correspondence inédite.' *Cahiers Charles Fourier* 6, 3–14. (in print)

Simon, Jules. 1860. *L'ouvrière.* Paris: Librairie de l'Hachette. Available at: http://gallicalabs.bnf.fr/ark:/12148/bpt6k29191z.r=Simon%20Jules%20l%27ouvriere [Accessed, 18-4-2015]

Tristan, Flora. 1843. Union ouvrière. Paris: Prévot Available at: http://gallicalabs.bnf.fr/ark:/12148/btv1b8626625v/f1.image [Accessed, 3-5-2015].

Voilquin, Suzanne. 1866. *Souvenirs d'une fille du peuple ou Saint-simonienne en Égypte.* Paris: Libraire E. Sauzet. Available at: http://gallicalabs.bnf.fr/ark:/12148/bpt6k111747w.r=Suzanne%20Voilquin [Accessed, 18-4-2015].

Voilquin, Suzanne. 1869. *Voyage en Russie,* edited by Maïté Albistur and Daniel Armogathe as *Memoires d'une saints-simonienne en Russie (1839–1846).* Paris: Éditions des femmes, 1977.

BIBLIOGRAPHY

Adler, Laure. 1979. A l'aube du féminisme: Les premières journalistes (1830–1850). Paris: Payot.

Ahmed, Sara. 2003. 'In the Name of Love'. *Borderlands, e-journal* 2 (3), 1–41. Available at http://www.borderlands.net.au/vol2no3_2003/ahmed_love.htm [Accessed 12-2-2015].

Ahmed, Sara. 2010. *The Promise of Happiness*. Durham, NC: Duke University Press.

Alexander, Lynn M. 2003. *Women, Work and Representation: Needlewomen in Victorian Art and Literature*. Athens: Ohio University Press.

Altman, Janet. 1982. *Epistolarity: Approaches to a form*. Columbus: Ohio State University Press.

Amann, Peter H. 1975. *Revolution and Mass Democracy*. New Jersey: Princeton University Press.

Amireh, Amal. 2000. *The Factory Girl and the Seamstress: Imagining Gender and Class in Nineteenth Century American Fiction*. New York and London: Garland Publishing.

Anderson, Bonnie S. 2000. *Joyous Greetings: The First International Women's Movement, 1830–1860*. New York: Oxford University Press.

Anderson, Linda. 2001. *Autobiography*. London: Routledge.

Anderson, Robert D. 1975. *Education in France, 1848–1870*. Oxford: Clarendon Press.

Albistur, Maïté. 1985. 'Une nouvelle demeure de Clio ou les archives Marie-Louise Bouglé', *Matériaux pour l'histoire de notre temps*, vol. 1, n° 1.

Arendt, Hannah. 1960. 'Action and "The Pursuit of Happiness"', unpublished lecture, American Political Science Association, New York. Library of Congress, *The Hannah Arendt Papers,* (Series: Speeches and Writings, File, 1923–1975).

Arendt, Hannah. 1968. *Men in Dark Times*. New York: Harvest Books.

Arendt, Hannah. 1972. 'On Violence'. In A. Hannah, *Crises of the republic,* 83–146. New York: Harcourt.

Arendt, Hannah. 1978. *The Jew as pariah*. Edited by Ron H. Feldman. New York: Grove Press.

Arendt, Hannah. 1981. *The Life of the Mind*. Edited by Mary Mc Carthy. Sections I and II, one volume edition. New York and London: Harcourt.

Arendt, Hannah. 1982. *Lectures on Kant's political philosophy*. Edited by Ronald Beiner. Brighton: The Harvester Press.

Arendt, Hannah. 1990. *On Revolution*. London: Penguin.

Arendt, Hannah. 1994a. 'Understanding and Politics (The Difficulties of Understanding)'. In *Essays in Understanding 1930–1954: Formation, Exile and Totalitarianism,* edited by Jerome Kohn, 307–27. New York: Schocken Books.

Arendt, Hannah. 1994b. 'What is Existential Philosophy?' In *Essays in Understanding 1930–1954: Formation, Exile and Totalitarianism,* edited by Jerome Kohn, 163–87. New York: Schocken Books.

Arendt, Hannah. 1996. *Love and St Augustine*, edited by Joanna V. Scott and Judith C. Stark. Chicago: University of Chicago Press.

Arendt, Hannah. 1998 [1958]. *The Human Condition*. Chicago: University of Chicago Press.

Arendt, Hannah. 2000. [1957] *Rahel Varnhagen: The Life of a Jewess,* edited by Liliane Weissberg, translated by Richard and Clara Winston. Baltimore and London: The Johns Hopkins University Press.

Arendt, Hannah. 2006a [1961]. 'The Concept of History' In Between Past and Future: Eight Exercises in Political Thought, by H. Arendt, 41–90. London: Penguin Books.

Arendt, Hannah. 2006b [1961]. 'What is Freedom?' In Between Past and Future: Eight Exercises in Political Thought, by H. Arendt, 142–69. London: Penguin Books.

Arendt, Hannah and Jaspers, Karl. 1993. *Correspondence, 1926–1969*, edited by Lotte Köhler and Hans Saner, translated by Robert and Rita Kimber. New York: Harcourt.

Baker, Vaughan, B. 1997. 'Jeanne Deroin: The Years in Exile'. In *Proceedings of the Western Association of French History*. Saskatoon, Saskatchewan, October 15–18, 1997, 1–16. [Archived paper, Bibliothèque Marguerite Durand, Broc. MF 1674].

Bakhtin, Mikhail. 1981. *The dialogic imagination: Four essays,* edited by M. Holquist. Austin: The University of Texas Press.

Barad, Karen. 2003. Posthumanist performativity: toward an understanding of how matter comes to matter. *Signs* 28(3): 801–31.

Barad, Karen. 2007. *Meeting the Universe Halfway: Quantum Physics and the Entanglement of Matter and Meaning.* Durham: Duke University Press.

Beckman, Frida. 2013. *Between Desire and Pleasure: A Deleuzian Theory of Sexuality.* Edinburgh: Edinburgh University Press.

Beecher, Jonathan and Bienvenu, Richard. 1971. Eds. *The Utopian Vision of Charles Fourier: Selected Texts on Work, Love, and Passionate Attraction.* Boston: Beacon Press.

Beecher, Jonathan. 1986. *Charles Fourier: The Visionary and His World.* Berkeley: University of California Press.

Beecher, Jonathan. 2000. 'Desirée Véret, or the Past Recaptured: Love, Memory and Socialism'. In *The Humanist Tradition in Modern France,* edited by K. Steven Vincent and Alison Klairmont-Lingo, 69–80. Wilmington: Scholarly Resources Books.

Beecher, Jonathan. 2001. *Victor Considerant and the Rise and Fall of French Romantic Socialism.* Berkeley: University of California Press.

Beik, Doris and Beik, Paul. 1993. 'Introduction to her life'. In *Flora Tristan, Utopian Feminist: Her Travel Diaries and Personal Crusade,* edited by Doris and Paul Beik, ix-xxi. Bloomington: Indiana University Press.

Bell, Susan. 2013. 'Seeing Narratives'. In *Doing Narrative Research,* 2nd edition, edited by Molly Andrews, Corinne Squire and Maria Tamboukou, 142–58. London: Sage.

Bell, Susan G. and Karen M. Offen. 1983. *Women, the Family and Freedom: 1750–1880.* Stanford: Stanford University Press.

Bergson, Henri. 1970. *Time and Free Will.* Translated by Frank L. Pogson. London: George Allen & Unwin.

Berrebi, Sophie. 2008. 'Jacques Rancière: Aesthetics is Politics'. In *Art and Research, a Journal of Ideas, Contexts and Methods,* 2(1), available on line, www.artandresearch.org.uk/v2n1/pdfs/berrebirev.pdf [Accessed, 9-9-2014].

Bezucha, Robert, J. 1974. *The Lyon Uprising of 1834: Social and Political Conflict in the Early July Monarchy.* Cambridge, MA: Harvard University Press.

Bidelman, Patrck K. 1976. 'The Politics of French Feminism: Léon Richer and the Ligue Française pour La Droits des Femmes, 1882–1891'. *Historical Reflections/ Réflexions Historiques* 3(1): 93–120.

Birrel, Ross. 2008. Jacques Rancière and The (Re)distribution of the Sensible: Five Lessons in Artistic Research. In *Art and Research, a Journal of Ideas, Contexts and Methods,* 2(1), available on line: www.artandresearch.org.uk/v2n1/pdfs/v2n1editorial.pdf [Accessed, 9-9-2014].

Blanchot, Maurice and Foucault, Michel. 1990. *Foucault, Blanchot.* Translated by Jeffrey Mehlman and Brian Massumi. New York: Zone Books.

Bouyssy, Maïté and Fauré, Christine. 2003. '1848 in Paris'. In *Political and Historical Encyclopaedia of Women,* edited by Christine Fauré, 294–317. New York: Routledge.

Braidotti, Rosi. 2000. 'The Way We Were: Some Post-structuralist Memoirs.' *Women's Studies International Forum* 23(6): 715–28.

Braidotti, Rosi. 2014. 'Thinking with an Accent: Françoise Collin, *Les cahiers du Grif,* and French Feminism'. Signs 39(3): 597–626.

Brown, Wendy. 1994. '"Supposing Truth Were a Woman...": Plato's Subversion of Masculine Discourse'. In *Feminist Interpretations of Plato,* edited by Nancy Tuana, 157–80. University Park: Pennsylvania State University Press.

Burton, Antoinette. 2005. Ed. *Archive Stories: Facts, Fictions and the Writing of History.* Durham: Duke University Press.

Butler, Judith. 2005. *Giving an account of oneself.* New York: Fordham University Press.

Carson, Anne. 1998. *Eros, the bittersweet.* London: Dalkey Archive Press.

Casey, Edward S. 1976. *Imagining: A Phenomenological Study.* Bloomington: Indiana University Press.

Casey, Edward, S. 2000. *Remembering: A Phenomenological Study.* Second Edition. Bloomington: Indiana University Press.

Cavarero, Adriana. 1995. *In Spite of Plato: A Feminist Rewriting of Ancient Philosophy,* translated by Serena Anderlini-D'Onofrio and Aine O'Healy. Cambridge: Polity Press.

Cavarero, Adriana. 2000 [1997]. *Relating Narratives: Storytelling and Selfhood,* translated by Paul A. Kottman. London: Routledge.

Christen, Carole. 2013. 'Popular education under the Restoration and the July Monarchy'. In *The French Revolution* [Online], available at: http://. lrf.revues.org/905 [Accessed 21-6-2014].

Coffin, Judith. 1996. *The Politics of Women's Work: The Parisian Garment Trades, 1750–1914.* Princeton: Princeton University Press.

Cosslett, Tess, Lury, Celia and Summerfield, Penny. Eds. 2000. *Feminism and Autobiography: Texts, Theories, Methods.* London: Routledge.

Cross, Máire and Tim Gray. 1992. *The Feminism of Flora Tristan.* London: Berg.

Cross, Fedelma, Máire. 2004. *The Letters in Flora Tristan's Politics, 1835–1844.* Basingstoke: Palgrave.

Crowston, Claire Haru. 2001. *Fabricating Women: The Seamstresses of Old Regime France, 1675–1791.* London and Durham: Duke University Press.

De Certeau, Michel. 1988a. *The Writing of History,* translated by Tom Conley. New York: Columbia University Press.

De Certeau, Michel. 1988b. *The Practice of Everyday Life,* translated by Steven F. Rendall. Oakland: University of California Press.

DeGroat, Judith, A. 1997. 'The Public Nature of Women's Work: Definitions and Debates during the Revolution of 1848.' *French Historical Studies,* 20(1): 31–47.

DeGroat, Judith, A. 2005. 'Ateliers nationaux des femmes'. In *Encyclopaedia of the Revolutions of 1848,* edited by James Chastain. Available on line at: http://www. ohio.edu/chastain/ac/ateliers.htm [Accessed, 19-2-2015]

DeLanda, Manuel. 2006. *A New Philosophy of Society: Assemblage Theory and Social Complexity.* London: Continuum.

Deleuze, Gilles. 1983 [1962]. *Nietzsche and Philosophy,* translated by Hugh Tomlinson. London: The Athlone Press.

Deleuze, Gilles. 1988. *Foucault.* Translated by Seán Hand. Minneapolis: University of Minnesota Press.

Deleuze, Gilles. 1992. 'What is a Dispositif?' In *Michel Foucault, Philosopher: Essays French and German,* edited and translated by Timothy J. Armstrong, 159–68. London: Harvester Wheatsheaf.

Deleuze, Gilles. 1993 [1988]. *The Fold: Leibniz and the Baroque,* translated by Tom Conley. Minneapolis: Minnesota of University Press.

Deleuze, Gilles. 1997. 'Desire and Pleasure'. In *Foucault and His Interlocutors,* edited by Arnold I. Davidson, translated by Daniel W. Smith, 183–92. Chicago and London: The University of Chicago Press.

Deleuze, Gilles. 2001 [1969]. *The Logic of Sense,* translated by Mark Lester. London: Continuum.

Deleuze, Gilles. 2004 [1968]. *Difference and Repetition,* translated by Paul Patton. London: Continuum.

Deleuze, Gilles and Guattari, Felix. 1988. [1980] *A Thousand Plateaus: Capitalism and Schizophrenia,* translated by Brian Massumi. London: The Athlone Press.

Deleuze, Gilles and Guattari Felix. 1994. *What is Philosophy?* Translated by Graham Burchell and Hugh Tomlinson. London, New York: Verso.

Denzin, Norman. 2009. 'The elephant in the living room: or extending the conversation about the politics of evidence'. *Qualitative Research,* 9(2): 139–60.

Derrida, Jaques. 1998. *Archive Fever,* translated by Eric Prenowitz. Chicago: The University of Chicago Press.

Descarries, Francine. 2014. 'Language is not Neutral: The Construction of Knowledge in the Social Sciences and Humanities' / 'Construction et Circulation des Idées: La Langue N'est Pas Neutre'. *Signs* 39(3): 564–69.

De Tocqueville, Alexis. 2009 [1969]. *Recollections: The French Revolution of 1848.* Edited by J. P. Mayer and A. P. Kerr, translated by George Lawrence. New Brunswick: Transaction Publishers.

Disch, Lisa, Jane. 1994. *Hannah Arendt and the Limits of Philosophy.* Ithaca and London: Cornell University Press.

Dixon-Fyle, Joyce. 2006. *Female Writers' Struggles for Rights and Education for Women in France (1848–1871).* New York: Peter Lang.

Dolphijn, Rick and van de Tuir, Iris. 2012. *New Materialism: Interviews and Cartographies.* Ann Arbor: Open Humanities Press.

Donnachie, Ian. 2000. *Robert Owen: Owen of New Lanark and New Harmony.* East Linton: Tuckwell Press.

Draper, Hal. 2011. *Women and Class: Towards a Socialist Feminism.* Alameda: Centre for Socialist History.

Eihner, Carolyn. 2014. 'In the Name of the Mother: Feminist Opposition to the Patronym in Nineteenth-Century France'. *Signs,* 39(3): 659–83.

Falk, Candace, Pateman, Barry and Moran, Jessica. 2003. Eds. *Emma Goldman: A Documentary History of the American Years.* Vol. 1: *Made for America, 1890–1901.* Urbana and Chicago: University of Illinois Press.

Falk, Candace, Pateman, Barry and Moran, Jessica. 2008. Eds. *Emma Goldman: A Documentary History of the American Years.* Vol. 2: *Making Speech Free, 1902–1909.* Urbana and Chicago: University of Illinois Press.

Falk, Candace and Pateman, Barry. 2012. Eds. *Emma Goldman: A Documentary History of the American Years.* Vol. 3: *Light and Shadows, 1910–1916.* Palo Alto: Stanford University Press.

Farge Arlette. 1989. *Le goût de l' archive.* Paris: Gallimard. Translated in English as *The Allure of the Archive,* 2013, by Thomas, S. Railton. New Haven & London: Yale University Press.

Fasel, George, W. 1968. 'The French Election of April 23, 1848: Suggestions for a Revision.' *French Historical Studies* 5(3): 285–98.

Featherstone, Michael. 2006. 'Archive'. *Theory, Culture and Society.* 23(2–3): 591–96.

Foucault, Michel. 1963. 'A Preface to transgression', translated by Donald F. Bouchard and Sherry Simon. In *Language, Counter-memory, Practice: selective essays and interviews,* edited by Donald F. Bouchard, 29–52. Ithaca: Cornell University Press.

Foucault, Michel. 1976. 'The political function of the intellectual', translated by Colin Gordon. *Radical Philosophy,* 17(Summer 1977): 12–14.

Foucault, Michel. 1979. *Discipline and Punish,* translated by Alan Sheridan. London: Penguin.

Foucault, Michel. 1980. 'The Confession of the Flesh', a conversation. In *Power/ Knowledge: Selected Interviews and other writings 1972–1977,* edited by Colin Gordon, 194–228. London: Harvester Wheatsheaf.

Foucault, Michel. 1986a. 'Nietzsche, Genealogy, History', translated by Donald. F. Bouchard and Sherry Simon. In *The Foucault Reader,* edited by Paul Rabinow, 76–100. Harmondsworth: Peregrine.

Foucault, Michel. 1986b. 'What is Enlightenement?', translated by Donald. F. Bouchard and Sherry Simon. In *The Foucault Reader,* edited by Paul Rabinow, 32–50. Harmondsworth: Peregrine.

Foucault, Michel. 1987. *Death and the Labyrinth: The World of Raymond Russel,* translated by Charles Ryas. London: The Athlone Press.

Foucault, Michel. 1988a.'The Concern for Truth'. In *Michel Foucault, Politics Philosophy, Culture,* edited by Lawrence D. Kritzman, 255–70. London: Routledge.

Foucault, Michel. 1988b. 'Technologies of the Self'. In *Technologies of the Self,* edited by H. Martin Luther, Gutman Huck, H. Hutton Patrick, 16–49. London: Tavistock.

Foucault, Michel. 1989 [1969]. *The Archaeology of Knowledge.* Translated by Alan Sheridan. London and New York: Routledge.

Foucault, Michel. 1991. 'The Ethic of Care for the Self as a Practice for Freedom'. In *The Final Foucault,* edited by James Bernauer and David Rasmussen, *1–20.* Cambridge, MA: MIT Press.

Foucault, Michel. 1996. *Foucault Live: Interviews 1961–1984,* edited by Sylvère Lotringer. New York: Semiotext(e).

Foucault, Michel. 1997. 'Self Writing'. In *Michel Foucault, Ethics, Subjectivity and Truth, the essential works of Michel Foucault, 1954–1984, vol. 1,* edited by Paul Rabinow, 207–22. Harmondsworth: Penguin.

Foucault, Michel. 2000. *The Order of Things.* Translated by Tavistock Publications. London: Routledge.

Foucault, Michel. 2001. *Fearless speech,* edited by Joseph Pearson. Los Angeles, CA: Semiotext(e).

Foucault, Michel. 2010. *The government of self and others: Lectures at the Collège de France 1982–1983.* Translated by Graham Burchell. Basingstoke: Palgrave.

Gagnier, Regenia. 1987. 'Social Atoms: Working-Class Autobiography, Subjectivity and Gender.' *Victorian Studies* 30(3): 335–63.

Gane, Mike. 1993. *Harmless Lovers: Gender Theory and Personal Relationships.* London: Routledge.

Garreau, Bernard-Marie. 1991. *Marguerite Audoux, la couturière des lettres.* Paris: Tallandier.

Garreau, Bernard-Marie. 2004. Ed. *Le Terroir de Marguerite Audoux : Actes du Colloque organisé par l'équipe.* Orleans: L'Harmatan.

Gatens, Moira and Lloyd Genevieve. 1999. Collective Imaginings: Spinoza Past and Present. London: Routledge.

Gordon, Felicia and Máire Cross. 1996. *Early French Feminists: A Passion for Liberty.* Cheltenham: Edward Elgar Publishing.

Gossez, Remi. 1967. *Les Ouvriers de Paris, 1848–1851. 2 vols.* La Roche-sur-Yon: Imprimerie de l'ouest.

Graham, Walter. 1925. 'Shelley and the Empire of the Nairs'. Publications of the Modern Language Association, PMLA 40(4): 881–91.

Green, Nancy. 1997. *Ready to Wear, Ready to Work: A Century of Industry Immigrants in Paris and New York.* Durham and London: Duke University Press.

Gilmore, Leigh. 1994. *Autobiographics: A feminist theory of women's self-representation.* Ithaca, NY: Cornell University Press.

Grogan, Susan. 2000. 'Playing the Princess': Flora Tristan, Performance and Female Moral Authority during the July Monarchy.' In *The New Biography: Performing Femininity in Nineteenth-Century France,* edited by Jo Burr Margadant, 72–98. Berkeley: University of California Press.

Grosz, Elizabeth. 2004. *The Nick of Time: Politics, Evolution and the Untimely.* Durham and London: Duke University Press.

Grosz, Elizabeth. 2005. *Time Travels: Feminism, Nature, Power.* Durham and London: Duke University Press.

Guaraldo, Olivia. 2001. Storylines: Politics, History and Narrative from an Arendtian Perspective. Jyväskyla: SoPhi.

Guaraldo, Olivia. 2012. 'Thinkers that Matter: On the Thought of Judith Butler and Adriana Cavarero'. *About Gender. International Journal of Gender Studies.* 1(1): 92–117.

Halewood, Michael. 2008. 'Introduction to a special section on Whitehead'. *Theory, Culture and Society,* 25(4): 1–14.

Halewood, Michael. 2013. *A. N. Whitehead and Social Theory.* London: Anthem Press.

Hallgren Hanna. 2015. 'Writing as a Method of Inquiry, a Study of Poetry, the Writing Process and the Possibilities of Reflexive Academic Writing'. In *Artistic Research: Yearbook 2015,* edited by Torbjörn Lind, 76–88. Stockholm: Swedish Research Council (Bilingual, Swedish and Englis).

Hammer, David. 2000. 'Freedom and fatefulness: Augustine, Arendt and the journey of memory', *Theory, Culture & Society* 17(2): 83–104.

Haraway, Dona. 1988. 'Situated Knowledges: The Science Question in Feminism and the Privilege of Partial Perspective. *Feminist Studies* 14(3): 575–99.

Haraway, Dona. 1992. 'The promises of monsters: a regenerative politics for inappropriate/d others. In *Cultural Studies,* edited by Lawrence Grossberg, Cary Nelson and Paula Treichler, 295–337. New York: Routledge.

Haraway, Dona. 1997. *Modest_Witness@Second_Millennium. FemaleMan_Meets_ OncoMouse: Feminism and Technoscience.* New York: Routledge.

Hardt, Michael. 2007. 'About Love'. Presentation for the European Graduate School. Available at: http://www.egs.edu/faculty/michael-hardt/videos/about-love [Accessed, 12-2-2015].

Hardt, Michael and Negri Antonio. 2005. *Multitude: War and Democracy in the Age of Empire.* New York: Penguin Press.

Harris, Beth. 2005. Ed. *Famine and Fashion.* Aldershot: Ashgate.

Heidegger, Martin. 2003 [1926]. *Being and Time,* translated by John Macquarrie and Edward Robinson. Oxford: Blackwell.

Hemmings, Clare. 2011. *Why Stories Matter: The Political Grammar of Feminist Theory.* Durham, NC: Duke University Press.

Hinchman, Lewis and Hinchman, Sandra. 1994. 'Existentialism politicized: Arendt's debt to Jaspers'. In *Hannah Arendt: Critical Essays,* edited by Lewis and Sandra Hinchman, 143–78. New York: State University of New York Press.

History of the Human Sciences, vol. 11(4), 1998 and vol. 12(2), 1999. London: Sage.

Hollis, Karyn. 2004. *Liberating Voices, Writing at the Bryn Mawr Summer School for Women Workers.* Carbondale: Southern Illinois University Press.

Honig, Bonnie. 1992. 'Toward an Agonistic Feminism: Hannah Arendt and the Politics of Identity'. In *Feminists theorize the political,* edited by Judith Butler and W. Scott Joan. 215–35. London: Routledge.

Honig Bonnie. 1995. Ed. *Feminist Interpretations of Hannah Arendt.* University Park, PA: Pennsylvania State University Press.

Hooks, bell. 1999. *Wounds of Passion: a writing life.* New York: Henry Holt and Comapany

Howarth, Thomas, E. B. 1961. *The Citizen-King.* London: Eyre & Spottiswoode.

Hughes, Christina. 2011. Salivary identities: the matter of affect. Subjectivity, 4(4): 413–33.

Hughes, Christina and Lury, Celia. 2013. 'Re-turning feminist methodologies: from a social to an ecological epistemology'. Gender and Education, 25(6): 786–99.

Humm, Maggie. 1989. 'Subjects in English: autobiography, women and education'. In *Teaching Women: Feminism and English Studies*, edited by Ann Thompson and Helen Wilcox. Manchester: Manchester University Press.

Irigaray, Luce. 1994. 'Sorcerer Love: A Reading of Plato's *Symposium,* Diotima's Speech. In *Feminist Interpretations of Plato,* edited by Nancy Tuana, 181–96. University Park: Pennsylvania State University Press.

James, William. 1912 [1807]. 'The Dilemma of Determinism'. In *The Will to believe and other essays,* 145–83. New York: Keagan Press.

Jones, Peter. 1991. *The 1848 Revolutions.* New York: Routledge, 2nd edition.

Kant, Immanuel. 2011 [1798]. 'The Contest of Faculties'. In *Kant, Political Writings,* edited by Hans S. Reiss, translated by H. B. Nisbet, 177–90. Cambridge: Cambridge University Press.

Kauffman, Linda, S. 1986. *Discourses of Desire: Gender, Genre and Epistolary Fictions.* Ithaca and London: Cornell University Press.

Keckley, Elizabeth. 2006 [1868]. *Behind the Scenes in the Lincoln White House. Memoirs of an African-American Seamstress.*

Kirch, Gesa. E and Rohan, Liz. 2008. *Beyond the Archives: Research as a Lived Process.* Carbondale: Southern Illinois University Press.

Klumpke, Anna. 2001. *Rosa Bonheur: The Artist's (Auto)Biography,* [Rosa Bonheur, sa vie et son oeuvre, 1908], translated by Gretchen van Slyke. Ann Arbor: The University of Michigan Press.

Kringelbach, Morten. 2009. *The Pleasure Centre.* New York: Oxford University Press.

Kristeva, Julia. 1981. 'Women's Time'. Translated by Alice Jardine and Harry Blake. *Signs: Journal of Women in Culture and Society.* 7(1): 13–35.

Kristeva, Julia. 2001a. *Life is a Narrative,* translated by Frank Collins. Toronto: University of Toronto Press.

Kristeva, Julia. 2001b. *Hannah Arendt,* translated by Ross Guberman. New York: Columbia University Press.

Lather, Patti. 2000. 'Reading the Image of Rigoberta Menchu: Undecidability and language lessons. *International Journal of Qualitative Srudies in Education.* 13(2): 153–62.

Latour, Bruno. 2005. *Reassembling the Social: An Introduction to Actor-Network Theory.* New York: Oxford University Press.

Lefebvre Henri. 1991. *The Production of Space* [1974], translated by Donald Nicholson-Smith. Oxford: Blackwell.

Lefebvre, Henri. 2004. *Rhythmanalysis: Space, Time and Everyday Life,* translated by Stuart Elden and Gerald Moore. London: Continuum.

Livingston, Beverly. 2007. 'Translator's Introduction'. In The Workers' Union by Flora Tristan, translated by Beverly Livingston. Chicago: University of Illinois Press.

Livholts, Mona and Tamboukou, Maria. 2015. *Discourse and Narrative Methods: Theoretical Departures, Analytical Strategies and Situated Writing.* London: Sage.

Lloyd, Genevieve. 1996. *Spinoza and the Ethics.* London: Routledge.

McQuillan, Martin. Ed. 2000. *The Narrative Reader*. Lincoln and London: Routledge.

MacCormack, Patricia. 2000. 'Pleasure, Perversion and Death: Three Lines of Flight for the Viewing Body.' Unpublished PhD thesis, Monash University, Australia. Available on-line at: http://arrow4.lib.monash.edu.au:8080/vital/access/manager/Repository/monash:5969 [Accessed, 7-2-2015].

Magraw, Roger. 1992. *A History of the French Working Class: The Age of Artisan Revolution, 1815–1871,* Volume I. Oxford: Blackwell.

Marx, Karl and Engels, Friedrich. 2002 [1848]. *The Communist Manifesto.* Translated by Samuel Moore. London: Penguin Classics.

Miller, Michael. 1981. *The Bon Marché: Bourgeois Culture and the Department Store, 1869–1920.* New Jersey: Princeton University Press.

Miller, Nancy, K. 2011. *What they saved: Pieces of a Jewish Past.* Lincoln: University of Nebraska Press.

Moe, Halvard. 2010. 'Everyone a pamphleteer? Reconsidering comparisons of mediated public participation in the print age and the digital era. *Media, Culture and Society,* 32(4): 691–700.

Moore, Niamh, Salter, Andrea, Stanley, Liz and Tamboukou, Maria. 2016. *The Archive Project: Archival Research in the Social Sciences.* Farnham: Ashgate, (forthcoming).

Moses, Clare Goldberg. 1984. *French Feminism in the Nineteenth Century.* New York: State University of New York Press.

Moses, Claire Goldberg and Rabine, Leslie Wahl. 1993. *Feminism, Socialism and French Romanticism.* Bloomington and Indianapolis: Indiana University Press.

Nietzsche, Friedrich W. 1990 [1895]. *Twilight Of The Idols or, How To Philosophize With A Hammer; The Anti-Christ,* translated by Reg, J. Hollingdale. London: Penguin.

Nye, Robert. 1998. *Masculinity and Male Codes of Honour in Modern France.* Berkeley: University of California Press.

Pesotta, Rose. 1958. *Days of Our Lives.* Boston: Excelsior Publishers.

Pesotta, Rose. 1987 [1944]. *Bread Upon the Waters.* Ithaca: Industrial and Labor Relations Press.

Pilbeam, Pamela. 1983. 'The "Three Glorious Days": The Revolution of 1830 in Provincial France'. *The Historical Journal* 26 (4): 831–44.

Pilbeam, Pamela. 2003. 'Jean Deroin: French Feminist and Socialist in Exile.' In *Exiles from European Revolutions: Refugees in Mid-Victorian England,* edited by Sabine Freitag, 275–94. New York: Berghahn Books.

Pilbeam, Pamela. 2014. *Saint-Simonians in Nineteenth Century France: From Free Love to Algeria.* Basingstoke: Palgrave.

Pinkney, David H. 1973. *The French Revolution of 1830.*

Planté, Christine. 1997. 'La Parole souverainement révoltante de Claire Démar'. In *Femmes dans la Cité,* 1815–1871, edited by Alain Corbin, Jaqueline Lalouette, Michèle Riot-Sarcey, 481–94. Paris: Créaphis.

Plummer, Ken. 2001. *Documents of Life.* London: Sage. New Jersey: Princeton University Press.

Popkin, Jeremy D. 2010. *Press, Revolution and Social Identities in France, 1830–1835.* Philadelphia: Pennsylvania University Press.

Ragon, Michel. 1974. *Histoire de la littérature prolétaire en France.* Paris: Albin Michel.

Rajchman, John. 1985. *Michel Foucault: The Freedom of Philosophy.* New York: Columbia University Press.

Rancière, Jacques. 2004. *The Politics of Aesthetics,* translated by Gabriel Rochill. London: Continuum.

Rancière, Jacques. 2008. 'Aesthetic Separation, Aesthetic Community: Scenes from the Aesthetic Regime of Art'. In *Art and Research, a Journal of Ideas, Contexts and Methods,* 2(1), available on line, www.artandresearch.org.uk/v2n1/pdfs/ranciere.pdf [Accessed, 9-9-2014].

Rancière, Jacques. 2011. *Staging the people: the proletarian and his double,* translated by David Fernbach. London: Verso.

Rancière, Jaques. 2012. *Proletarian nights: the workers' dream in nineteenth-century France,* translated by John Drury. London: Verso.

Raymond, Joad. 2003. *Pamphlets and Pamphleteering in Early Modern Britain.* Cambridge: Cambridge University Press.

Reid, Donald. 2012. Introduction. In Jaques Rancière, *Proletarian nights: the workers' dream in nineteenth-century France,* translated by John Drury, xiii–xxxv. London: Verso.

Richard, Oliver A. 1964. *Charles Nodier: Pilot of Romanticism.* Syracuse: Syracuse University Press.

Riessman-Kohler Catherine. 1990. *Divorce Talk. Women and Men Make Sense of Personal Relationships.* New Brunswick and London: Rutgers University Press.

Riessman-Kohler Catherine. 2008. *Narrative Methods for the Human Sciences.* London: Sage.

Riley, Denise. 1988. *'Am I That Name?': Feminism and the Category of 'Women' in History.* London: Macmillan.

Riot-Sarcey, Michèle. 1989. 'Une vie publique privée d'histoire: Jeanne Deroin ou l'oubli de soi'. Cahiers du CEDREF (Centre d'Enseignement, de Documentation et de Recherches pour les Etudes Féministes), No. 1, Silence émancipation des femmes entre privé et public, Paris: Editions de Université de Paris VIII.

Riot-Sarcey, Michèle. 1994. *La démocratie à l'épreuve des femmes: Trois figures critiques du pouvoir 1830–1848.* Paris: Editions Albin Michel.

Riot-Sarcey, Michèle. 1998. *Le réel de l'utopie: Essai sur le politique au XIXe siècle.* Paris: Editions Albin Michel.

Robinson, Keith. 2003. 'The Passion and the Pleasure: Foucault's Art of not Being Oneself'. *Theory, Culture and Society,* 20(2): 119–44.

Rogers Helen. 1997. '"The Good Are Not Always Powerful, Nor the Powerful Always Good": The Politics of Women's Needlework in Mid-Victorian London'. *Victorian Studies* 40(1): 589–623.

Rousseau, Jean-Jaques. 1979 [1762]. *Emile or, On Education,* translated by Alan Bloom. NewYork: Basic Books.

Rowbotham, Sheila. 1973. *Hidden from History: 300 Years of Women's Oppression and the Fight Against it.* London: Pluto Press.

Rowbotham, Sheila. 1993. 'A New Vision of Society: Women Clothing Workers and the Revolution 1848 in France'. In *Chic Thrilles: A Fashion Reader,* edited by Juliet Ash and Elizabeth Wilson, 189–98. Berkeley: University of California Press.

Rowbotham. Sheila. 2014. *Women, Resistance and Revolution: A History of Women and Revolution in the Modern World.* London: Verso

Ruddick, Susan. 2010. 'The Politics of Affect: Spinoza in the work of Negri and Deleuze'. *Theory, Culture and Society,* 27(4): 21–45.

Sapori. Michelle. 2010. *Rose Bertin: Couturière de Marie-Antoinette.* Versailles: Editions Perrin.

Schwartz, Leonard. 2009. 'A conversation with Michael Hardt on the Politics of Love'. *Interval(les)* II(2)–III(1), 810–21.

Scott, Joan W. 1987. 'New Documents on the Lives of French Women: The Journal of Caroline B., 1864–1868. *Signs: Journal of Women in Culture and Society* 12(3): 568–72.

Scott, Joan W. 1988. *Gender and the Politics of History.* New York: Columbia University Press.

Scott, Joan W. 1996. *Only Paradoxes to offer: French Feminists and the Rights of Man.* Cambridge MA: Harvard University Press.

Scott, Joanna.,V. and Stark, Judith.C. 1996. 'Preface: rediscovering love and St Augustine'. In *Love and St Augustine* by Hannah Arendt, edited by J. V. Scott and J. C. Stark, vii-xvii. Chicago: University of Chicago Press.

Secomb, Linnell. 2007. *Philosophy and Love: From Plato to Popular Culture.* Bloomington: Indiana University Press.

Serrière, Michel. 1981. 'Jeanne Deroin' in *Femmes et travail,* edited by Romorantin, Lantenay, 8–41. Paris: Editions Martinsart.

Shaviro, Steven. 2012.*Without Criteria: Kant, Whitehead, Deleuze and Aesthetics.* Cambridge, MA: The MIT Press.

Smith, Sidonie and Watson, Julia. 1998. Eds *Women, Autobiography, Theory: A Reader.* Madison: University of Wisconsin Press.

Souriau, Étienne. 2009. [1956] *Du mode d'existence de l'œuvre à faire.* In *Les différents modes d'existence,* suivi de *De l'œuvre à faire,* presented and introduced by Isabelle Stengers and Bruno Latour, 195–217. Paris: Presses Universitaires de France.

Spinoza, Benedict de. 1996 [1677]. *Ethics.* London: Penguin.

Stanley, Liz. 1984. *The Diaries of Hanna Cullwick, Victorian Maidservant.* New Brunswick: Rutgers University Press.

Stanley, Liz. 1992. *The Auto/biographical I.* Manchester: Manchester University Press.

Stanley, Liz. 2013. 'Introduction: Documents of Life and Critical Humanism in a Narrative and Biographical Frame. In *Documents of Life Revisited: Narrative and Biographical Methodology for a 21st Century Critical Humanism,* edited by Liz Stanley, 3–16. Farnham: Ashgate.

Stanley, Liz. (2016). 'Archival Methodology Inside the Black Box: Archigraphics and Archival Research'. In *The Archive Project: Archival Research in the Social*

Sciences, co-authored by Niamh Moore, Andrea Salter, Liz Stanley and Maria Tamboukou. Farnham: Ashgate (forthcoming).

Stanley, Liz and Salter, Andrea. 2014. *The World's Great Question: Olive Schreiner's South African Letters.* Cape Town: Van Riebeeck Society.

Stanley, Liz, Salter, Andrea, Dampier, Helen. 2013a. 'The work of making and the work it does: Cultural sociology and "beinging-into-being" the cultural assemblage of the Olive Schreiner letters'. *Cultural Sociology* 7: 287–302.

Stanley, Liz, Salter, Andrea, Dampier, Helen. 2013b. 'Olive Schreiner, Epistolary Practices and Microhistories: A Cultural Entrepreneur in an Historical Landscape' *J. Cultural & Social History* 10: 577–97.

Steedman, Carolyn. 1989. 'Women's Biography and Autobiography: Forms of History, Histories of Form'. In *From My Guy to Sci-Fi: Genre and Women's Writing in the Postmodern World,* edited by Helen Carr, 9–111. London: Pandora.

Steedman, Carolyn. 2001. *Dust.* Manchester: Manchester University Press.

Stengers, Isabelle. 2011. *Thinking with Whitehead,* translated by Michael Chase. Cambridge, MA: Harvard University Press.

Stoler, Anne, Laura. 2009. *Along the Archival Grain: Epistemic Anxieties and Colonial Common Sense* Princeton: Princeton University Press.

Sullerot, Evelyne. 1968. *Histoire et sociologie du travail féminin.* Paris: Editions Gonthier.

Swindells, Julia 1985. *Victorian Writing and Working Women, The Other Side of Silence.* Cambridge: Polity Press

Tamboukou, Maria. 2003a. *Women, Education and the Self: A Foucauldian Perspective.* Basingstoke: Palgrave.

Tamboukou, Maria. 2003b. 'Interrogating "the emotional turn": making connections with Foucault and Deleuze'. *European Journal of Psychotherapy, Counselling and Health*, 6(3): 209–23.

Tamboukou, Maria. 2008. 'Re-imagining the narratable subject'. *Qualitative Research* 8(3): 283–92.

Tamboukou, Maria. 2009. 'Leaving the self, Nomadic passages in the memoir of a woman artist. *Australian Feminist Studies*, 24:61, 307–24.

Tamboukou, Maria. 2010a. *In the Fold Between Power and Desire: Women Artists' Narratives.* Newcastle-upon-Tyne: Cambridge Scholars Publishing.

Tamboukou, Maria. 2010b. *Nomadic Narratives, Visual Forces: Gwen John's letters and paintings.* New York: Peter Lang.

Tamboukou, Maria. 2010c. 'Relational Narratives: Autobiography and the Portrait'. *Women Studies International Forum* 33: 170–79.

Tamboukou, Maria. 2012a. 'History and Ethnography: interfaces and juxtapositions'. In *Handbook of Qualitative Research in Education,* edited by Sara Delamont, 136–52. Northampton (MA) and Cheltenham (UK): Edward Elgar.

Tamboukou, Maria. 2012b 'Truth telling in Foucault and Arendt: Parrhesia, the Pariah and Academics in *Dark Times*'. *Journal of Education Policy*, 27(6): 849–65.

Tamboukou, Maria. 2013a. 'Good night and good-bye: temporal and spatial rhythms in piecing together Emma Goldman's auto/biographical fragments'. BSA *Auto/biography Yearbook.* Vol. VI, 17–31.

Tamboukou, Maria. 2013b. 'Love, Narratives, Politics: Encounters between Hannah Arendt and Rosa Luxemburg'. *Theory, Culture and Society* 30(1): 35–56.

Tamboukou, Maria. 2013c. 'Educating the seamstress: studying and writing the memory of work'. *History of Education* 42(4): 509–27.

Tamboukou, Maria. 2014a. 'Narrative Personae and Visual Signs: Reading Leonard's intimate photo-memoir'. *a/b: Auto/Biography Studies* 29(1): 27–49.

Tamboukou, Maria. 2014b. 'Archival research: unravelling space/time/matter entanglements and fragments. *Qualitative Research* 14(5): 617–33.

Tamboukou, Maria. 2014c. 'Imagining and living the revolution: an Arendtian reading of Rosa Luxemburg's letters and writings'. *Feminist Review* 106: 27–42.

Tamboukou, Maria. 2014d. The female self as punctum: Fannia Cohn's archival technologies of the self. BSA Auto/biography Yearbook. Vol. VII, 99–113.

Tamboukou, Maria. 2014e. 'The autobiographical you: letters in the gendered politics of the labour movement'. *Journal of Gender Studies.* (on-line first, doi.10.1080/09589236.2014.957169.

Tamboukou, Maria. 2015a. 'The Artpolitics of May Stevens' work: disrupting the distribution of the sensible'. *Women's Studies International Forum* 48, 39–46.

Tamboukou, Maria. 2015b. 'Becomings: Narrative Entanglements and Microsociology' [44 paragraphs]. Forum Qualitative Sozialforschung / Forum: Qualitative Social Research, 16(1), Art. 19, http://nbn-resolving.de/urn:nbn:de:0114-fqs1501193.

Tamboukou, Maria. 2015c. The work of memory: embodiment, materiality and home in Jeanne Bouvier's autobiographical writing. *Women's History Review* (on-line first).

Tamboukou, Maria. 2016. *Gendering the memory of work.* London: Routledge (forthcoming).

Taylor, Barbara. 1983. *Eva and the New Jerusalem.* London: Virago.

Thomas, Edith. 1948. *Les Femmes de 1848.* Paris: Presses Universitaires de France.

Thomas, Edith. 2007 [1967]. *The Women Incendiaries,* translated by James and Starr Atkinson. Chicago: Haymarket Books.

Traugott, Mark. 1993. Ed. The French Worker: Autobiographies from the Early Industrial Era. Translated by M. Traugott. Berkeley: University of California Press.

Tristan, Flora. 2007 [1843]. *The Workers' Union.* Translated by Beverly Livingston. Chicago: University of Illinois Press.

Valles Martínez, Miguel S. (2011). Archival and Biographical Research Sensitivity: A European Perspective from Spain [38 paragraphs]. Forum Qualitative Sozialforschung / Forum: Qualitative Social Research, 12(3), Art. 2, http://nbn-resolving.de/urn:nbn:de:0114-fqs110327.

Valles, Miguel S., Corti, Louise, Tamboukou, Maria, & Baer, Alejandro. (2011). Qualitative Archives and Biographical Research Methods. An Introduction to the *FQS* Special Issue [19 paragraphs]. Forum Qualitative Sozialforschung / Forum: Qualitative Social Research, 12(3), Art. 8, http://nbn-resolving.de/urn:nbn:de:0114-fqs110381 .

Vapnek, Lara. 2013. 'The 1919 International Congress of Working Women: Transnational Debates on the Woman Worker'. *Journal of Women's History* 26(1): 160–84.

Varikas, Eleni. 2010. 'The outcasts of the world-Images of the pariah'. *Estudos Avançados* 24(69): 31–60.

Veyne, Paul. 1997. 'Foucault Revolutionizes History'. In *Foucault and his interlocutors,* edited by Arnold, I., Davidson, 146–82. Chicago: The University of Chicago Press.

Voss-Hubbard, Anke. 1995. '"No Document-No History": Mary Ritter Beard and the Early History of Women's Archives'. *The American Archivist* 58(1): 16–30.

Walkley, Christina. 1981. *The Ghost in the Looking Glass: the Victorian Seamstress.* London: Peter Owen.

White, Hayden. 1987. *The Content of the Form: Narrative Discourse and Historical Representation.* Baltimore, MD: Johns Hopkins University Press.

Whitehead, Alfred, North. 1958. [1927] *Symbolism: Its meaning and effect.* New York: Fordham University Press.

Whitehead, Alfred, North. 1964 [1920]. *The Concept of Nature.* Cambridge: Cambridge University Press.

Whitehead, Alfred, North. 1967a [1925]. *Science and the Modern World.* New York: Free Press.

Whitehead, Alfred, North. 1967b [1933]. *Adventures of Ideas.* New York: Free Press.

Whitehead, Alfred, North. 1967c [1929]. *The Aims of Education.* New York: Free Press.

Whitehead, Alfred, North. 1968 [1938]. *Modes of Thought.* New York: Free Press.

Whitehead, Alfred, North. 1985 [1929]. *Process and Reality* [Corrected Edition], edited by David Ray Griffin and Donald W. Sheburne. New York: The Free Press.

Wilkinson, Eleanor. 2013. 'Love in the Multitude?' A Feminist Critique of love as a political concept.' In *Love: A Question for Feminism in the Twenty-First Century,* edited by Anna G. Jónasdóttir and Ann Ferguson, 237–49. London: Routledge.

Young-Bruehl, Elisabeth. 1982. *Hannah Arendt: For Love of the World.* New Haven, CT: Yale University Press.

Zandy, Janet. 1990. Ed. *Calling Home, Working-Class Women's Writings.* New Brunswick: Rutgers University Press.

Zerilli, Linda. 1982. 'Motionless Idols and Virtuous Moyjres: Women, Art and Politics in France: 1789–1848. *Berkeley Journal of Sociology* 27: 89–125.

Zévaès, Alexandre. 1924. 'Les proscrits français en 1848 et 1851 à Londres' In *La Révolution de 1848 et les révolutions du XIXe siècle, 1830-1848-1870: Bulletin de la Société d'histoire de la Révolution de 1848* (20) 1923–1924, 345–75.

Index

227

About the Author

Maria Tamboukou (BA, MA, PhD) is Professor of Feminist Studies, co-director of the Centre for Narrative Research at the University of East London, UK and co-editor of the journal *Gender and Education*. Her research activity develops in the areas of critical feminisms, auto/biographical narratives and studies in neo-materialism. Writing feminist genealogies is the central focus of her work. She is the author of 5 books, more than 60 journal articles, and has co-edited 3 volumes on research methods. Recent publications include the books *In the Fold Between Power and Desire* and *Discourse and Narrative Methods*.